# Royal Family,
## Royal Lovers

The family of King James, showing both those dead and alive,
in an engraving by Willem van de Passe (1622–1624).
Courtesy of the Folger Shakespeare Library.

Standing *l to r* are Charles, Henry, Anne, James, Elizabeth and Frederick,
and the grandchildren. Seated on the floor are Mary and Sophia.

# Royal Family, Royal Lovers

## King James of England and Scotland

David M. Bergeron

University of Missouri Press

Columbia and London

Copyright © 1991 by
The Curators of the University of Missouri
University of Missouri Press, Columbia, Missouri 65201
Printed and bound in the United States of America
5   4   3   2   1        95   94   93   92   91

Library of Congress Cataloging-in-Publication Data

Bergeron, David Moore.
  Royal family, royal lovers : King James of England and Scotland /
David M. Bergeron.
      p.        cm.
  Includes bibliographical references and index.
  ISBN 0-8262-0783-9
  1. James I, King of England, 1566–1625.  2. Great Britain—
History—James I, 1603–1625.  3. Scotland—History—James VI,
1567–1625.  4. Great Britain—Kings and rulers—Biography.
5. Scotland—Kings and rulers—Biography.  6. Stuart, House of.
I. Title.
DA391.B47    1991
941.06′1′092—dc20
[B]                                                                        91-9282
                                                                              CIP


∞™This paper meets the requirements of the
American National Standard for Permanence of Paper
for Printed Library Materials, Z39.48, 1984.


Designer: Elizabeth K. Fett
Typesetter: Connell-Zeko Type & Graphics
Printer: Thomson-Shore, Inc.
Binder: Thomson-Shore, Inc.
Typeface: Palatino

*To My Mother and
the Memory of My Father*

# Contents

# *Preface*

$O$n a recent transatlantic flight, I happened to glance at the reading material of a nearby passenger. My eye fell on a full-page advertisement for a book on the "secret lives" of English royalty. Prominently displayed was a photograph of King James I of England with the odd date of 1611 and an enticing caption: "The king whose wife chose his lovers." This misleading statement corresponded to the sensational tabloid in which the item appeared. But the episode suggested that maybe I was on to a topic of popular interest. How rare to have the subject of one's scholarly research blaring from a suggestive advertisement. I knew from my research, however, that only a huge leap away from the evidence could enable one to make such a claim about James and his queen.

My interest in King James goes back for some time. As a teacher of Shakespeare and Renaissance literature, I have had to know about this king. I am struck that we ordinarily refer to the era in which Shakespeare wrote as the "Elizabethan" period, although nearly half of his plays were written during James's reign in England. Eventually I wrote *Shakespeare's Romances and the Royal Family* (1985) in an attempt to understand Shakespeare's final plays in light of their focus on royal families. The only such family that Shakespeare could have had immediate knowledge of was James's. I discovered that this Stuart royal family would not let me go. The more I learned, the more I wanted to know about this fascinating group of people. The present book offers what I have learned about them. Francis Bacon surely understood the power of this king when he wrote to James in 1616 and said that the king "besides his active and politic virtues is the best pen of kings, much more the best subject of a pen."

In the process I have enjoyed the benefits of support from the University of Kansas in the form of a General Research Fund grant and a sabbatical leave in 1989–1990 in which I was able to finish the book. I also received the Balfour Jeffrey Higuchi Research Achievement Award in 1987, which greatly facilitated an important research trip to England and Scotland.

I thank the museums, galleries, and libraries that have made the illustrations available and have given permission to reproduce them. The staffs and resources of several libraries have been essential for this project: the British Library, Institute of Historical Research, Public Record Office, National Library of Scotland, Folger Shakespeare Library, Watson Library of the University of Kansas, and the Department of Special Collections, Spencer Research Library, University of Kansas. Even if I hadn't been working on this particular project, I would have enjoyed working in these wonderful repositories. It was especially exciting to examine original letters of King James and other members of his family; at such moments I felt rather close to them.

Speaking of pleasures, I get to record the active efforts of a large group of people who read part or all of this manuscript and offered their helpful advice. Each brought a special perspective that enriched my thinking and writing. These friends include: Richard Hardin, Geraldo U. de Sousa, Frank Murphy, Daryl Palmer, Carolyn Doty, John Kenyon, Arthur Kinney, John Veal, Richard DeMolen, and Jeanne Roberts. They will understand if I did not always follow their suggestions. For special technical assistance I thank Roger Johnson, John Veal, and Paula Malone, who cheerfully and skillfully presided over the wonders of word processing and without whose aid I would be months away from finishing. My friends Cheryl Lester and Philip Barnard kindly checked my French translations and smoothed out some rough spots. I am grateful to my friend Bruce Smith, who sent appropriate sections of his forthcoming book so that I could benefit from his exciting work even before it is published. From early on in this project I received invaluable support and incisive criticism from Frank Murphy. Geraldo Sousa has helped in innumerable ways, even including specific research assistance. Many other people have expressed interest, asked questions, and offered support.

Because this is a book about a family, I have had much occasion to think of families that I know, especially my own and one in Brazil that means much to me. It is easy to see why literary artists also share a fascination with families. I have felt a poignant regret for King James, who never knew the love of a mother or father or brother or sister. With respect and love I recall my parents.

# Royal Family,
## Royal Lovers

*Chapter One*

# Introduction

## A True Novel

*I*n the hour of his death in 1625, James I, King of England, lay speechless. A contemporary account reports: "The king lay all the time of his sickness almost silent. What he spake was to litle purpose. . . . He lay speechless from the Fryday at night till the Lord's day following, to witt, the 27th of Marche, groning and sighing heavilie." Eventually six large silver candlesticks, which Prince Charles had bought in Spain in 1623, filled with wax tapers, surrounded the body as they burned all night—mute testimony to the life that was. James's loquacious, verbose, bawdy, and at times eloquent voice lay stilled. As Northumberland reported of the dead John of Gaunt in Shakespeare's *Richard II,* "His tongue is now a stringless instrument." The vibrant candles pushed back the darkness, but James would have life no more. The eloquence of James, as praised by Francis Bacon, "flowing as from a Fountain, and yet streaming and branching it self into Natures Order, ful of Facility and Felicity," had become in late March 1625 a mere memory.[1]

Silence becomes a useful metaphor by which to characterize and analyze an important part of this Stuart royal family's life together. Of course much action and much speech dominated their lives, as in any family; but one observes the cumulative power of silence—not a golden silence, as the cliché would have it, but one born of tension, disaffection, intimidation, and insensitivity. I do not imply that the family members stopped talking to one another; instead, I refer to the silence that can reign even in the midst of torrents of speech. Its presence profoundly shaped the stir of ordinary and extraordinary life within James's royal family.

A few examples, which will be developed more fully in the chapters to come, suggest the centrality of silence in the Stuart family. Separated from his mother when barely a year old, James would experience an uneasy relationship with her, dominated by a mistrust, even though words of affection often flowed through their personal letters. Imprisoned in England, Mary Queen of Scots lived expectant that her only child would somehow rescue her. But James sent conflicting signals to Queen Elizabeth and her government, enabling them to decide that if Mary were executed, James would not respond in any threatening way. Having done little to prevent the execution of his mother, James shed few tears when the executioner's blade snapped her life.

In the face of death James often responded with silence. Prince Henry's illness and death offer a case in point. James and his queen, Anne, absented themselves from the bedside of their dying teenage son, and James did not even attend the funeral. Similarly, when, after going mad in the Tower where she had been imprisoned by James, Arbella Stuart finally died in 1615, James exhibited no response to the death of this cousin, who had formed close relationships to other members of the family. James had treated her with contempt and turned a deaf ear to her increasingly desperate pleas that she be given her estate and be allowed to marry the man she loved. When Queen Anne died in 1619, James had little to say, indulged in an embarrassing hunt for funds to pay for her funeral, and once again did not attend the funeral.

Moments of silence troubled the lives of the royal children. One catches in the genuinely loving letters that passed between brother and sister, Prince Henry and Princess Elizabeth, an occasional note of despair over their enforced absences from one another and finally the inadequacy of letter writing to compensate for silence. After Henry's death, Elizabeth married in February 1613 and left England, never to return during her father's lifetime. In fact, she was absent from her native land for nearly fifty years. She often felt abandoned by the father who would not rescue her and her husband from the snares of the Thirty Years War and exile.

Just before departing Scotland in 1603 to become king of England, James spoke to the great Kirk of Edinburgh, promising to "visite you every three years at least, or oftner as I shall have occasion; (for so have I written in my Book directed to my Sonne, and it were a shame to me not to perform that, which I have written)." Though he had instructed Henry in the pages of *Basilicon Doron* not to neglect Scotland, James himself returned to Scotland only once after going to England. The 1617 trip reinforces a certain gap between the word and the deed—a silence inadequately explained. His early experience in England contains telling images of silence. For example, he delayed his 1603 arrival in London in order to avoid Queen Elizabeth's funeral. Unfortunately, his first months in London witnessed an outbreak of the plague; therefore, on his coronation day, "the streets, by reason of the plague, became almost desolat." When on March 15, 1604, James made his official royal entry through the streets of London and enjoyed one of the most spectacular pageants ever seen in that city, James had nothing to say—all in great contrast to his predecessor. An eyewitness account in fact says that the king rode through the streets frowning. A silent king amid an adoring public produces an unsteady tension.[2]

These examples offer only a partial picture; but they serve here to prepare us to see the entire family—its failures, frustrations, and pains, as well as its triumphs, achievements, and pleasures. The metaphor of silence underscores the remoteness that pervades the life of the royal family. A vital clue to an early understanding of James can be found in a letter that he wrote to the people of Scotland as he readied himself to sail to Denmark in 1589 to claim Anne as his bride. He explained his apparent delay in getting married—he was twenty-three already: "The reasons were that I was alone, without father or mother, brother or sister, king of this realm and heir apparent of England." In a word, James did not truly know what a family was. Cut off from routine family involvement, James, though surrounded by much noise, some adulation, and occasional threats, lived in a kind of silent world, untouched by a love that may occur in family bonds. Small wonder that he had such difficulty in understanding what it meant to be a husband and a father. He looked at the canvas of familial experience, and it stared back in unrelieved whiteness.[3]

Into such silent space steps the biographer or historian. Analyzing Joseph-François Lafitau's eighteenth-century *Moeurs des sauvages*, Michel de Certeau comments on the place and function of the writer: "Silence reigns on this stage. How could it be otherwise, where the breaking apart of bodies (individual and social), creates the space and condition of writing?" Certeau adds, "The mutism of monuments and customs allows writing to inhabit their silence." The Stuart royal family can no longer speak directly to us. Instead, we hold in our hands the testimony of letters, dispatches, reports, gossip: monuments that prompt analysis and writing, as we move into the space between us and the royal family.[4]

What do we mean by "family" and "royal family?" This question may be answered in several different ways, including social structure, historical information, and emotional or psychological bonds. Mark Poster, for example, offers a simple but compelling definition of the family as "the place from which one desperately seeks escape and the place to which one longingly seeks refuge." This paradox corresponds with what can be observed in the Stuart royal family, especially in James himself, who sought escape from the familial ties with his mother, for example, but who also took great refuge in the political strength that his own family provided. Ambivalence characterizes much of the Stuart family's reaction to its own structure. Poster's concept takes us away from the definition of family only by size or kinship and points in the direction of the psychological dimensions shared by a group known as family. But to answer what constitutes a family also requires pertinent knowledge of the historical era, recognizing that family life at the end of the twentieth century bears only general parallels to that of the sixteenth and seventeenth centuries. And to be a member of a royal family complicates the issue further.[5]

Several historical and critical studies assist in the task of understanding the family in earlier centuries. Observing that most historical studies were published after 1960, Michael Anderson discusses the various "schools" and analyzes their contributions and limitations. He groups them as psychohistory, demographic history, "sentiments" school, and household economics approach. D. H. J. Morgan, in a more recent book, makes a similar assessment. As early as 1978, Mark Poster in the preface to his *Critical Theory of the Family* had examined the major historical studies on the family, such as those by Phillipe Ariès, Peter Laslett, and Edward Shorter, noting their respective achievements and deficiencies. He contends that "the history of the family is discontinuous, involving several distinct family structures, each with its own emotional pattern." His model of the life and structure of the aristocratic family corresponds closely to what we observe in the Stuart royal family, only it raises such a life to a higher power.[6]

Despite the many studies of families and the periodical called *Journal of Family History*, begun in 1976, we still have no thorough treatment of the concept or even the practice of what it meant to be a "royal" family. Charles Carlton's book on *Royal Childhoods* with its chapter on Charles I disappoints because it does not adequately explore the ramifications of such family life. Patrick Morrah in his study of Charles's family devotes only two pages to some generalizations about what a royal family implies. He claims, "Throughout most of the century in which the Stuarts ruled England the [royal] family lived in amity." This broad assertion will need to be assessed.[7]

Additional historical information can come from Ariès's book *Centuries of Childhood,* which examines the centrality of the child in delineating family life, arguing that the concept of the family is "inseparable from the concept of childhood." He says that the child was virtually unrecognized in the Middle Ages as a significant member of the family but was "discovered" in the seventeenth century. Ariès concludes: "Between the end of the Middle Ages and the seventeenth century, the child had won a place beside his parents to which he could not lay claim at a time when it was customary to entrust him to strangers. This return of the children to the home was a great event: it gave the seventeenth-century family its principal characteristic, which distinguished it from the medieval family." But as Richard DeMolen has noted, the concepts of childhood that Ariès delineates can be found firmly in place in the *sixteenth* century in the writings of Erasmus and in certain church practices. These scholarly works demonstrate persuasively the crucial importance of children, signaling a major break with the past. In a royal family that importance increases because the children become pawns in royal matchmaking and dynasty-creating activities, and they represent the hope of a peaceful succession—an immediate political strength that James brought with him from Scotland to England. The child will presumably succeed the parent as sovereign—a source of assurance but also of tension.[8]

The birth of a child, the death of a child, the marriage of a child have profound consequences in James's family because they intersect the political world in ways that no ordinary family, even most aristocratic families, experiences. The intertwined nature, the mingled yarn (to which Shakespeare refers) of domestic and public life becomes a major theme in analyzing the Stuart royal family. James says to his son Henry in the dedication of *Basilicon Doron:* "For I protest before that great God, I had rather not be a Father, and childlesse, then be a Father of wicked children." Probably any father could make such a statement; but for James this emotional concern has special political resonance: his children stand in line to succeed him. What if they should rebel against him? What if they deliberately rival him? What if they seem more attractive than he? Such worries in fact consume the royal father. Paradoxically, James gains a political advantage from his children and simultaneously feels threatened by them. This Stuart royal family, composed of father, mother, and three surviving children (Henry, Elizabeth, and Charles), constitutes indeed the space where the generations confront one another and thereby define themselves.[9]

Especially in a royal family genealogy is destiny, as Jonathan Goldberg has reminded us. James recalled in the Star Chamber in June 1616 that he was "lineally descended" from King Henry VII, the first Tudor king, and that his claim to the English crown was double. Politically one asserts legitimacy: no less so in the royal family. One recalls Mary's subtly compelling her husband Darnley to admit that he was indeed the father of the newborn son James. This clarified the legitimate status of the royal child and removed any potential doubts about his eventual rightful claim to the throne. If one can in a way control genealogy, one can control destiny: witness the seriousness of marriage negotiations on behalf of the royal children. Similar to the pattern in aristocratic families, marriage in the royal family became far more a political matter than a romantic one. Haggling over dowries transcended other considerations. The royal child, often impassive and silent, watched as his or her parents and other statesmen plotted to arrange the most lucrative and politically viable marriage possible. We will see in the case of Prince Charles what silliness and yet what politically explosive consequences resulted from marriage negotiations for him. Nothing less than the future lay at stake.[10]

Opening several other historical issues, Lawrence Stone's *The Family, Sex and Marriage in England, 1500–1800* emphasizes the transient nature of families, subject as they were to oppressive mortality. High infant mortality rate and low life expectancy ensured a constant presence of death, which undermined any strong emotional links among family members, generating what Stone calls "lack of affect." He enumerates four practices that encourage such emotional distance: "the lack of a unique mother figure in the first two years of life [the wet-nurse syndrome], the constant loss of close relatives, siblings, parents, nurses and friends through premature death, the physical imprisonment of the infant in tight swaddling-clothes in early months, and the deliberate breaking of the child's will." Stone's analysis reveals an unrelieved silence and distance in family relationships; such is often apparent in the Stuart royal family, whatever the precise cause.[11]

But an understanding of the late sixteenth and early seventeenth centuries through historical records and the literature raises questions about this presumed "psychic numbing." One hears in a letter from the countess of Buckingham to her son something quite different. She wrote to him on April 6, 1623, hoping to share his company "before it bee longe to keepe me company in this sollitarie life for I can say now as I could never I am without husband childe grand-child or kine." And she signed the letter, "I am as I have always bene Your most affectionate loving Mother till death." Recognizing the presence of death led, at least in a number of instances, to closer family bonds rather than distance, as Stone had argued.[12]

That James's apparent lack of response to the death of his child does not grow out of understood or expected behavior for a sovereign can be seen in an opposite response by Henry VII. In 1502 his elder son Arthur died at Ludlow Castle. An anonymous source reports:

> When his grace understood that sorrowful heavy tidings, he sent for the queen, saying that he and his queen would take the painful sorrows together. After that she was come and saw the king her lord, and that natural and painful sorrow, . . . she with full great and constant com-fortable words besought his grace that he would first after God remem-ber the weal of his own noble person, the comfort of his realm and of her. . . . After that she departed and came to her own chamber, natural and motherly remembrance of that great loss smote her so sorrowful to the heart that those about her were feign to send for the king to comfort her.

Here king and queen share in their royal grief, drawing together for sustaining comfort. We recall also the close bonds in Sir Thomas More's family and especially his unstinted delight in and devotion to his children.[13]

Family in the earlier centuries can also be defined by its patri-archal structure. Stone observes, "The growth of patriarchy was deliberately encouraged by the new Renaissance state on the tradi-tional grounds that the subordination of the family to its head is analogous to . . . subordination of subjects to the sovereign." Gor-don Schochet adds, "It is no exaggeration to state that virtually all social relationships—not merely those between fathers and children and magistrates and subjects—were regarded as patriarchial or familial in essence." James insisted from the moment that he arrived in England that he was "father" of the country. He shifted the meta-phor slightly in his March 19, 1604, address to Parliament in which he likened himself to the husband of the kingdom: "I am the Hus-band, and all the whole Isle is my lawfull Wife; I am the Head, and it is my Body." In 1610 he told Parliament, "Kings are also compared to Fathers of families: for a King is trewly *Parens patriae*, the politique father of his people." As late as 1624, James still insisted to Parlia-ment: "I am the Husband, and you the Wife; and it is subject to the

Wife to be jealous of her Husband." If the king was father to the country, James was also clearly head of an actual royal family. Metaphor and reality collapsed in his person.[14]

James liked to emphasize his role as father because it offered a sharp contrast to the several previous childless sovereigns of England. His status as royal father, secure in succession, offered him political and ideological advantages that he would exploit. Francis Bacon in the dedication of the *Advancement of Learning* (1605) to King James drew the distinction between the situation of James and that of his predecessor. Bacon notes:

> Queen Elizabeth, rather a sojourner in the world than an inhabitant, in respect of her unmarried life, was an ornament to her own times and prospered them in many ways. But to your Majesty (whom God in His goodness has already blessed with so much royal issue, worthy to continue and represent you for ever, and whose youthful and fruitful bed still promises more) it is proper . . . to extend your care to those things which all memory may preserve and which are in their nature eternal.

James, no mere sojourner, gains an additional advantage because of his progeny; he provides the kingdom what no recent English sovereign had: three children who offer the potential of a stable political world. Certainly the prospects in 1605 looked especially hopeful.[15]

A contemporary document that skillfully sums up seventeenth-century ideas about patriarchy is Robert Filmer's *Patriarcha*, which, though not published until 1680, had been in existence no later than midcentury. Filmer had been a student at Cambridge in 1604, was knighted by Charles I, and died in 1653. As he writes, he explicitly has an eye on King James and the king's own pronouncements on patriarchy and kingship. Filmer argues that no matter how a king becomes king, he "hath the Right of a Father over many a Gray-headed Multitude, and hath the Title of *Pater Patriae*." The authority of the father derives from the decalogue's admonition to "honour thy father." The king's authority "is the only Right and Natural Authority of a Supreme Father." Filmer adds: "If we compare the Natural Rights of a Father with those of a King, we find them all one, without any difference at all, but only in Latitude or Extent of them: as the Father over one Family, so the King as Father over many Families extends his care to preserve, feed, cloth, instruct and defend the whole Commonwealth. . . . all the Duties of a King are summed up in an Universal Fatherly Care of his People." Under such terms patriarchy resonates with benign good will—small wonder that James likened himself to a politic father of his people.[16]

The sovereign arrives, in Filmer's terms, with the natural right of a supreme father—hence the familial metaphors that govern James's concept of his kingly rights and functions. As Goldberg observes: "In these metaphors, James mystified and politicized the body. With the language of the family, James made powerful assertions." The ideology of patriarchy governs the politics of family life in the seventeenth century, most evident in the royal family.[17]

Another set of metaphors indicates how this Stuart royal family presented itself to the public: the theater. Queen Elizabeth told a deputation of Lords and Commons in 1586, "We princes are set on stages in the sight and view of all the world duly observed." King James wrote in the *Basilicon Doron*, "A King is as one set on a stage, whose smallest actions and gestures, all the people gazinglie doe beholde." Such a concept fits James's understanding of the position and importance of the sovereign perfectly. The theater metaphor seems apt for a royal family conscious of its public function and one able to exploit this situation. The danger of this particular metaphor is that the king and other members of the royal family only play their roles, fulfilling expectations but with little substantial character. The metaphor takes a paradoxical twist as James in fact often withdraws from public display, much preferring to hunt with a few companions rather than to face the stare of the public.[18]

The theatrical metaphor, Stephen Greenblatt points out, was Thomas More's favorite: "It is the point in which the disparate and seemingly discontinuous aspects of his existence come together, touch, and resonate." In the discussion of More's "self-fashioning," Greenblatt asserts that the quintessential sign of power "is the ability to impose one's fictions upon the world." James spent his life imposing his fictions on the world: his role of sovereign subsumes concepts and practices of self-fashioning. Whether through civic pageants, coronation ceremonies, or daily obeisance shown to him, the king and his public collaborated in an elaborate theatrical experience. Similarly, other members of the royal family participated also as the citizenry beheld them on a stage.[19]

But all is not self-fashioning, the self-conscious dramatic pose; rather, as Alan Liu observes, "Without both these concepts of subject *and* action, of identities on display and practices creative of such modes of self-fashioning as display itself, there could be no fully satisfying historical explanation." If the royal family exists on a stage, they also have a backstage existence, a private life that necessarily and inevitably intersects and even at times contradicts the public role—a series of actions that may lead to their public position. As Goldberg and others have noted, little in the way of privacy exists for the royal family (indeed for most families): they lead their lives in public. True, but private emotions, inner secrets, and moments of special intimacy also occur. One can imagine that the wealth of letters that survives for the Stuart royal family may result in part from an attempt at personal expression, even if some of the letters were destined to become public. An inescapable paradox results: the private life of the Jacobean royal family seems assured of becoming known. Therefore the emphasis will be on the royal *family,* as opposed to the royal *court* in the attempt to discern and explore the private, familial life. The court calls attention to the public and political life of this family. Finally, of course, one cannot divorce public from private, especially for a royal family. The metaphors and ideology of patriarchy and theater underscore ways in which the Stuart royal family's life translates from private to state politics—and back again.[20]

In the pages that follow, we will examine a particular royal family, learning that it often included many other people, it followed the practice of sending away its children, it negotiated carefully for their marriages, it maintained many separate residences, and it remained ever conscious of its public role. Therefore, regardless of personal feelings, the family could come together for public occasions and provide the image desired by society. Any political family understands the requirement that its members sometimes subordinate feelings in order to serve a political goal. Built into the construct of a royal family, therefore, lies an inherent tension between private feelings and public responsibilities. Words and ceremonies may at moments only mask the silence of private hearts.

The focus of this book necessarily falls on James himself, assessing his role successively as son, husband, father, and lover. Was James the "wisest fool in Christendom," as Henry IV of France charged; or was he "Solomon," as many insisted? Did James truly regret the execution of his mother, or did he see her death as easing his path to the English throne? Were James and his wife a "matchless pair," as one contemporary writer claimed; or were they merely tolerant of each other for political purposes? Was James the amiable and loving father that his children sometimes asserted, or was he the father who ignored most of their needs? Was James's arguable homosexuality in conflict with his role as head of a family? To attempt answers to these questions opens the family to the rich paradoxes that it contains.

Such questions may be phrased in a slightly different way. The simplest and yet the most all-encompassing question is: in what way can the Stuart royal family be regarded as a *family*? Is a family a group of people merely united by blood relationship? What kinds of emotional bonds existed among the family? Death visited this royal family several times, often unexpectedly. Did the presence of death seriously change feelings or responses to each other? Did it exacerbate a condition that Stone calls "psychic numbing"? The family maintained separate residences; does that pattern imply anything about family life? How can one sift out politics from the private lives of the family? What personalities did these people exhibit—in private and in public? What does marriage mean or signify in the royal family? What is the status of the royal children within the family; do they move to the forefront of consideration, as Ariès argues? Did James's penchant for male favorites expand or threaten the royal family? The narrative that ensues will provide answers and thereby help define this unusual institution known as a royal family.

This book proceeds chronologically, dividing the family's life roughly into three periods: 1566–1603 (Scotland), 1603–1613 (first decade in England), and 1613–1625 (disintegration and death). James's family has a narrative life that unfolds more richly if explored chronologically. Day by day and year by year this family came into being, fought its battles, solidified its position, and then disintegrated. At any given moment it might differ radically from what it had been: personalities evolve, and events intervene. No smooth line of transition can be discerned but rather fits and starts—signs of a family growing and changing.

Born in June 1566, James had by a year later been crowned king of Scotland because his mother, Mary, had been driven into exile and imprisonment in England. The Scottish period clearly formed many of the patterns, personal and political, that would govern the rest of James's life. He established himself as husband to Anne of Denmark and father of three surviving children, and yet he engaged in an ongoing struggle with Anne over control of the children, especially Henry. He brought stability to Scotland and pursued his dream of peacemaker king, but he could not manage finances. He wrote poetry and prose tracts, some clearly directed to family or friends. He discovered love, and yet he silently watched his mother's fateful demise. He indulged his passion for male favorites and apparently saw no conflict between that and family or governmental responsibilities. By 1603, James had reached a major goal: the throne of England. He later in 1616 analyzed his own condition when he became king of England: "I was an old King, past middle aage, and practised in governement ever sithence I was twelve yeeres olde." All his life James would be a king, and he understood that role far better than the task of being husband and parent.[21]

The first decade in England saw moments of great triumph (coronation, investiture of a prince, marriage of a princess) and others of profound sadness (deaths of royal children and departure of the princess from her homeland). The royal family arrived in England clearly expecting it to be a kind of Promised Land, and the English responded to them with great enthusiasm and genuine joy. George Marcelline observed that Anne helped bring stability to the kingdom by the birth of children, setting "us above the winds, as safe sheltred from all stormes, by the firme assurances of so faire a succession." James had peacefully gained the English throne and brought with him the seeds of potential succession. But that very seeming permanence foundered on the deaths of royal children. By 1613, the family had begun to reverse the process of formation and to move instead toward disintegration. Death rather than birth became the challenging and disruptive force.[22]

This process accelerated in the final years leading up to James's death in March 1625, complicated by James's involvement with his greatest favorite George Villiers, duke of Buckingham. Ironically, James eventually developed an attachment to Buckingham's wife and children that surpassed what he had formed with his own children. They became for him a substitute family. The king's predicament in 1623 seemed particularly precarious: Princess Elizabeth and her husband were in exile in Holland, having been forced from Bohemia and from her husband's German state; Prince Charles and Buckingham were on a rather pointless and potentially dangerous mission in Spain, attempting to further marriage negotiations for Charles and the Infanta; Prince Henry and Queen Anne had died. A poignant silence threatened to overcome James. In his final months he went through the motions of ruling but not much more; the power had already shifted to Charles and Buckingham. James, who had all his life been a ruler, alternated between indifference about his function as husband and father and an apparently genuine concern for the well-being of his wife and children. But as one who had never known the love of a brother or a sister, or a father or a mother, he never fully grasped what family bonds might mean.

A Dr. Morley from Oxford offered an epitaph for James. He included the following admonition: "Princes are Gods; o doe not then, / Rake in their graves to prove them men." The archaeological diggings in the following chapters have been undertaken not to demonstrate that James was a man and not a god, for that is self-evident. Rather, in attempting to provide a family portrait, one must capture the Stuart royal family at its best, but also peer into the darker corners of their lives, seeking not scandal but completeness. This family at moments resembles one of those perspective paintings that the Renaissance so enjoyed, such as the picture of Edward VI in the National Portrait Gallery in London or Holbein's famous painting *The Ambassadors.* Looked at from certain angles, the family seems at best distorted and chaotic; looked at yet another way, it may seem clear and the rough places plain. To gain the fullest perspective we will move around the family, looking inward, at moments drawing in very close and searching for the personal qualities that made this particular group of people a family.[23]

Historical assumptions govern the approach. Shakespeare's contemporary Philip Sidney in his *Apology for Poetry* took an especially dim view of historians, preferring, understandably, the function of poets who can give us a golden world. Sidney offers an unflattering portrait of the historian as one "loden with old Mouse-eaten records, authorising himselfe (for the most part) upon other histories, whose greatest authorities are built upon the notable foundation of Hearesay." This historian, Sidney asserts, picks truth "out of partiality." A hundred years after Sidney, Thomas Frankland in the preface to his *Annals* (1681) wrote, "It is the Genuine Character of an Historian to be bold and honest, not timerous to speak the Truth, and to be veracious in what he says." Roger Coke at the end of the seventeenth century endorsed Frankland's "sacred" vision of the historian when he wrote: "That to compose Histories is sacred, and not to be undertaken but with an upright Mind, and undefiled Hands." These writers certainly offer alternative views of history.[24]

Yet another perspective comes from Francis Bacon, King James's attorney general and eventually Lord High Chancellor, who thought deeply about the function of history and offered some skillful practices of it. In his *Advancement of Learning* (1605) and especially in its revised and expanded form *De Augmentis Scientiarum* (1623), Bacon outlined the kinds and functions of history. Unlike Sidney, he took the purposes of history quite seriously; but unlike Frankland and Coke, Bacon did not assign sacred importance to the writing of history. In fact he says at the opening of book 3, chapter 1 of *De Augmentis:* "All History, excellent King, walks upon the earth, and performs the office rather of a guide than of a light." According to Bacon's system, this study of the Stuart family may be designated as "civil" history. Bacon complains about the relative lack of contemporary "lives," a type of "perfect" history. Emphasizing the function of narrative in writing history, Bacon argues that "though very wise history is pregnant (as it were) with political precepts and warnings, yet the writer himself should not play the midwife." This biography of the Stuart royal family emphasizes the narrative of their lives and pays less attention to court politics.[25]

Like literary artists, historians "fictionalize" history by giving the accumulated facts some coherent shape or a narrative structure. Hayden White has written compellingly about such issues in his *Tropics of Discourse* in which he emphasizes the textual and literary nature of history and notes how the historian interprets in ways similar to those of the literary artist. He comments, "Histories, then, are not only about events but also about the possible sets of relationships that those events can be demonstrated to figure." History involves as well personal relationships among the characters of history. Louis Mink persuasively argues for the importance of narrative as a primary cognitive instrument by which we understand ourselves and our past. He says, "Narrative form as it is exhibited in both history and fiction is particularly important as a rival to theoretical explanation or understanding." Historical writing shapes the untold story of the past. Mink suggests that historical narratives "are capable of *displacing* each other," but "narrative fictions . . . do not displace each other." Imaginative fiction is unique, while differing versions of historical narratives may simultaneously exist. However we view the matter, "narrative form in history, as in fiction, is an artifice, the product of individual imagination." Offering what then was a competent summary of James's life, Godfrey Davies fifty years ago suggested that the single epithet that could characterize James might well be "unkingly." Davies notes, "Always undignified in public, he appeared an odd mixture of a formal pedagogue and a fussy paterfamilias, of a philosopher and a jester." Then in a kind of inspired afterthought, Davies exclaims, "How happy he might have been, in the realm of fiction." Davies intends a clear distinction between "history" and "fiction"; but that line is sometimes rather unclear, and surely the lives of the Stuart royal family contain a fictional element. Even as James and the royal family may have fashioned themselves, the historian from the vantage point of the present fashions their lives into a narrative, seeing and constructing their story in ways which they could not.[26]

Though Sidney condemned historians for providing only a partial truth, White embraces that idea as a fundamental axiom of all that a historian can ever pretend to do. He observes, "Our *explanations* of historical structures and processes are thus determined more by what we leave out of our representations than by what we put in." The "brutal capacity" to exclude facts White sees as the hallmark of a historian's tact and understanding. Paul Veyne believes that "history is mutilated knowledge." We know what it is still possible to know, based on surviving remnants. Or to put the issue in Albert Cook's terms: "All history writing must be synecdochic," even though it aspires to the complete account. Far more material exists than can reasonably be incorporated in telling the story of James's family. One can hope to have kept the right things, but the truth can only be partial and incomplete.[27]

In this fictionalized and necessarily incomplete historical account one also engages in interpretation, as White suggests: "A historical narrative is thus necessarily a mixture of adequately and inadequately explained events, a congeries of established and inferred facts, at once a representation that is an interpretation and an interpretation that passes for an explanation." History does not consist of reciting facts; rather, it involves interpretation as the historian revolves around the axes of explanation and interpretation. He or she frequently chooses a narrative structure by which and through which to resolve this tension. White insists that "there can be no explanation in history without a story, so too there can be no story without a plot." Veyne also underscores the importance of such a plot: "Facts do not exist in isolation, in the sense that the fabric of history is what we shall call a plot. . . . The word 'plot' has the advantage of reminding us that what the historian studies is as human as a play or a novel." History is, Veyne suggests, "a true novel." Further, it is, as Certeau reminds us, a fiction of the past that can only be constructed in the present.[28]

If thinking about the special nature of royal history, we can confront the questions posed by Louis Marin, who writes about the French court. He asks: "How does the King place himself in the acts of history?" "What representation of his power—image, symbol—is published in his history's account?" The first refers to the sovereign's action—and I include the whole royal family—that is, his self-conscious attempts to represent himself, encompassing at moments theatricality. The second question points to the role of the historian/biographer who must confront yet another question: what constitutes royal historiography? Such historical writing may of course be thinly disguised propaganda, special pleading, self-indulgent sentimentality, blatant cheerleading, or fashioning the story to suit royal ideology. The closer the historian lives in time to the sovereign, the greater the chance for such aberrations. Marin especially focuses on the royal historian *appointed* by the king to write his history. Such a person did not exist in the Stuart court. Marin adds, "The product of the historian's writing is a monument to the King, an architecture of signs subsisting for the future, a memory in perpetuity written so as to assure an eternal present for the royal act." In other words, "Royal history is the product of the force of narrative power applied to the manifestations of political omnipotence."[29]

Not authorized by the Stuart royal family and living a safe distance in time from them, I do not encounter the potential risk of failing to serve their needs and thereby gaining their ire—or worse. My royal history need not respond to the immediate demands of monarchical ideology. Nevertheless, I recognize that narrative must confront the political power of the Stuart royal family. Through preserved letters and accounts of speeches, we hear something of their own potent voices in the first person. Their story, however, will primarily unfold in the third-person rendering—the traditional place of the historian. The third person allows adequate space for the true novel of this family, the representation of their lives.

I propose a narrative account of James's royal family, a textualizing of their historical lives, in part because the self-conscious and at moments theatrical awareness of fulfilling their roles as family members lends itself to a narrative rendering. The narrative will unfold chronologically, as sketched above. But this story also has a plot, not merely a chronicle of events in sequence, but a shape. The shape of that plot I will call *ironic*. Northrop Frye wrote a number of years ago: "As structure, the central principle of ironic myth is best approached as a parody of romance: the application of romantic mythical forms to a more realistic content which fits them in unexpected ways." He added, "Irony with little satire is the non-heroic residue of tragedy, centering on a theme of puzzled defeat." The Stuart royal family offers the "non-heroic residue of tragedy" with a "theme of puzzled defeat." Frustrated desires and goals, the inability to achieve some final reconciliation, and the lack of redemption characterize much that happens in the life of James's family. Its life mocks romance; it shatters romantic illusions. A large gap exists between intentions and fulfillment: a young prince, intended to be heir, falls prey to unexpected death; a young princess marries a German prince in a stunning ceremony, only to find herself a prisoner of European wars; a king-father, noted for his peacemaking, gets his country caught in a war as his life ends; a queen-mother, determined to nurture her young children, finds herself estranged from them, shut out of their care.[30]

At moments the gap between expectation and reality invited satiric treatment. The theater itself on occasion took such swipes at

James and his court, as in Thomas Middleton's *A Game at Chess.* Anthony Weldon offers a bitingly satiric portrait of James's trip to Scotland in 1617 (see chapter 4). Another contemporary comments on the parodic portraits of James seen in European capitals in the 1620s:

> They picture the King in one place with a Scabberd without a Sword. In another place with a Sword that no body could draw out, though divers stand pulling at it. At *Bruxels* they painted him with his pockets hanging out, and never a penny in them. . . . In *Antwerp* they pictured the Queen of *Bohemia* like a poor *Irish Mantler,* with her hair hanging about her ears, and her child at her back, with the King her father carrying the *Cradle* after her.

This unflattering picture illustrates the situation of James, penniless and unable or unwilling to enter battle in order to rescue his daughter. James, of course, often parodied himself by his liberality from a treasury that remained nearly empty.[31]

He often aggravated the gap between word and deed. For example, just a year before he died, James addressed Parliament, seeking its advice about a course of action regarding the Spanish match and the plight of the Palatinate. And he analyzed his position as ruler: "I can truly say, and will avouch it before the Seat of God and Angels, that King never governed with a purer, sincerer, and more incorrupt heart than I have done, far from all will and meaning of the least error or imperfection of my Reign." Hearing this speech, one cannot resist the idea of a fiction, for James surely creates one of and for himself. Those listening in Parliament would have had difficulty in accepting this at its face value. They could not have missed the ironic distance between what James said and what in fact existed.[32]

The Stuart royal family, a mixture of competing sounds, a tissue of conflicting problems, contains romance but also its opposite held in an unsteady tension. Ironies and paradoxes abound. The paradox of absence and presence, already figured in the metaphor of silence, dominates. This paradox grows out of jealousy and neglect. James, for example, was by nature jealous of the family members but simultaneously neglectful of them, a man torn by conflicting and largely irreconcilable desires. Tragic and comic plots twist themselves through the life of the Stuart royal family; irony remains the common denominator.

If drama is "history made visible," as Francis Bacon says in his *De Augmentis,* then surely one can say that history makes a drama visible; in this case, a drama of the royal family. The web of its life, as Shakespeare would observe, is a mingled yarn, good and ill together.

Or, as Margaret tells her sister Helen in E. M. Forster's *Howards End:* "Differences—eternal differences, planted by God in a single family, so that there may always be colours; sorrow perhaps, but colour in the daily grey." Differences, of course, may lead to ironies; they certainly add color to James's family. This family understands the need for public statements and appearances that satisfy public expectation, even though such self-conscious statements may differ from personal feelings. Exploring the family's personal and private life will enable us to see behind the scenes of their drama, to see the actors unguarded as they make ready to enter the public stage. Through such an investigation we may come closer to a Jonsonian satire than to a Shakespearean romantic comedy. Refracted through an ironic prism, the Stuart royal family will both dazzle and dismay. Its sounds of tinkling bells and clanging cymbals signify everything, even when they fall silent.[33]

*Chapter Two*

# Scotland (1566–1603)

## *Coffers of Perplexity*

$S$oaring high above the city on volcanic rock, the impregnable Edinburgh Castle witnessed in early summer 1566 the birth of James. In contrast to the massive castle, the room in which Mary gave birth to her only child is pitifully small—a tiny space against a large world. The security of the castle masked the troubles that mother and son would endure. James's cries at birth on June 19 shattered the silence of an expectant castle. Mary had fulfilled a major role of a sovereign: she had produced an heir.

Just a few months earlier in March, down the Royal Mile from the castle, Mary had watched in horror as her husband, Darnley, and other conspirators in a struggle for power killed her secretary David Riccio in the Palace of Holyroodhouse. They threatened her, Darnley holding her arms, and apparently hoped to induce a miscarriage. From that horrifying experience Mary lost whatever shred of respect she still had for her husband; she seemed all the more determined to give birth to her child successfully. The episode of Riccio's murder reminds us of the cruel and brutal world that James had entered. Fierce castles set against the sky served necessity, not aesthetics. A tiny baby faced an uncertain life, one bereft of the nurture of his parents.

By 1603 this once infant prince had become not only king of a stable Scotland but also king-designate of England. In this formative period of life in Scotland, James developed, struggled with the personal and political dilemmas of his mother, shook off his regents, became king in his own right, discovered love in the person of Esmé Stuart and then in Anne of Denmark, became a husband, and then father to three surviving children. All of these things happened against a backdrop of political turmoil and confusion. The raging bonfires and rattling cannon shot that greeted James's birth gave way to a fitful silence of uncertainty. But by the time he left Scotland to go to England, the thirty-seven-year-old king had much to be proud of, not the least of which was the royal family—a personal and political reality that made him especially attractive as the new king of England, the man who would designate himself as the king of Great Britain. He had moved from the tiny room of his birth in Edinburgh Castle to a very large stage indeed: a major player in the political theater of Europe.

Had we been able to stand on the ramparts of the castle on that June morning in 1566, we might have wondered about the future of this child. Several centuries removed from that moment and armed with evidence, we attempt to define who this James was and became. In so doing, we explore how he functioned as a member of a royal family, the one that he belonged to as a matter of birth and the one he helped create. We note, for example, that only when the issue of his mother's fate was settled did James seriously contemplate marriage, even though some of his counselors had been urging it as early as 1582. The death of his mother released James in many ways, but paradoxically it haunted him with a sense of guilt that he kept trying to assuage. The joyous births of his royal children also carried many tensions and uncertainties, seriously affecting James's relationship with his wife. The seeds of joy existed in an uneasy solution with the seeds of discontent throughout this Scottish period. Patterns of jealousy and neglect, absence and presence, asserted themselves in this period. The decade from the late 1570s to the late 1580s was the most crucial, including—as we shall see—the assumption of power, experiences of love, death, and marriage.

Having successfully given birth, having compelled Darnley to admit that he was the father of James, and having asserted that this baby would one day unite Scotland and England, Mary began preparations for his baptism, which finally took place in the Chapel Royal at Stirling Castle on December 17, 1566. Queen Elizabeth, named as one of the godparents, sent a representative and an impressive gold font as a gift. The ceremony was conducted according to Catholic rites—an offense to Elizabeth and to the Scottish Reformers. In the service the priest called out the baby's name: "Charles James, James Charles." The seeming reversibility of his name, though apparently merely following the rites, raises a teasing question about identity. Fireworks and other festivities concluded the celebration.[1]

This baptism, a religious and political event, brings into focus several themes we will be able to trace throughout James's life. James's father was absent from the baptism: unwittingly James began a life-time of being alone and abandoned. Several matters come into focus at the baptismal font. First, the absent father raises concern about James's nurture as a child and his lack of experience in understanding family life. The Catholic ritual introduces a religious tension that James as ruler would face throughout his career. Elizabeth as god-parent began her intimate involvement in the life and destiny of James. When the fireworks and feasting ended, the disquieting fact remained that baptism, which underscores family ties, seems a bit incomplete in this case.

Events in early 1567 moved quickly and decisively. Though apparently suffering from syphilis, which would have been fatal in that era, Darnley nevertheless died in what Bingham calls a "premeditated but mysterious end," an explosion on February 10 that claimed his life. His death, or murder, to be precise, had Mary's tacit approval. She was free now to pursue her new passion, the earl of Bothwell. Indeed, in a Protestant ceremony in May, they were married. But the moral and political consequences of this marriage forced both of them into separate exile. In fact, the Scottish lords required Mary to abdicate the throne in favor of her infant son. She fled from Scotland, never to see her son again. Within the space of a few fateful months, the little prince had lost his father by death and his mother by expulsion. Therefore, on July 29, 1567, outside the castle walls at Stirling and down the hill at the Church of the Holy Rude, the thirteen-month-old child became King James VI of Scotland. The fiery reformer John Knox preached at the coronation—no Catholic rites this time. Ironically, James followed the pattern of his mother, who herself had been crowned at nine months of age in 1543. The beautiful parish church in Stirling witnessed a profound change in the life and government of Scotland in 1567 and of course in the life of James. Until his death in 1625, he would carry with him the title and responsibilities of a king.[2]

Our knowledge of James's early years remains fragmentary. In early 1567, Mary placed James into the custody of the earl of Mar and his household, to be kept at Stirling Castle. As a contemporary noted: "The Earle of Marr was esteemed a trustie man, whose predecessors had oft been trusted with the tuition of the kings, in there infancie." The earl's family was as close as James would come to understanding family life. His upbringing was stern and sometimes severe but not without some degree of affection. A contemporary observer reported that James always called the countess of Mar "his

Lady-Minnie," meaning "Mama." Probably the earliest surviving letter in James's own hand is one addressed to Annabel Erskine, countess of Mar:

> Lady Minny,
> This is to show you that I have received your fruit and thanks you therefore, and is ready for mee when ye please to send them, and shall gif as few by me as I may. And I will not trouble you farther till meeting which shall be as shortly as I may.

Late in his career in Scotland, James wrote to the then earl of Mar, the son of his guardian, pointedly reminding him, "Youre self had the honour to be brocht up with me." James remained on friendly terms with most of the immediate members of this family.[3]

While in their care, James received letters from his mother, as did the countess also. They reflect Mary's genuine concern for the well-being of her child. In January 1570, Mary wrote to the countess, "Thinking now tyme that he begyn to learne to knaw sum thing of reiding and wryting, we have send hym ane A.B.C. and example how to forme his lettres." In addition she sent some clothing and a saddle. She asked that her servants might see James and report back to her. In a postscript she added: "I pray you read this letter here inclosed to my son, and remembering 'auld gudewill and service profest to me, quhairupon I have done for zour husband and zow [you]. Remember hym yat he hes a mother that he awes obedience and luif to.'" She closed by again urging the countess to remind James of his duty and to pray for his mother. Thus, the absent mother sought to make her presence felt in her son's life, with the Mar household serving as intermediary between parent and child and as surrogate family.[4]

Reports from the time show James as a precocious young boy, given to scholarly if not pedantic pursuits. The churchman Andrew Melville and his nephew James Melville visited Stirling Castle in 1574 and encountered the little king there. James Melville described James as "the sweetest sight in Europe that day, for strange and extraordinar gifts of ingyne [wit], judgement, memory, and langage. I hard him discours, walking up and doune in the auld Lady Marr's hand, of knawlage and ignorance, to my great mervell and astonishment." Other stories tell of his great facility with languages, as he moved effortlessly among several languages, especially Latin and French. In fact, James once complained that his tutors made him speak Latin before he could speak Scots.[5]

While in the care of the earl of Mar, James began his formal education at about age four. George Buchanan and Peter Young became his tutors: Buchanan the old, irascible scholar and Young the pleas-

James at the age of eight (1574), attributed to R. Lockey. National Portrait Gallery.

ant, compassionate junior man. A difficult and demanding regimen of studies steeped in the classical tradition greeted James every day. Buchanan was a fierce taskmaster, one who, unfortunately, had come to detest James's mother and did not hide his feelings from James or anyone else. Buchanan also seems to have been a misogynist; doubtless his dim view of women spilled over into James's education as well. Some evidence indicates that Buchanan did not hesitate to whip the young king severely—small wonder that, years later in England, James could still tremble at the recollection of his old tutor. But he also boasted of having studied with such a great scholar.

Young apparently recognized that James was still a little boy who needed to be treated accordingly. He was to serve James in many capacities throughout the rest of his life, having earned James's respect and affection. Young left behind a rather fascinating catalog of the books in the royal library, revealing, among other things, the royal predilection for things French. Young also recorded some witty sayings of the little James. Together Buchanan and Young formed an impressive team and instilled in James his persistent love of learning. He shared his education with four other young boys in the Mar household, including the young earl of Mar. One day as they indulged in some frivolity and inadvertently disturbed Buchanan, he emerged and beat the king, who was rescued by the countess of Mar. "She rebuked Buchanan for 'laying hands on the Lord's Anointed' "; but the old tutor "who found Lady Mar's sentiment offensive, coarsely retorted, 'I have whipped his arse, you can kiss it if you like.' "[6]

When James became king as an infant, he was, of course, incapable of ruling; therefore a series of four regents ruled Scotland in his behalf. Each had considerable difficulty in holding the country together and solidifying rule in James's name. His uncle, the earl of Moray, became the first regent. Moray was assassinated in 1570, and James's grandfather, the earl of Lennox succeeded him. He was shot in the back, and the five-year-old James watched in horror as men brought him into Stirling Castle. James long remembered the sight of his mortally wounded grandfather. Moray and Lennox became victims of internecine battles among the Scottish lords, some of the struggles caused by conflicting views about the rights and fate of Mary. James's guardian, the earl of Mar, became the third regent, the only one to die of natural causes. His regency lasted little more than a year. By 1572, James and the country had already had three regents. The earl of Morton was the obvious successor to Mar, for he had long been a power in the court, had supported the other regents, and had helped lead in the overthrow of Mary. A harsh, blunt man, he, for the most part, worked for James's benefit; but his enemies grew in number, and criticism increased.

Under pressure Morton resigned his regency in March 1578; James now assumed responsibility for the government. The 1578–1579 period marked one of several pivotal moments in James's life in Scotland, certainly the most significant politically and personally since his coronation. He began to rule on his own authority, albeit tentatively and cautiously at first. In 1579, two important events influenced his development as king and as an emerging adult: the royal entry pageant in Edinburgh in October and the arrival at court that fall of James's French cousin, Esmé Stuart d'Aubigny. Though the regency period had ended, James lacked sufficient strength and skill to rule effectively by himself. Indeed, various groups vied to control him. Even Morton, though removed from office, reasserted control over James. James was to witness several bloody feuds, including one at Stirling Castle, before the government achieved some semblance of stability. Small wonder that he lived in fear for his own life. Brutality and violence defined much of James's world with little countering forces of respect and love. The prospects for the twelve-year-old king seemed at best uncertain.

In the first civic pageant of his reign, James made an official royal entry into Edinburgh in mid-October 1579. This public display marked the country's acceptance and celebration of its adolescent king. Crowds lining Edinburgh's streets shouted approval and conferred a degree of legitimacy on James. Having been too young when crowned king for such a display, James now gathered unto himself the citizens' adulation. This occasion signaled the end of the regency and the beginning of James's emergence as a king exercising his own power. The pageant contained scenes from religion, history, mythology, and allegory. At the West Port, for example, James saw a tableau portraying the "Wisdom of Solomon." A globe device opened, and a child presented the king the keys to Edinburgh. Justice, Peace, Plenty, and Policy greeted James at the old Tolbooth; and Religion led him to St. Giles Cathedral for a service. Emerging from the church, James saw Bacchus and a fountain flowing with wine. Before reaching Holyroodhouse, the king also saw a representation of former kings of Scotland. Along Canongate he witnessed a tableau for the abolition of the pope and the mass. Echoing the 1561 pageant for Mary, this pageant for James, whatever its artistic merit, marked a rite of passage for the young king: he moved among public display and accepted the recognition of his kingship and power.[7]

In that same autumn of 1579 Esmé Stuart entered James's private life with unexpected force. This handsome, sophisticated thirty-seven-year-old Frenchman was the son of John Stuart, brother of James's grandfather and onetime regent the earl of Lennox, and was thus first cousin to James's father, Darnley. Esmé Stuart arrived in Scotland in September, apparently under the control of the Guise faction in France, with three goals in mind: to promote closer ties between France and Scotland, to encourage and support Catholicism, and to assist the cause of the imprisoned Mary. Ironically, James had been encouraged to invite Esmé to Scotland in the spring of 1579 by a number of his counselors in the hope that Esmé might provide James with some political guidance, skills, and knowledge—a kind of regent for a teenager yet unsure of himself. But Esmé arrived on Scottish shores ready to do the bidding of a foreign government, contrary to what James needed.

An early account captured the scene and impact of the first meeting between the French courtier and the young king. In the Presence Chamber of Stirling Castle, Esmé entered and immediately prostrated himself before James, wishing for him perpetual felicity. The report recorded James's reaction: "No sooner did the young King see him, but in that hee was so neare allyed in bloud, of so renouned a Family, eminent ornaments of body and minde, tooke him up and embraced him in a most amorous manner, conferred on him presently a rich inheritance; and that he might be imployed in state-affairs, elected him one of his honourable Privy Counsell, Gentleman of his Bed-chamber, and Governour of *Dumbarton* Castle." No one can accuse James of being reticent. His reaction to Esmé was immediate and intense.[8]

In one sense James was unprepared for Esmé, his attractiveness and courtly manner; James simply had not seen such refined qualities in Scotland. But in another way, James was prepared and ready for someone like Esmé Stuart: all of his life and experience up to that point had readied him. Surrounded mainly by rough, gruff counselors whom James feared rather than loved (the regents, for example), bereft of parental love and care, trapped in a world of stark violence, James welcomed Esmé as a force of springtime. That gray world of youthful uncertainty now acquired color. James began to understand love in a different way.

Perhaps because of his youth and his inexperience in such matters, James loved absolutely, not knowing restraint or caution. Esmé opened James to a quality of loving that James had not known. As a result, James, like Othello, loved not wisely but too well. He showered gifts and titles on Esmé Stuart without reservation. The culmination came when James named him duke of Lennox—the only duke in Scotland. He also loved demandingly; as Caroline Bingham observes, "He expected d'Aubigny [Esmé] to supply everything that he had always lacked and everything that he was now beginning to need: to be his family, his beloved, his friend, his mentor and counsellor, and his constant companion." Esmé responded ably to these demands.[9]

During the spring and fall of 1580, the English ambassador to Scotland, Robert Bowes, nervously recorded the developing relationship between James and Lennox. He seemed especially struck that Lennox's absences from court did not abate James's affection for him. Even Lennox had worried about that possibility. Though subdued by absence, such love did not die out. Bowes wrote to the earl of Leicester on May 16, 1580: "But at his access [Lennox's return], . . . it is like to kindle again and to come to the former course, against which few or none will set themselves. He professes in words sufficient to be religious and to do good offices with all loyalty to the King, realm, and maintenance of the amity." Bowes wrote to Burghley and Walsingham on June 3, 1580, that Lennox had returned to court, pleased at James's reception of him, "for he thought that his former absence and other meanes had abated the Kings favor towardes hym. But since his last retorne he fyndeth hymself recovered and renughtt [renewed] to his former grace." In July, Bowes wrote the same English authorities: "Lennox greatnes is exceedingly increased, as the King so much affectioned to him as he is onely delighted with his company; and thereby he carryeth the sway." A few months later in September, Bowes seemed increasingly alarmed: "But Lennox standeth so highe in the King's favor and stronge in counsell as fewe or none will openly withstand any thing that he wold have forwards." Thus those who would dare to challenge Lennox remained uncertain about gathering support at home or abroad. Bowes attributed this increasing political problem to James's "younge yeres and strange affection to Lennox." Bowes saw no remedy to Lennox's political power, which Queen Elizabeth and her government increasingly feared, in part because they could not control James and regarded Lennox with fear and suspicion.[10]

Lennox, who had left a staunchly Catholic wife and children behind in France, faced a difficult situation. How could he fulfill his presumed obligation to his French supporters? He clearly understood, grasped, and used his ever-enlarging political power. Curiously, one of the persons whom he had been sent to help, namely Mary, looked upon him with suspicion. At any rate, Lennox must have found himself torn between his initial purpose and a young king who obviously worshiped him. To fulfill his plan would be to betray James, of whom he had become genuinely fond. He did, however, open communication with Mary and encouraged James to write to her. Such gestures led Mary in 1581 to proffer the idea of an "Association" in which she and James would jointly rule. Perhaps prompted by Lennox, James first favored the proposal. But his counselors were horrified, and eventually Lennox turned against the idea also. This episode offers a measure of how difficult his predicament was.[11]

While James and Lennox enjoyed each other's company at Stirling, Edinburgh, and other places during progresses, the Kirk of Scotland launched virulent attacks on Lennox, especially his Catholicism. Finally in 1580, James sent Lennox to Edinburgh for several months to be instructed by churchmen. James himself had spent much time with Lennox arguing and discussing theology. Clearly Lennox's future remained limited so long as he held to his Catholic faith. He did relent, under the sway of the Kirk, and announced that he had been converted to Protestantism. Such a decision thrilled James and only deepened his love for Lennox. The Kirk could not quite figure out how to respond: the man had accepted its religion, and it could not openly express doubt about his sincerity. Certainly his conversion looked suspiciously expedient, but we do know that he died a Protestant in France, to the chagrin of his wife. Perhaps James's love had indeed begun to affect him.

Jealous of their positions, power, and prerogatives, the lords of Scotland became alarmed by Lennox's power and his sway over the king. Little by little they began to collaborate in ways to get rid of Lennox. They were startled at how swiftly James, at Lennox's insistence, moved to try to execute the old earl of Morton, the former regent, in 1581. He had been accused by James Stewart, earl of Arran, of involvement in the plot to kill Darnley. Technically, he was innocent, though he surely knew about this plot. His execution struck terror in the noblemen. This episode probably reflected Lennox's power at its zenith; in fact, Morton had been one of the few remaining obstacles, and therefore Lennox was eager to have him removed. In small and large ways the lords sought to undercut that power.

One issue that rankled some at court was James's personal behavior with Lennox, though had Lennox not enjoyed increasing authority, these noblemen would probably have ignored the matter. One recalls the case of Edward II and his love for Gaveston. Whatever the noblemen's outrage about the presumed moral offense, the real issue was power—who would control the king. If the question is, did James and Lennox have a homosexual relationship, the answer is probably yes. Certainly some contemporaries thought that the nature of their relationship. The historian David Willson cites several sources. Moysie says that James "having conceived an inward affection to the Lord d'Aubigny [Lennox], entered in great familiarity and quiet purposes with him," a code for sexual relations. The clergyman John Hacket, in his *Scrinia Reserata,* says that James "from the time he was 14 Years old and no more, that is, when the Lord *Aubigny* came into *Scotland,* . . . even then he began . . . to clasp some one *Gratioso* in the Embraces of his great Love, above all others." The Scottish clergy declared "that the Duke of Lennox went about to draw the King to carnal lust."[12]

In any event, one cannot assess James's personal life and his family relationships without somehow confronting the matter of his homosexuality. That he preferred the company of attractive young men cannot be doubted. But many difficulties inhere in trying to define a person's sexuality in earlier centuries. To begin with, as John Boswell notes, the "word 'homosexual,' despite its air of antiquity, was actually coined in the late nineteenth century by German psychologists, [and] introduced into English only at the beginning of the present century." Although anachronistic, we use homosexual as a convenient term in discussing earlier periods. Building on Michel Foucault's multivolume *History of Sexuality* and other works, Bruce Smith skillfully examines homosexual desire as found in English Renaissance literature. He points out that "in the sixteenth and seventeenth centuries, sexuality was not, as it is for us, the starting point for anyone's self-definition. . . . No one in England during the sixteenth or seventeenth centuries would have thought of himself as 'gay' or 'homosexual' for the simple reason that those categories of self-definition did not exist." James would have been mystified by such terms. He himself used the term *sodomy* in *Basilicon Doron* as one of the crimes never to be forgiven. But one cannot be sure what James meant by that term, for Smith notes Simon Forman's example in which the word includes certain kinds of heterosexual acts as well.[13]

We do know that homosexual acts were forbidden and illegal. One need go no farther for evidence than Edinburgh in 1570 when two men accused of sodomy were burned at the stake. Alan Bray in a book that focuses on Renaissance England discusses society's strictures against homosexual acts. But he also demonstrates that homosexual practice existed with the tacit consent of the same society that condemned it. Smith puts the legal issues in perspective when he notes: "During the forty-five years of Elizabeth's reign and the twenty-three years of James I's reign only six men are recorded as having been indicted for sodomy in the Home County assizes. The record on convictions is even more astonishing. During the same sixty-eight-year period there was but one conviction for sodomy." Some act of violent abuse was apparently required before the legal system took much notice of homosexual practice.[14]

Eve Sedgwick has called attention to a whole range of same-sex relationships, which she defines as "homosocial"—a useful term to characterize James's lifelong interest in other men, not all of these relationships having a sexual dimension. Sedgwick hypothesizes, "In any male-dominated society, there is a special relationship between male homosocial (*including* homosexual) bonds and the institutions for maintaining and transmitting patriarchal power over women: a relationship founded on an inherent and potentially active structural congruence." This obviously does not mean that patriarchal societies necessarily give rise to male homosexuality; rather, the political and social institutions in such a society enable, encourage, and possibly require strong homosocial bonds. Certainly James's experience in Scotland and later in England bears this out. From infancy he lived in a male-dominated world. In an observation that has implications for James, Sedgwick notes, "The importance of women (not merely of 'the feminine' but of actual women as well) in the etiology and the continuing experience of male homosexuality is just as vexed a question as the importance of other men in male heterosexuality." James's relationships with his mother, his wife, Anne, and his cousin, Queen Elizabeth, demonstrate just how vexing the matter is. Smith offers this astute analysis: "In terms of the male power-structure of English Renaissance society, James' homosexuality may be the equivalent of Elizabeth's virginity: the erotic seal of men's political transactions with one another."[15]

Modern historians have been troubled by James's apparent homosexuality: some have ignored it, some have been coy, and some have acknowledged it. Willson offers what may be a representative judgment: "The two [James and Lennox] formed a striking contrast; the elegant French courtier and the awkward and ungainly lad. James did not learn good manners from d'Aubigny, whose influence was rather upon his character, his morals, his political philosophy. And without exception that influence was malignant." That seems a rather harsh judgment—after all Lennox treated James like an adult with love and respect. He opened James's starved life to the challenges and demands of love. Lennox made his share of mistakes, and something duplicitous governed some of his actions, but to find his influence on James as totally "malignant" skews the historical record itself. Certainly James himself would not agree that Lennox's effect on him was malignant. Godfrey Davies raises the troublesome issue in this way: "The King's extreme partiality for his favorites, and the unseemly embraces he bestowed on them in public, naturally has given rise to suspicions, or even charges, that his behavior in private was still worse." Reviewing the charge of a possible homosexual angle to the Gowrie conspiracy of 1600, Davies concludes: "Surely, however, on a candid review of the evidence, the verdict likely to be given when James is charged with unnatural vices is 'not guilty'—even 'not proven' seems unfair." Most recently, Maurice Lee claims that "whatever sexual element this love [between James and Lennox] contained was certainly subconscious." Clearly James's homosexuality does not define him, any more than some of his other attributes do; but to ignore the subject or to brush it aside quickly produces an incomplete history.[16]

Those opposed to Lennox came together in 1582 and waited for their chance to strike; they included James's former playmate the earl of Mar, Lord Lindsay, the master of Glamis, the earls of Glencairn, Bothwell, Angus, Gowrie, and others. Somewhat surprisingly, this group enjoyed the support of the Scottish Kirk. Stirred by rumors of Lennox's involvement in Catholic plots and by increasing animosity from church leaders, these men made their plans. Their opportunity came in late summer 1582. James and Lennox on progress to Perth in July planned some kind of countercoup to split the opposition; they parted company in early August, planning to rendezvous soon in Edinburgh.

The "Lords Enterprisers," as the conspirators called themselves, isolated James outside Perth while he was hunting; Gowrie invited James to rest at the castle of Ruthven. On the evening of August 22, James, sensing no trouble, accepted. But when he tried to leave the next morning, several of the lords barred his way in an ironic reversal of hospitality. James may have felt like Duncan welcomed into the hospitable confines of Macbeth's castle. Lulled into a false sense of security, James now found himself a trapped prisoner. He screamed, he wept, he cursed—all to no avail. The lord of Ruthven had been successful.

The conspirators had driven a wedge between James and Lennox: that which they could not accomplish by any other means they succeeded in doing by trickery and brute force. James would never see Lennox again. Lennox had fled to Dumbarton for safety; James fully expected Lennox to rescue him, but that never happened. The Lords Enterprisers insisted that James require Lennox to leave Scotland. James, powerless, acquiesced. Reports from Bowes back to England reveal that those who saw James realized that his love for Lennox had not abated: "He [James] keipeth his affecion still fastened to the duke." George Carey reported similarly to Burghley, having seen James on September 12. James would not allow his soul to be captured; and surely he and Lennox, who established secret communication, believed that Lennox at some point in the future would be recalled to Scotland. On December 21, Lennox began his journey toward France, first going to England. He felt altogether destitute, devoid of friends and supporters, no longer a power in Scotland, banished from the presence of one whom he clearly loved.[17]

Two poignant letters survive that Lennox wrote immediately before his departure in December. He was worried that James had begun to believe the terrible stories being told about his faithlessness: he feared the loss of James's love. He wrote to James on December 18: "For whatever might happen to me, I shall always be your very faithful servant; and although there might be still this misfortune that you might wish to banish me from your good graces, yet in spite of all you will be always my true master, and he alone in this world whom my heart is resolved to serve. And would to God that my breast might be split open so that it might be seen what is engraven therein." Lennox continued, "I have such extreme regret that I desire to die rather than to live, fearing that that has been the occasion of your no longer loving me." He closed the letter by asking some favors, "out of love to me (if you still love me a little)." Clearly, both men felt deeply and painfully the effect of their separation and Lennox's impending banishment.[18]

With James imprisoned and Lennox banished to France, they faced a bleak midwinter indeed. Each bided his time, waiting to be reunited. Henry Cobham reported to Walsingham in England on February 11, 1583: "The bishop of St. Andrews has written to D'Aubigny that the King continues his affection to him, having of late drunk to him, when none of the lords standing by would seem to like thereof; wherewith the King moved after he had drunk, and hurled the rest over his shoulder." Broken by his experiences and largely spurned in his native France, Lennox eventually succumbed to illness and died on May 26, 1583. Lennox's last letter to James, no longer extant, actually arrived after his death. James was incredulous at reports of Lennox's death and unable to accept the possibility.

Those around him were reluctant to provide confirmation. Finally, James accepted Lennox's death. In early summer, still a virtual prisoner and now dispossessed forever of Lennox, James must have looked out and seen only winter. He felt terribly alone. A powerful and poignant silence now ruled his heart.[19]

Whatever self-pity existed, James did not indulge it long. To his credit, part of his response to Lennox's death was to devise a plan of escape from his captors. Just days after his seventeenth birthday in June 1583, James skillfully gave his captors the slip, they having grown lax about security. He rallied supporters and former friends of Lennox at St. Andrews and reasserted his authority. After ten months of captivity, he outsmarted the jealous Protestant lords, who fled when they realized what had happened. What an education James had received about the consequences of love and about the difficulty of ruling the Scottish lords. As part of his political revenge, James invited the nine-year-old son of Lennox, Ludovic Stuart, to Scotland to claim his father's rights. The son arrived in November and became a mainstay of the court until his death in 1624.

In the fall of 1583, James completed the grief process by writing a poem, entitled *Phoenix*, about Lennox. James, who for the rest of his life would have trouble confronting death, found a medium through which to discharge his feelings. In this elaborate allegory James likened Lennox to the phoenix, which has female identity. By choosing a female bird to represent his love for Lennox, James may simply have been trying to cloud the topicality of the poem. Such a choice may also reflect some sexual confusion on James's part: that is, an unwillingness or inability to confront the homoerotic feelings for his French cousin, at least in artistic expression. One recalls, for example, how Michelangelo struggled with his homosexual feelings, sometimes using his art or public statements to conceal his actual feelings, recognizing the difficulty of public scrutiny of his private life. Later, Michelangelo's great-nephew for publication purposes changed the genders in his uncle's poetry to deflect their erotic nature toward women.[20]

James refers to his tale as "Ane Tragedie" about death. "But I lament my *Phoenix* rare," the poet says. He describes the qualities of this wonderful bird and its arrival "into this land" and how he encountered her, "I knew that she was sum / Rare stranger foule." But the admiration that this bird has stirred in others changes to envy. James clearly alludes to his and Lennox's enemies. In the fiction of the poem he names three of them: "Thir ware, the *Rauin*, the *Stain-*

*chell*, & the *Gled*, / With other kynds, whome in this malice bred"—
apparent references to the earls of Angus, Gowrie, and Mar. The
bird becomes their "commoun prey." In the central stanza the poet
claims that the bird came to him for safe refuge.

> Yet they followed fast
> Till she betuix my leggs her selfe did cast,
> For saving her from these, which her opprest,
> Whose hote pursute, her suffred not to rest.

The poet suffers with the bird, "Whyles they made to bleid / My
leggs." Finally the bird flees and goes homeward. The poet eagerly
awaits news of her fate and learns of her death, "Whose end dois
now begin / My woes: her death makes lyfe to greif in me." He
lashes at the devils of darkness that have caused this tragedy. But in
the final stanza of the main poem, the poet alludes to the offspring
of the phoenix (Ludovic Stuart). In "L'envoy" James sees the potential comedy arising from this tragedy: "Let them be now, to make
ane *Phoenix* new / Even of this worme of *Phoenix* ashe which grew."
If this happens, "My tragedie a comike end will have."[21]

No one else in James's life prompted such a poetic response from
him. We may call it adolescent sentimentality, if we like, but something powerful and stirring flows through this poem. The author
has cased in his fiction profound feelings for one whom he loved
and lost—this one, like the phoenix, who brought so much color
into his life. Reading James's poem makes it all the more difficult to
refer to Lennox as a totally "malignant" influence on James. James's
*Phoenix* recalls a lament of many centuries earlier: David's response
to the deaths of Saul and Jonathan in 1 Samuel 1:1–27. David wrote a
poem and commanded that it should be taught to the people:

> O Jonathan, laid low in death!
> I grieve for you, Jonathan my brother;
> dear and delightful you were to me;
> your love for me was wonderful,
> surpassing the love of women. (verses 25–26)

Through the skillful allegory of *Phoenix*, James documents the wonderful love he has known, cut short by brute force and malice. Out
of heartache he created compelling poetry.

Even at the height of his involvement with Lennox, James, a man
of seemingly unending contradictions, had been attracted to James
Stewart, earl of Arran. Arran and Lennox vied for James's attention. Eventually James succeeded in reconciling the two, and Arran

became allied with Lennox. Arran was handsome, assertive, dashing, and also "arrogant and rapacious," as Akrigg calls him. James never had an intense relationship with him, but he did name him his chief minister after the successful escape in 1583—an unfortunate political choice. Queen Elizabeth helped engineer Arran's downfall and replacement in 1585.[22]

Later in the decade James again linked up with an unreliable lord, this time the Catholic George Gordon, earl of Huntly. Even when James learned in February 1589 that Huntly was part of a group of Scottish Catholic lords who had written to Phillip II of Spain promising help should he invade Scotland, he imposed only minor punishment. Thomas Fowler reported to Walsingham on March 1, 1589: "The next day the King went to the castle to dinner, where he entertained Huntly as well and kindly as ever, yea he kissed him at times to the amazement of many." Two weeks later Fowler observed that the "King hath a strange, extraordinary affection to Huntly, such as is yet unremoveable." In a long letter James instructed Huntly on how to repent his faults because "ye have offended two persons in me, a particular friend and a general Christian king." A string of rhetorical questions focuses on Huntly's disloyalty. James wrote, "How many million of times, and specially that night in the cabinet, after that suspicion among you in the abbey, did I not then, I say, amongst innumerable other times resolve you that ye could not both trow [trust] me and those busy reporters about you." Despite Huntly's attractiveness and his nod in the direction of religious conversion, James eventually had to face Huntly's disloyalty. Even so, Huntly, charged with treason, received a light sentence, to the chagrin of Elizabeth and the Scottish Kirk. Certainly neither Arran nor Huntly ever served or loved James as devotedly as Lennox had. James's personal desires and interests clearly interfered with political judgment; in part James paid the political price of his desire for love. His life resonates with the irony of frustrated and irreconcilable desires.[23]

James was no more successful in resolving problems with Mary, his mother. He found himself in a dilemma from which he could not easily emerge unscathed. The parent-child relationship fascinates in part because most of it evolved over long distance and separation. As noted earlier, before James was a year old, his mother had left him, forced to abdicate in his favor. She assumed for a long time that her son would by some means rescue her from English imprisonment and that she might be restored to the Scottish throne. In the vast silence of their lives, James nevertheless heard some voices, especially the sirenlike call of the English throne. He came to understand that such a prize might well be within his grasp; two women constituted the only major obstacles: Elizabeth and his mother. In the events that unfold in the 1580s, one has difficulty in determining who desired Mary's death more—Elizabeth or James.

To the portraits of the young precocious boy and the teenage lover trying to negotiate the minefields of love and politics we can add the James who reached adult status in the mid-1580s. The decade of the 1580s included the loss of Lennox, the execution of Mary, and marriage to Anne. Probably no other decade in James's personal life surpassed this one in importance. We catch a wonderful picture of James in 1584 in the report by the Frenchman, Fontenay, who had been on a mission for Mary. He visited James in Scotland and wrote a long letter to Mary, appending his most trenchant analysis in a secret note to his brother-in-law Nau. The document, dating from August 15, 1584, incisively assesses James's strengths and liabilities and reveals much about the mother-son relationship.

Fontenay touches on everything from James's physical qualities to his mental skills. He asserts that James has "three parts of the soul in perfection. He grasps and understands quickly; he judges carefully and with reasonable discourses; he restrains himself well and for long." Fontenay admires James's knowledge and his facility in languages but notes his awkwardness in manners, especially "in the company of women." Although still fearful of the great lords, James nevertheless "likes very much to be considered brave and to be feared." James likes hunting "above all the pleasures of this world," and he hates dancing and music. In light of what we already know about James, he has a somewhat peculiar or misguided moral streak: he hates "all wantonness at Court, be it in discourses of love or in curiosity of habits, not being about to see above all *ear-rings.*" Perhaps the result of a childhood illness, "his gait is bad, composed of erratic steps, and he tramps about even in his room." Although he has a weak body, he "is in no wise delicate." "In short, to tell you in one word, he is an old young man"—the aging process doubtless aggravated by his responsibilities and fearful experiences.[24]

According to Fontenay, James has three bad qualities that impair his rule: "The first is his ignorance and lack of knowledge of his poverty and his little strength, promising too much of himself. . . . The second, that he loves indiscretely and inadvisedly in spite of his subjects. . . . The third is that he is too lazy and too thoughtless over his affairs, too willing and devoted to his pleasure, especially hunting." If the English had wanted to know about the effect of James's personality on his rule, they need have looked no farther

An imagined scene of James and his mother Mary, Queen of Scots (1583). Courtesy of His Grace the Duke of Atholl, Blair Castle.

than this perceptive commentary of 1584; they would come to say precisely the same things about James in the seventeenth century. Only one thing truly astonished Fontenay during his interview with James: "He has never inquired anything of the Queen [Mary] or of her health, or her treatment, her servants, her living and eating, her recreation, or anything similar." In the presence of an official emissary from his mother, James had nothing to say or to ask about her. Small wonder that the Frenchman found such silence astonishing. We might share that incredulity.

The silent portraits of James and Mary that stare at us from the anonymous fanciful painting of 1583 (from the collection of the duke of Atholl at Blair Castle) reveal, perhaps unwittingly, much about the mother-son relationship. Obviously, as Jonathan Goldberg has noted, one face served as model for both. They seem interchangeable, inextricably linked to one another and therefore in a sense indistinguishable, rather like Rosencrantz and Guildenstern in *Hamlet*. The son is the mirror of his mother and vice versa. How appropriate that the crown seems to float between them as if capable of lighting on one or the other. And, of course, in 1583 that issue seemed as yet unresolved: Mary was queen of Scotland, and James was king of Scotland and actually ruling (perhaps indicated by his hand's grasping a sword). The identical smiles of mother and son hint at some kind of secret, but ironically not one shared. In the picture James, though an adolescent, is larger than Mary—again perhaps the artist's rendering of who actually had power. Interestingly, they do not look at one another but at some unseen third object. This mythical painting of a presumed meeting of mother and son underscores what we already know: the eyes look elsewhere, the mouths are closed, and silence reigns. The First Gentleman reports of the reunion of father (Leontes) and daughter (Perdita) in *The Winter's Tale:* "There was speech in their dumbness, language in their very gesture." This "dumb" picture of Mary and James does speak about the distance and silence of their relationship.[25]

Mother and son corresponded somewhat regularly, as extant letters demonstrate. But in this correspondence cordiality and sincerity ebb and flow. Genuine affection seems ready to burst through, only to be dashed by some real or imagined slight that leads to pique. As noted earlier, Mary wrote to the countess of Mar and sent along books to assist James in learning to read and write. She also wrote to James in January 1570 and sent him a book to help him learn arithmetic. More important, these tangible reminders came from her with the desire that he should remember and honor her, his "loving moder." She reminds him that she gave birth to him, "Hir yat [that] hes borne zow in hir sydes." Mary even wrote Elizabeth in 1571, wishing that she might hear from her child, who should fulfill his duty.[26]

A report in 1579 illustrates how James sometimes reacted to the letters: "[James] stormed vehemently thereat; insomuch as they would neither entertaine those haughty Letters, nor messenger; both because that instead of writing to the King, she had writ to the Prince, as in diminution to his authority, especially seeing the King was lawfully enthroned by her consent." By January 1581, James wrote to thank his mother for a ring that she had sent and referred to the "honour and the duty" that he owes her. He also made a point of signing the letter "Jaques R." In a letter of August 17, 1581, James claimed to be pleased to learn that Mary was in better health and offered assurance: "I will always bear you the honour and duty that I owe you, and I will obey you in everything that it pleases you to honour me with your commandments." Duty may exist in the eye of the beholder. One catches a hint of the formulaic nature of some of this writing, especially from James.[27]

At the instigation of her French supporters, Mary in 1581 floated the idea of an "Association" in which she and James would share the rule of Scotland. Given that Lennox enjoyed the height of power and influence at that time and that he sympathized with Mary, the plan received serious consideration well into 1582; but resistance built, and the plan did not materialize. The demands of his mother and his love of Lennox pulled James in different directions. Mary wrote in April 1582, wishing again that she might visit James. She complained about the irregularity of their correspondence: "My dear son, the state in which I have been thirteen years heretofore without having had almost any news from you nor you of mine." For some reason feeling kindly disposed toward Elizabeth, Mary urged James to regard Elizabeth "as to your second mother." Perhaps this admonition only reminds us how cheap words could become. After all, James and Mary were, practically speaking, strangers, who— despite being nearest of kin—knew no reinforcement of common living. Their love, however understood, experienced a breach.[28]

James did respond to Mary in a letter dated May 28, 1582. He had apparently just received several letters from her, including the April one. He wrote explicitly about the Association idea of joint rule, and he insisted that he would "follow the overtures that it has pleased you to make touching our union and association." But he wanted the plan spelled out in detail in writing; then James would "cause the lords of my Council to consent thereto." That, of course, did not happen. He noted the recent reconciliation of Lennox and Arran: "Both [will] strive for the accomplishment of our union, you being able to assure yourself of not having anyone in Scotland who may be more affectionate." James closed the main part of the letter by praying God "that he will give you happy and long life." Hesitancy and events—James's capture and Lennox's banishment— spelled temporary doom for the Association.[29]

But that did not keep Mary from continuing to push the idea, as we learn from documents of the French court in January 1583. Bowes provides an even more detailed account in a report to Walsingham, dated May 1, 1583. In a long interview, the ambassador and the king discussed the concept of the Association and all the various strings that Mary had attached to it. James began to realize that not only would Mary be equal to him in authority but also she would "have the chief place before him"; this James regarded as dangerous. He insisted that his mother had initiated the whole idea of the Association and that Lennox, reading over the proposals, had begun to perceive problems in what she outlined. Lennox had explored the gap between James's meaning and what Mary actually proposed. James also recalled that "he should be a suitor and mean to her Majesty [Elizabeth] for his mother's liberty" and that "he should not marry without the advices of her Majesty and herself [Mary]." James assured Bowes, knowing that his words would speedily travel to Elizabeth, that he understood that by "his mother's offers . . . she seeketh to have a quality and joint interest with him in those weighty matters, and prefereth herself before him in the same, with such prejudice and danger to him and his estate as he cannot agree to join with her therein." James's position became that the Association would not exist. Mary would take longer to come to this recognition.[30]

After crying out about her miserable conditions and expressing concern for her son, Mary in an interview with William Wand in April 1584 responded to various questions about her son by saying "that she knew nothing of her son's doings." She spoke more truly than she perhaps intended. Each at great distance tried to interpret the other, having only letters and reports from visitors. Even if there was no deceit intended on either side, misunderstandings could easily occur. In a letter to his mother, tentatively dated July 1584, James refers to the visit of Fontenay and takes delight in "the incomprehensible maternal affection that it pleases you to continue in my respect." We may take that statement with some irony if James refers to the visit discussed earlier in this chapter, the visit in which James never asked anything about his mother—a silence noted by Fontenay. James becomes enthusiastic about the Association ("our perfect union and association") and goes into some detail about how he will prepare his subjects for the ratification of the proposal. He will send to her a statement of his intentions and also "require of the Queen of England your deliverance, for which I wish above all the happiness of this world." He closes by wishing for her a long and happy life in perfect health. Many of these words will ironically reverberate through history.[31]

In March 1585, James concluded with his council that the Association idea was dead. Archibald Douglas reported the decision: the "Association desired by his mother should not be granted nor spoken of hereafter." As Antonia Fraser observes, "At first Mary, in her pathetic desire to protect the image of her son in her own mind, even tried to persuade herself that the betrayal could be blamed on Gray." She threatened to disinherit James and give his crown to someone else. Fraser records the passionate postscript that Mary added to a letter: "I am so grievously offended at my heart at the impiety and ingratitude that my child has been constrained to commit against me, by this letter which Gray made him write." James's apparent support of the Association, documented in his letter of just a few months earlier, evaporated like a sudden summer shower. Mary had reason to feel betrayed. Fraser concludes, "But in the delicate game of Anglo-Scottish relations, James had discovered that whereas he held some of the cards and Elizabeth held some of the others Mary held none at all." Through her copious tears Mary doubtless saw the handwriting on the wall: James would betray her if it suited his purpose. The Association matter became—in retrospect—a kind of dry run for Mary's trial. Not only had Mary lost an important political struggle, she also lost her illusion about her only child. During the summer of 1585 she cried out that her son was a usurper and that he had dealt with her "unkindly" by his letters. " 'Yet,' said she, 'the love of a mother is tender.' " Those final words sound like a desperate attempt to hang on to an idealized view of the mother-child relationship. Like her son at Ruthven in 1582, Mary, also imprisoned, must have felt utterly alone, seeing no exit from the predicament and tortured by the recognition of her son's "impiety and ingratitude."[32]

For Mary, of course, things went from bad to worse—1586 sealed her fate. An amusing incident in February 1586 may shed light on the political context in Scotland in which James now functioned. He ordered the ministers of Edinburgh to pray for his mother and for her deliverance. They refused. Finally James appointed the archbishop of St. Andrews to preach in St. Giles Cathedral in Edinburgh, but the archbishop found the pulpit occupied by John Cowper, who threatened the king when ordered to step down. "There arose a wonderful cry in the church, chiefly by the women. They rose from their stools and cried to the King, Oh! God, what is this?" With the help of guards the archbishop gained a place in the pulpit. "He prays for the Queen according to command. He kept close to the King's heels, afraid of being stoned." Prayers rose up for Mary amid a disgruntled rabble of people.[33]

While ordering that prayers be offered for the release of his mother, James took practical and economic steps to assure his own survival, regardless of what would happen to Mary. We can call James's action political cunning or unfeeling betrayal, and we would be correct. In July 1586, authorities signed a formal alliance between England and Scotland. It guaranteed James a yearly pension of £4,000 from Elizabeth (he had expected £5,000) and, more important, tacitly assured him of a clear claim to the English throne. Such political actions helped make his mother increasingly irrelevant. Instead of an Association with Mary, there would be an alliance with Elizabeth. James had chosen what he saw as the future.

Mary's approval of the "Babington Plot," a plan by insistent Catholics to assassinate Elizabeth and free Mary, determined her final destiny. Unknown to her, all her correspondence was read and made known to Walsingham and his forces. No secrets existed. She had been set up and trapped. On August 3, 1586, Mary was arrested for plotting against the life of Elizabeth. Not foreseeing the potential danger to his mother, James wrote to Walsingham on September 9 and praised him for exposing "foul conspiracies as have been of late haply discovered amongst you." The French ambassador to Scotland, Courcelles, reported to his king on October 4 of James's railing against his mother, whom he loved "as much as nature and dutie bounde him." He accused her of trying to unseat him. His conclusion: "It was meete for her to medle with nothinge but prayer and servinge of God." By October 15, Mary stood trial at Fotheringhay Castle, and she was soon found guilty.[34]

James sent emissaries, such as Patrick Gray and William Keith, to intervene in behalf of his convicted mother; but he also sent conflicting signals, letting Elizabeth and her government understand that there would be no severe repercussions should Mary be executed. In Scotland, James threatened revenge if anything happened to his mother, at one point asserting that he and five thousand would "revenge his Grace's mother's scaith." The lords undergirded James's vengeful resolve. Enraged at one point by the accusation that he had not acted forcefully enough to protect his mother, James retorted: "For proof how I have in every thing discharged my duty towards her, our correspondence since my succession to the throne shall be laid before the highest tribunal of this realm, and copied." No evidence survives that he ever made good on this boast. In fact, the whole thing looks like an empty theatrical gesture which James could make with reasonable confidence that no one would dare call his bluff. No risk existed that these secret and private letters would be offered to a public audience that might disseminate them. Such action would violate a cardinal principle of James's understanding of kingship: the necessity of secrets. As James once wrote to Elizabeth, "For ye know dead letters cannot answer no questions."[35]

James wrote the earl of Leicester twice in December 1586 seeking his assistance. In the letter of December 15, James laid bare his concern: to protect his claim to the English throne. He denied any knowledge of his mother's complicity in foreign plots; indeed, he emphasized, "My religion ever moved me to hate her course, although my honour constrains me to insist for her life." In a statement of revealing and bracing honesty James wrote: "How fond [foolish] and inconstant I were if I should prefer my mother to the title let all men judge." Although James was not a party to any effort on Mary's part to snatch the English throne ("the title"), the statement also seems to say that James would be foolish to prefer his mother over his own claim to the title. Goldberg reminds us, "There can be no such thing as an unambiguous expression of power, for it is precisely in ambiguity that power resides." The French ambassador in a late December dispatch made clear that James would make no move to revenge unless the queen "deprive him of his right to that crowne." Mary's death, the ambassador reported, "though it may be greevouse unto him, [the Scots] may . . . with such occassyones as time may presente, excuse the execution"—the time-heals-all-wounds syndrome, in this case masking cold-blooded calculation. Leicester's letter of December 31 reinforced what James had already perceived: "If what I hear is true, Mary's will would dispossess you, both of the crown of Scotland and of your claim to that of England." He confirmed James's judgment: "Her case is not worth the losing of such a friend as the Queen of England, and her friendship may easily be had and kept, and also easily lost." These haunting if honest words rang out the old year of 1586 and spelled the doom that awaited Mary in early 1587.[36]

James wrote Elizabeth one final time, January 26, 1587, in an attempt to have her spare his mother's life, a letter striking for its dispassionate tone. One recalls Troilus's complaint, "Words, words, mere words, no matter from the heart." The letter scored debater's points in urging Elizabeth to be a merciful ruler when mercy is least expected and reminded her of the moral and legal precedent that would be set if she executed another sovereign. In a moment of special pleading he insisted on his constancy in these matters and said, "I pray you not to take me to be a chameleon." Mary had another perspective. Even as James's January letter made its way to Elizabeth, Mary told any who would listen that "her saide son, and all that ar dealaris in his effairis, [are] oppen leyarris and dowble dealarris." Though separated by hundreds of miles and not communicating with one another, mother and son nevertheless responded to the same topic simultaneously: James insisting that he is no chameleon, and Mary calling him a liar and a double dealer.[37]

Nothing could now prevent her execution. In a scene replete

with theatrical implications Mary, dressed in black, on the morning of February 8 made her way to the appointed scaffold. Fraser's long description captures the scene superbly. In some accounts Mary asks to be remembered to her son. After speeches and prayers the inevitable moment had come: Mary lowered her head on the block, and the executioner's blade claimed her life. The nightmare of her soul had ended; she was released from the prison of this world. As news of her execution reached London, "bells were rung from all the churches for 24 hours, and towards evening bonfires were lighted in the streets . . . at every corner and cross-road."[38]

No bonfires burned in Edinburgh—only momentary fires of passion. Lord Scrope reported to Walsingham on February 21, 1587, that when James understood the message that "his mother was in truth put to death, he not only took that news very grievously and offensively, but also gave out in secret speeches that he could not digest the same or leave it unrevenged." Other accounts paint a rather different picture of James's reaction. Pury Ogilive observed to Archibald Douglas, March 2: *"Last of all I will assure you that the King moved never his countenance at the rehearsal of his mother's execution, nor leaves not his pastime and hunting more than of before."* David Calderwood said: "When the king heard of the executioun, he could not conceale his inward joy, howbeit outwardlie he seemed to be sorrowfull. . . . He said that night to some few that were beside him, 'I am now sole king.' " When Elizabeth wrote to him on February 14 about "that miserable accident which farre contrary to my meening hath bene befallen" and insisted on her innocence, James responded demurely in a late February letter and accepted her explanation. He continued to thrash about for a while threatening revenge, but he put on black mourning clothes instead of a sword, as many had urged.[39]

James had no intention of avenging his mother's death; he had truly come to desire it. A manuscript document in fact outlines James's reasons for not responding to his mother's death with force, beginning with a reference to "my tendre youth not trained up in dexteritie of Armes." James noted also, "the divers factions of Spirituall and Morall Estats every one regarding himselfe and not me." He had been counseled for the sake of the security of his estate not to avenge Mary's execution. Such security "could never have bene without factions if she had beene left alive." Finally, James commented on "the puisance of England which may worke a contrarie faction of my owne subjectes against all my intentes." This realistic political assessment confirms James's reticence. Whatever filial affection he may have felt for this mother-stranger who sent books for him to learn reading and arithmetic and sent gifts of rings and saddles had long since vanished. He would build no fire of revenge; he would remain silent.[40]

With Mary dead and his path thereby eased toward the English throne, James nevertheless remained troubled by her execution and his part in it. His reaction all the way through 1612 suggests that he could not readily assuage his guilt about her. No longer a force in his personal and political life, she lingered in his psychological life as he attempted in several ways to revise history to suit the image of himself as a dutiful son. Here we find another example of James's attempt to impose his fiction on the world, a sign of his authority and power, and to create a romantic narrative to replace the tragic and damning world. James the writer and poet would represent himself in a new familial fiction as a son who valiantly tried to save his mother. It may be that James came to think more kindly about his mother after her death. Of course, as noted earlier, James had little basis for knowing how to be a son, how to respond to parents: that part of family existence remained a vacuum to him. Thus, somewhat surprisingly, in 1596 James took exception to part of Edmund Spenser's *The Faerie Queene*. Books 4 through 6 of the poem appeared that year, and James thought an episode in book 5 insulted his mother.

The English ambassador, Bowes, reported to Burghley on November 12, 1596:

> The King has conceived great offense against Edward [*sic*] Spenser (Spencer) publishing in print in the second part of the Fairy Queen and 9th chapter some dishonourable effects (as the King deems thereof) against himself and his mother deceased. He alleged that this book was passed with privilege of her Majesty's Commissioners. . . . But therein I have (I think) satisfied him that it is not given out with such privilege. Yet he still desires that Edward Spenser for this fault may be duly tried and punished.

This remarkable document lets us know, if nothing else, that James as a reader of poetic texts fancied himself an interpreter of literature. Also, the reaction reveals that James would assert his authority as king. The politics of the family required that he protect the memory of his mother, albeit after the fact. The document demonstrates his vigilance to any slight; and James's reaction casts a suspicious eye toward Elizabeth, who seems to have countenanced the poem: after all, she is the Fairy Queen of the poem in its allegorical development.[41]

The offending passage comes in book 5, canto 9, stanzas 25–50.

The scene focuses on the trial of Duessa (presumably Mary) presided over by Mercilla (Elizabeth). James made the topical identification and smarted from it. The prisoner Duessa enters in stanza 38, "A Ladie of great countenance and place, /. . . But blotted with condition vile and base." Zeal presents the charges against her, the "many haynous crymes" of which she is guilty, especially her attempt to deprive "*Mercilla* of her crowne, by her aspyred, / That she [Duessa] might it unto her selfe deryve." That in a nutshell is the critical issue of Mary's trial of October 1586. Allegorical representations of Murder, Sedition, Incontinency, Adultery, and Impiety confront her in a spirit of recognition. The trial breaks off as Mercilla withdraws— recall Elizabeth's "absence" from Mary's trial. In canto 10 we learn of the decision to execute Duessa. Goldberg argues that in 1596, "James wished to extend his innocence to his mother; having sacrificed her, he now wished to redeem her—at the poet's expense." Kill the messenger, James seems to say, as if somehow by punishing the poet Spenser, James would be absolved of his complicity and guilt. The poet remained free to speak the truth, though James desired to revise history to suit his own image.[42]

When James wrote his *Basilicon Doron* in 1599 as a guidebook of rule for his son Prince Henry, he alluded to his mother. In the address "To the Reader," which appeared first in the 1603 edition, James asserted that he never found any subjects so "stedfastly true to me in al my troubles, as these that constantly kept their alleageance to her in her time." James's memory failed him, or else he again revised history. Catholic sympathizers of Mary regularly caused problems for James. For Henry's edification James contrasted his marriage to Anne with the marriage of his grandfather James V, "the reward of his incontinencie." His grandfather left behind a double curse: "both a Woman of sexe, & a newe borne babe of age to raigne over them." He thereby referred to Mary. Interestingly, James made no comment about Mary's disastrous marriages—perhaps again an attempt to erase that memory. He boasted to Henry, "I have ever thoght it the duetie of a worthie Prince, rather with a pike, then a pen, to write his just revenge." James did not think so in 1587. Even in *Basilicon Doron* James could not resist the "write/right" pun. For James, writing made right: the pen, not the pike, would work revenge for his mother's horror. The pen enabled the king to impose a fiction on the world, whereas the pike would have required action in the world. These references to his mother indicate that something disquieting about her rankled James's soul.[43]

When James wrote William Keith in November 1586, he used an

image that captures much of the essence of his relationship to Elizabeth: "And would God she might see the inward parts of my heart where she should see a great jewel of honesty toward her locked up in a coffer of perplexity, she only having the key which by her good behaviour in this case may open the same." James put his finger on the central question of interpretation, as he and Elizabeth each tried to fathom the other. In his "Chinese-box" metaphor, one has to penetrate the heart, then find the "jewel of honesty," only to discover that it is "locked up in a coffer of perplexity." Presumably Elizabeth possessed the key, but that remains doubtful. James raised to a high art the posture of inscrutability: it exists as a means of defining his power. Ambiguity and contradictions characterize statecraft. Elizabeth also greatly desired to control her cousin; their alliance of July 1586 assured that she had James basically where she wanted him, while he received monetary benefits and clear access to the English title. As early as 1573, the young child wrote to Elizabeth as the "Princess under God whom he most leaneth unto for help."[44]

Patrick Gray reported to Elizabeth in January 1585 that James's disposition "at this time is such to your majesty as though he were your natural son." We recall Mary's admonition that James should regard Elizabeth as his "second mother." In some of his letters James indeed addressed Elizabeth in that style. In August 1585, for example, James referred to her as "Madame and mother" and closed the letter, "Your most loving and devoted brother and son, James R." He begged her in another letter "to continue still my loving mother as I shall be your devoted son." More often he referred to her as "sister." The point remains: James saw or sought some kind of close familial relationship with his cousin: he endowed her with characteristics of a nurturing mother or caring sister, neither of which he had. Typical of James, he seemed rather confused about human relationships. Of course, in one sense Elizabeth could possibly have been mother, sister, and cousin simultaneously—at least as a fiction in James's mind, in the same way that Elizabeth in Spenser's *Faerie Queene* could be represented as the Fairy Queen, Belphoebe, and Mercilla all in the same poem as different manifestations of the same person. But in actual, familial relationships one might be expected to clarify the other person's status.[45]

In many ways Elizabeth functioned as surrogate family for one who knew neither father nor mother, brother nor sister. We remind ourselves that James's image of the queen came as the product of discourse—letters exchanged, messages sent. Having never met his cousin, James created an image of her, rather as he had of his own mother, through documents that came to him—the raw materials that fed his imagination. In a 1586 document in which Elizabeth assured James of an annual pension and of his potential claim to the English throne, she also used familial terms, claiming to have had "a speciall and motherlye cair over our said darrest brother and cousing ever since his byrthe, respecting him as our owne sone." When James made the political decision to abandon Mary's idea of Association and to embrace the alliance with England, he essentially accepted the mother-substitute in preference to his natural mother. This accounts at least in part for his silence concerning his mother's trial and execution.[46]

This issue gains another interesting dimension when we discover that in August 1586 James had apparently made an offer of marriage to Elizabeth. In a long discussion with Archibald Douglas on the subject of marriage, James said: "It is true that of ourself we were never minded to make marriage suddenly, unless it might produce surety to her Majesty's state and apparent benefit to that whole realm. Which we think might best have been performed, if it might have liked her Majesty of the completing of that marriage with herself whereunto we could never find her inclined." James told Douglas to pass along such secret information to the earl of Leicester. The twenty-year-old James seriously, one assumes, proposed marriage to the fifty-three-year-old Elizabeth, underscoring that when they occur, royal marriages take place for political reasons. This same August, Mary had been charged with treason and was facing a trial. No event more clearly reflects James's calculated abandonment of his natural mother and his attempt to ingratiate himself further with Elizabeth. Since James never met Elizabeth, he seemed to have trouble deciding whether she was his sister, mother, or possible wife. She existed as a political reality but otherwise as an idealized figment of his imagination. One can never be quite sure which one, James or Elizabeth, resided in a "coffer of perplexity."[47]

Another major chapter of James's life opened in 1589: his marriage to Anne of Denmark. One historian claims, "King James's marriage to Anne of Denmark in 1589, the one romantic episode of his life, forms a human and pleasant interlude in the turmoil and self-seeking of his reign in Scotland." Scarcely can the marriage to Anne be regarded as the "one romantic episode" in James's life in Scotland; nor, as we shall see, can that marriage be accurately or completely defined as a "pleasant interlude." That very much depends at what moment one tries to capture that relationship. As James had his irreconcilable conflicts of conscience in his relationships with Mary and Elizabeth, much the same can be claimed for his life with Anne. Early 1589, as we recall, had seen James's fascination with the treasonous Huntly. Only by the summer had James decided to proceed with marriage, a decision largely governed by politics and economics.[48]

James's counselors had been urging marriage for some time—as early as 1582—in order to bring additional stability to the kingdom with the possibility of a royal family, hence natural successors to James as rulers of Scotland. These advisers sensed a vulnerability to their sovereign without a supporting cast of immediate royal family—a problem no less acute south of their border in England, where Elizabeth's counselors increasingly agonized over the succession issue. In 1587 James took some preliminary action by dispatching emissaries, one to Denmark and one to France, "to treat upon a matche to the king." The king did this on March 26, Calderwood says, "whill as yitt the memorie of the executioun of his mother was recent in men's mindes." This action confirms the view that his mother's death had in part a liberating effect on James. He seemed unready to confront the question of marriage until his mother no longer existed as an immediate personal and political problem for him. Perhaps James had something specifically in mind when he later wrote to his son on the subject of marriage in the *Basilicon Doron,* "First of all consider, that Mariage is the greatest earthly felicitie or miserie, that can come to a man." Certainly his marriage to Anne seems another of those ironic experiences: unfulfilled hopes that fall far short of the ideal or of expectation. Life for James often seems to have been lived in the gap between idealized concept and reality; the form of life never quite suits the conceit.[49]

By late spring 1589 James and his advisors had focused on two likely candidates: the countess of Navarre of France and Anne. Thomas Fowler in a report to Walsingham outlined the relative merits—for example, each had money—but rather favored Navarre because she was older and might be able to control James's prodigal spending. William Asheby told Walsingham on July 22 that James "is but a cold wooer," making it difficult to know whether he is hastening or delaying the negotiations. Asheby accurately reported: "He is not hasty of marriage, but will match with the Danes to please his boroughs and merchants." One notes with interest that the discussions often referred to the possibility of James's marrying either "Denmark" or "France." Such designations reveal much about the nature of royal marriages because matters of politics, dynasty, and money govern the arrangements. James's bride would be marrying Scotland as well as James. A good marriage meant one that involved a substantial dowry and one in which the king did not marry beneath his station.[50]

A charming, but probably doubtful, story from Sir James Melville has James withdrawing for fifteen days of contemplation and devout prayer only to emerge and announce that he had chosen to marry Denmark. James sent George Keith, the earl of Marischal, to complete the negotiations in Denmark and to serve as proxy at a wedding ceremony on August 20. James drove a hard and shrewd bargain and gained a large dowry, though not as much as his original exorbitant demands had been. By the time August rolled around, James had convinced himself that he was in love with the fourteen-year-old Anne. The same Asheby reports that James is "now far in love with the princess of Denmark, hearing of her beauty and virtues and her affection towards him." Having gazed on her picture and heard reports of her beauty, James became convinced that he was in love with Anne, whom he had yet to meet.[51]

On September 1, 1589, the youthful Anne set sail from Denmark on a ship named *Gideon* for the coast of Scotland. Unfortunately, nature did not cooperate. Violent tempests at sea banged her ship and the accompanying ones. With good reason she feared for her safety. Being tossed unceremoniously and dangerously on a violent sea, Anne may well have had many second thoughts about the agreement to marry the King of Scotland. On one occasion the fleet spotted the Scottish coast but could not land. Eventually they had to give up and return to Scandinavia. Anne came close to realizing her goal only to be driven back. This experience may serve as an appropriate image for her eventual relationship with James. Certainly many tempests occurred, some at her own instigation; and she never obtained the coast of marital bliss.

Asheby reported to Walsingham on September 24: "The King, as a true lover, wholly passionate, and half out of patience with the wind and weather, is troubled that he hath been so long without intelligence of the fleet." James wrote a letter to Anne during this uncertain period as she wandered about on the sea and he had no information. He tells her, "My resultant anguish, and the fear which ceaselessly pierces my heart, has driven me to despatch a messenger to seek for you, both to bring me news of you and to give you the same of me." He prays that she may have a safe arrival. James gets even more zealous in a poem he wrote about the situation, "A complaint against the contrary Wyndes that hindered the Queene to come to Scotland from Denmark," included in a collection entitled

*Amatoria.* In this two-sonnet poem James laments the fate of his loved one, although he focuses mainly on his own suffering. He blames Cupid: "Through deadlie shott alive I daylie dye / I frie in flammes of that envenomed darte / . . . The fever hath infected everie parte / My bones are dried." James appears every bit the languishing lover. As he had with regard to his mother and Elizabeth, James created a fiction about Anne, a romantic fiction to displace the silent reality.[52]

He finally decided in October to send a flotilla to fetch Anne and bring her to Scotland; but when he learned the likely cost of such an endeavor, he knew that he could not afford it—once again lack of money circumscribed James's ambition. So he chose a scaled-down operation and determined to make the journey himself. Asheby mythologized the decision, when he wrote to Elizabeth on October 23: James has committed himself "and all his hopes 'Leanderlike to the waves of the ocean, and all for his beloved Eroes sake.'" James would have been pleased with that image. Just before James boldly set sail, he wrote an important letter to the "People of Scotland." In this document James explains his motives for marrying, as well as the reasons for his seeming delay. Poignantly, James offers explanation: "The reasons were that I was alone, without father or mother, brother or sister, king of this realm and heir apparent of England. This my nakedness made me to be weak and my enemies stark." Some had wondered if James "were a barren stock." He has hastened the treaty; but, "as to my own nature, God is my witness I could have abstained longer." James belabors the fact that he alone has made the decision about going to Denmark; he even tells us where (Craigmillar) he made the decision. He carefully provides for the functioning of his government in his absence. He promises to return, "God willing, within the space of twenty days, wind and weather serving." Leaving about October 23, 1589, James would not return until May 1590. But this letter attests to James's maturity as a ruler, whatever one may think of his impulsiveness as a lover. With the young duke of Lennox in charge, supported by the earl of Bothwell and others, Scotland remained quiet. Calderwood indeed says, with unintended irony, that the country "was never in greater peace than during his [James's] absence."[53]

In a few days, James and his entourage landed safely on the coast of Norway. From there they made their way to Oslo, where Anne awaited. James and Anne got along well from their first meeting. Though already married by proxy, they were married in a ceremony in Oslo on November 23, 1589. From there they went on to Anne's native Denmark, where James met her mother in Elsinore at Kronberg Castle. Another wedding ceremony took place on January 21, this one according to Lutheran rites. No sovereign of Scotland had ever been more thoroughly married. At the kind invitation of Anne's family, James decided to spend the winter in Copenhagen. Scotland must have seemed far away, making it possible to devote little attention to problems. He and Anne enjoyed a seemingly endless round of feasts, celebrations, entertainments, and travels. James also spent time lecturing to Danish theologians and visiting the great astronomer Tycho Brahe.

James was in love, this time with Anne—exactly ten years after he first became involved with Esmé Stuart. James enjoyed the pleasant familial life that he found in Anne's home, a household presided over by her mother, accompanied by Anne's three sisters and three brothers. He enjoyed all the feasting and drinking. He even found time to write poems to or about Anne. In a sonnet about his voyage to Denmark, he urges the "Inconstant wynds": "Go Calme your selfs, be constant by your kynds / let not your stormes nor Chainge or cross my scope." In another sonnet, "To the Queene," he claims: "As on the wings of your enchanting fame / I was transported ou'r the stormie seas." He ascribes to Anne great power over his life:

> Your smiling is an antidote againes
> The Melancholie that oppresseth me
> And when a raging wrathe into me raignes
> Your loving lookes may make me calme to be
> How oft yow see me have an heavie hart
> Remember then sweete Doctour on your art.

One notes that James focuses on what Anne can do for him. In such flushes of joy James and Anne finally departed Denmark on April 21, 1590, and landed at Leith on May 1. For the second time in her life the young Anne left behind family and comfort; she would never see her mother again. From out of a loving and nurturing family she went with James to establish one of their own.[54]

Anne was an instant success in Scotland; her attractiveness and kind manner endeared her immediately to the people. With great excitement her coronation took place on May 17 in a seven-hour ceremony; and two days later, her official royal entry pageant occurred in Edinburgh. Anne found there pageant devices closely resembling those that had greeted James in 1579. Allegorical, mythological, and historical figures also confronted Anne. She received the keys to Edinburgh from a young boy who emerged from a globe device; she

saw the Nine Muses on a scaffold at the Butter Trone. In full icon-
ographical costume the Four Cardinal Virtues greeted Anne at the
Tolbooth. She attended worship at St. Giles, and afterward saw Bacchus and Ceres as well as representations of all the previous kings of
Scotland. At the Nether Bow a tableau depicted the marriage of James
and Anne, and singing of psalms closed the pageant. As with James,
so here: the city honored Anne and in a sense ratified her coronation, acknowledging that she now ruled with James.[55]

But feasting in Copenhagen and pageants in Edinburgh do not a
marriage make. As pageants fade, so does the early flush of romantic enthusiasm. Anne, who as a child had been nurtured first in her
grandparents' home and then in her mother's and always with her
brothers and sisters, found herself far removed from the warmth of
her family. She had much reason to be disappointed in what she
found in Scotland; the landscape and royal palaces appeared unduly
bleak and clearly impoverished. Her husband, rather uncouth of
manner and given to lecturing her, often seemed indifferent to her
needs and intent on controlling her. Anne did dabble somewhat in
politics and sharpened her disdain for Maitland and the earl of Mar.

In 1593, Anne became pregnant, and the impending royal birth
spurred new joy. But the births of royal children also carry some liabilities, and James and Anne would spend valuable time in Scotland
bickering over the destiny of these children. Anne, who had spent
her childhood in happy family surroundings, wanted to fulfill her
maternal instincts and nurture her own children. James, unfortunately, had other ideas; he wanted to be sure that he controlled the
royal children. Their ensuing struggle epitomized the incompati-
bility of this husband and wife. Anne could not reconcile the gap
between her desires and what she was allowed to do in the care of
their children.

Storms punctuated the calm of the marital relationship. In exas-
peration James wrote to Robert Bruce in June 1593 about Anne,
already presumably pregnant, who insisted on riding: "My wife
has this day given command to her servants to make all things ready
for her riding against Tuesday next, and she has said to myself flatly
that she will ride." Obviously, her insistence displeased James. Both
were capable of great stubbornness. By December of that year, perhaps in anticipation of the royal birth, James and Anne enjoyed
moments of tranquillity. The English ambassador, Bowes, reported
to Burghley: "I am informed that the King and Queen entered yester-
night into a very loving band, whereby the King has received the
Queen's promise to concur with and further his actions and courses,

which he protests shall be godly, princely and honourable." In return, James gave Anne "the greatest part of his jewels." But the union of husband and wife dissolved, unable to find a permanent stability. Like the Nile, their relationship ebbed and flowed, promising harvest and yet causing flooding. Caesar says in *Antony and Cleopatra:* "Yet if I knew / What hoop should hold us staunch, from edge to edge / O'th' world I would pursue it." A hoop to bind James and Anne remained especially elusive.[56]

Instead of a hoop, the children would provide still another snare. At Stirling Castle, Prince Henry was born on February 19, 1594. The expanding royal family would never be quite the same again. Rejoicing and relief greeted Henry's birth. James doubtless saw the event as providing him with another angle toward the English throne; it also fulfilled his kingly obligation to Scotland: he had provided a successor. For the first time in nearly thirty years the Scottish people could focus on the significance and possibilities of a royal child.

Shortly after Henry's birth, James made an eminently sensible decision that nevertheless caused insuperable harm and generated an ongoing struggle with Anne. James decided to place his son in the care of the earl of Mar and his mother, the countess of Mar, in Stirling Castle. The order, given with the advice of James's counselors, "constitutes and ordains the said John earl of Mar Keeper and Governor to the said Prince within the Castle of Stirling with enjoyment of such honours, privileges and commodities as he, his father and grandfather enjoyed of before." James gave the earl all the power that he needed to fulfill this important royal responsibility. Having himself spent his infancy and early childhood in the Mar household, James thought it natural that his son should also have such an upbringing. The Mar family was, after all, the only family that James had known. In part, James simply followed the common aristocratic practice of sending children away from their natural home. The fact of a royal child necessitated special concern for his personal safety. Such a procedure also assured James ultimate control over the destiny of the child, a prerogative that he insisted on asserting. By dint of experience, tradition, and desire for control, James took such action eventually for all his children. He apparently had no other models or ideas about the nurturing of children. Anne, on the other hand, possessed other ideas, having herself experienced genuine family life. She and James fought over the issue of Henry's rearing for a decade. To be denied care and nurture of her child shocked and angered Anne.[57]

Such a battleground served to magnify other problems that might have remained inconsequential. Even as James and Anne led the preparation for Henry's baptism, tension filled their relationship. Enlarging and rebuilding the Chapel Royal at Stirling took much longer than expected, but James wanted to show Europe that he was monarch of a major country. As a result, he had to spend money that he did not have. He struck a financial deal with merchants of Edinburgh, using money that Anne had brought as her dowry. In April, Bowes recorded her displeasure. An ominous note sounds from John Colville, who wrote to Robert Cecil, July 26, 1594: "It is certain that the King has conceived a great jealousy of the Queen, which burns the more the more he covers it. . . . and the end can be no less tragical than was betwixt his parents." A few days later Colville added that James "repents" all the plans for the elaborate baptism and that because of his jealousy "he begins to doubt of the child. . . . That matter takes deep root on both sides." These perceptive, if somewhat disconcerting, comments touch on a central axis of James's response toward his family: jealousy and negligence. Perhaps because he had been a king all his life, he had difficulty sharing that center of attention with other members of his family. But jealousy, as Colville notes, takes deep roots.[58]

Lamenting the great cost, regretting the convocation of foreign emissaries, even questioning the paternity of his son, James nevertheless went ahead with Henry's baptism on August 30, 1594, in the newly refurbished chapel. The earl of Sussex served as Queen Elizabeth's representative; she had shrewdly been named godmother for Henry. For the first time in Scottish history a royal child's baptism followed Protestant rites. At the baptismal font his name was given as "Frederick Henry, Henry Frederick." On the plain below the castle a mock battle took place between Turks and Christians as part of the festivities. The final banquet in the Great Hall included a number of pageant devices, such as a chariot occupied by Ceres, Fecundity, Faith, Liberality, Concord, and Perseverance, all appropriately costumed. Faith carried a basin in her hands, which were joined together "with this sentence *Boni alumna conjugii*," the fosterers and nurse of a blessed marriage. One wonders what glances may have been exchanged between James and Anne as they looked at Faith. In a ship, sea figures, such as Neptune, Arion, and Thetis, supposedly hinted at the sea voyage of James to fetch his new bride. Such an occasion and such festivities show us the royal family united in the baptism of their first child, in marked contrast to that scene in 1566 at James's own baptism. The public nature of the royal family shines with a special brilliance, despite whatever private quarrels may have been underway. Throughout the remainder of their lives this Stuart royal family summoned its reservoir of determination and fulfilled the public's expectations in such ceremonies. On September 9, Anne dutifully sent a letter to Elizabeth kindly thanking her for a generous gift for the baptism and her favorable disposition toward them. Anne wrote, "It hes plesed God to bliss us in our sone, so neir in bloode belangin to your self." Pleasantries masked for a while resentments that have already begun to fester.[59]

But conflict ruled again in 1595; battle lines solidified. Anne had one goal: gain control of Henry and remove him from the earl of Mar's custody. James had one goal: to prevent the success of Anne's plan. Diplomatic reports throughout the year bristle with the passion that each partner in the marriage expended in the cause. Something fundamental was going on here: James and Anne were fighting to define themselves as family and as husband and wife. They etched a psychological battlefield that would forever lurk in their consciousness. Pettiness often governed their actions, but each had some solid reasoning on his or her side. Anne wanted to be a mother to her child; James wanted to offer maximum security and protection to this fragile infant: the future of the country was at stake. Their actions mock romance; the frustrated and irreconcilable desires appear as the residue of tragedy. After a few short years of married life James and Anne stood at a crisis point, a crossroads of sorts: this experience shaped their future as husband and wife. Beneath the glitter of royal palaces, stalwart castles, and outward displays of civility, a husband and wife engaged in a decidedly human struggle over a child.

On March 4, 1595, Roger Aston wrote to Bowes: "The Queen has made a motion to the King that she may have the keeping of the Prince and the castle of Edinburgh. This has troubled the King these four days past very mightily, and he is highly offended with the plot-layers of this course." James apparently saw in these plans hints of his overthrow. Aston wrote later that Anne thought that those who would hinder her love cared nothing for the king, herself, or the Prince. Momentary quietness prevailed during part of June. But Aston reported to George Nicolson, June 17: "The King is in such rage that such news is in the country that I believe that motion [Anne's cause] will not be made again. The Queen bears a great grudge against Mar and would not give him her presence"—a quietness as result of exhaustion. A new strategy developed: James "entertains the Queen very lovingly and uses means to draw her off that course"; Anne, as

Aston wrote to Bowes, "entertains the King in all love and obedience, thinking thereby to come the sooner to her intent": kill with
kindness. This familial relationship increasingly defined itself in a
fiction of appearing to be pleasant, as both husband and wife engaged in a certain amount of mythmaking. Contradictions abounded
in this family as in the political world itself. James insisted that should
he die, the earl of Mar should still keep Henry. At the end of June,
Anne raised the forbidden topic again, "thinking she had the King
in a good humour"; because everyone in Scotland, England, and
Denmark now knew of the struggle over the prince, Anne insisted
that her honor was at stake. Nicolson reported James's reaction:
"The King replied that he regarded her honour and the safety of
the Prince as much as she, and would, if he saw cause, yield to
her, adding that he would satisfy any of this land, as she should
please. . . . But he has utterly refused her motion and continues his
promises to Mar." Anne next pretended illness in order to draw
James to her and thereby persuade him on the issue. "For prevent-
ing thereof the King will not come to the Queen," as Nicolson wrote
to Bowes on July 12.[60]

In late July, James wrote to the earl of Mar, reinforcing their understanding of the care of Prince Henry: "This present therefore
shall be a warrant unto you not to deliver him out of your hands
except I command you with my own mouth, and being in such company as I myself shall best like of—otherwise not to deliver him for
any charge or message that can come from me. And, in case God
call me at any time, that neither for Queen nor Estates' pleasure ye
deliver him till he be eighteen years of age and that he command
you himself." The king's will could not be stated more clearly. But
Aston reported an episode on July 31 that took place in Edinburgh.
Anne broached the forbidden subject; and James responded: " 'My
hartt, I am sorry you should be persuaded to move me to thatt wich
wil be the destrocsion of me and my blod.' Whereupon the Queen
fell to tears and so left off that purpose." James also had harsh words
for Chancellor Maitland, worried that some would decide that he
could not control his wife, "and that night passed from him in some
passion."[61]

The spring and summer of quarreling gave way to a more tran-
quil autumn. Though Anne would not even speak to Mar, "she entertains the King more lovingly than ever she did," so reported
Aston to Bowes on September 22. A month later Aston added: "The
Queen gives herself altogether to please the King and there was
never greater love than at this time." On December 1, Nicolson

wrote to Bowes: "To-morrow the King rides to Linlithgow with purpose upon declaring to the Queen . . . his agreements which he has made . . . to get her to go to Stirling to see the young Prince and after to bring her hither [Edinburgh] to stay here this winter." We must remind ourselves that not only did Anne not have control over Henry, she often could not even see him. The controversy spilled over into 1596—indeed for years to come—as James also got advice from Queen Elizabeth, urging him to persist in the custody of Henry.[62]

Jealousy and stubbornness prevented James and Anne from reaching a sensible compromise that might have brought some mutual harmony into their marriage. James's vision of politics clearly collided with human concerns, and familial love suffered. One cannot be sure about exactly when James wrote his poem "A Satire against Woemen"; but it could easily have come from this period, if he needed any special impetus to write on this subject. The poem is something of a tour de force with most of the opening thirty-five lines beginning with the word "As." In comparison to the animals of earth, air, and sea, women come off rather badly. In one sense, however, women merely follow their nature:

> Even so all wemen are of nature vaine
> And can not keep no secrett unrevealed
> And where as once they doe concaive disdaine
> They are unable to be reconcealed
> Fullfild with talke and clatters but respect
> And often tymes of small or none effect.

This poem starkly contrasts with the amatory poems written to Anne earlier. Perhaps this satire emerged from James's experience. Writing about the failure of reconciliation, as in the above stanza, James clearly knew whereof he spoke. His pen captured the irony in his own existence; perhaps he wrote his revenge.[63]

Soon Anne was pregnant again, and royal domestic life focused on that situation. On August 19, 1596, Anne gave birth to a daughter at Dunfermline Palace, a child named Elizabeth in honor of the queen of England. Bowes reported to Burghley on October 4: James "desired me to recommend to her Majesty the hearty requests of himself and the Queen here, praying her to accept their dedication of this princess to her, to give name to her and to dispose of all things therein as she shall like." Though Bowes thinks that Anne will determine the custody of their daughter, James apparently made the decision to place the young Elizabeth in the household of Lord and

Lady Livingstone at Linlithgow Palace. Elizabeth's baptism at Holyroodhouse on November 28 was a meager affair, especially by contrast to Henry's. James knew what he was doing when he named the child Elizabeth, thereby tightening his grasp on the succession to the English throne. In 1598 another daughter, named Margaret after James's grandmother Margaret Tudor, was born; she lived only two years. Surprisingly little appears in the records about these two children, apparently because they faded soon from the Scottish public eye and never became the focus of controversy that Henry had.[64]

The "Gowrie Conspiracy" of August 1600 remains a mystery. We have only James's version of events, a version that the ministers in Edinburgh and Anne found unbelievable. James was apparently lured to Gowrie House by a strange tale of a man who had found a pot of gold. Why James would go to this place, the scene of his capture and imprisonment in 1582, defies explanation. After dinner, James followed Alexander Ruthven into a room in the turret of the house. Whatever happened, James panicked and shouted "Treason." His page entered, slew Ruthven, and subsequently his brother the earl of Gowrie, who had come to find out what was happening. In any event, James escaped unscathed, and that fifth day in August became one regularly celebrated in honor of the king's deliverance. The whole story strikes one as bizarre: was it another attempted kidnapping of James, or was it James's plan to destroy the Ruthven descendants of those who had imprisoned him in 1582? Only James survived the initial provocation, but his story encourages doubt.[65]

Renewed tension had been percolating between Anne and James, as he threatened to take all the royal children to his own safekeeping. In late October 1600, Nicolson reported to Cecil that James and Anne seemed to be getting along very well. James's statement "that he had the best wife of her that was in the world, is by some wondered at, by others suspected to be for disguising of some secret intentions, by some well thought on, by others to be outward and not inward." The words and actions of James and Anne constitute a living contradiction, capable of multiple interpretations, a fundamental irony that threads its way through this royal family. Three days later the Master of Gray noted that the "King and Queen are in very evil menage" and included this incident: "At public table she said to him that he was advised to imprison her, but willed him to beware what he 'mintit' at for she was not the earl of Gowrie. He said he believed she was mad." But the next day, November 1, they again appeared at peace with each other, though what lingers here is Anne's possible role in the Gowrie Conspiracy—another mystery.

As Aston wrote to Cecil: "What the Queen's part was in the matter, God knows. The presumptions were great both by letters and tokens." Beatrice Ruthven, sister of the slain brothers, had been a lady-in-waiting for Anne and remained her friend. James, probably wisely, chose to ignore whatever he had learned about Anne's involvement in the conspiracy. They seemed determined to make their lives a mock romance; certainly those around them perceived such a quality in their marriage.[66]

On November 19, 1600, Anne gave birth to a son, to be named Charles after one of James's names. James visited her at Dunfermline after the birth. Nicolson says that "they never loved better." But in a few weeks Nicolson observed: "The Queen being advertised that the King, in his secret dislike of her, did also dislike this newborn son and therefore cared not with how little honour it should be baptised." Anne urged James to postpone the baptism until spring, when her brother, King Christian IV of Denmark, could attend. But the plans for a December 1600 baptism went ahead. Nicolson added: "The Queen comes not to it." The royal family had traveled a long and rather perilous distance from the spectacle and interest that Henry's baptism provoked in 1594. Here, Anne claimed that she will not even attend the baptism of her latest born. As we will see several times in the future, Anne would respond to familial and political strife by strategically absenting herself—a potent weapon in her arsenal. Not being present at the child's baptism struck a blow at any ordinary concept of familial communion and celebration. Paradoxically, Nicolson added further: "She makes much of the child as she was not wont to do of any and intends to keep and make him serve her turn in these matters. Always I remit these matters to the sequel." What a wise last sentence by Nicolson. No sooner do we think that we have an understanding of this royal couple, but everything changes. As it turned out, the weak and sickly Charles went to live in the household of Alexander Seton, Lord Fyvie.[67]

Even the birth of another child could be used as a pretext to continue the quest for control of Henry. The last royal child born in Scotland was Robert, born in January 1602. Anne decided to use his baptism as an opportunity "to have the Prince from the earl of Mar," as Gray wrote to Cecil on February 10. She did not succeed, and by May, Robert was deathly ill. Thomas Douglas wrote to Cecil that Anne, seeing the king's melancholy, told James that if God should take Robert, they would have another child because she believed that she was pregnant. "At which words the King forgot all his melancholy and rode presently to Stirling where now he is." Both parents seemed genuinely moved by the loss of Robert. Nicolson reported to Cecil the reaction to Robert's death: "The King and especially the Queen were so exceeding sorrowful for his loss as yet they rest scarce quieted from their sorrow. For the Queen's comfort it is meant that the young Prince shall be brought from Stirling to the Queen to Falkland . . . and to remain there . . . some few days with his mother." Prince Henry therefore came at last to comfort his mother, a poignant moment that James at least allowed. Such action fulfills the spirit of a letter that Henry wrote his mother while still in Scotland. Writing from Stirling, Henry noted his mother's illness, which has prevented her visiting him. He added: "Bot because I am the zounger man I culd be weill content to tak the travell, and as I promise be my other letter, sall be maist willing quhen the kings ma. [majesty] will grant me leve to come." Henry indicated that he had sent a gift of a hound: "I hope ye giff sall not be sa mickle respected as the hawt [heart] of ye gever, quhilk is disposed to obey and serve zour ma. in all points, and sall continew by the grace of God, quhom I beseih to preserve zour g. [grace] in gud helth."[68]

From this tragedy of 1602 the royal family moved to a moment of great excitement and promise: James's becoming king of England. The speedy Carey reached James at Holyroodhouse Palace on March 26, 1603, and told him of Elizabeth's death and his proclamation as their new king. Standing in those rooms of the old palace, James must have felt an enormous sense of relief: he had outlived Elizabeth and removed every obstacle that might have lain in his path to the English throne. A childhood dream and an adult strategy had at last been fulfilled. Out of his mother's death and his marriage and births of children had come this much-coveted prize. What lay before the Stuart royal family seemed like a land of dreams.

James began the extensive preparations for the journey to London. He decided to leave the family behind for a while—Anne, after all, was pregnant. James had to prepare the government to function effectively in his absence; and, as we recall, he had promised the Kirk of Edinburgh that he would return regularly to visit. Before he left on April 5, he wrote a letter to Prince Henry, knowing they would be separated for a while. The letter begins: "That I see you not before my parting, impute it to this great occasion wherein time is so precious, but that shall (by God's grace) shortly be recompensed by your coming to me shortly and continual residence with me ever after." James also sent Henry a newly published copy of *Basilicon Doron*, the first public edition of March 1603, though written in late 1598. James dedicated the book to Henry and offered therein his instructions on how to govern. He explained one of his reasons for such a book: "Because my affaires will not permit me ever to be present with you, I ordaine to be a resident faithfull admonisher of you. And becaus the houre of death is uncertaine to me, as unto all fleshe, I leave it as my Testament & latter-will unto you." Interestingly, both the 1603 letter and the dedication to *Basilicon Doron* attempt to confront the problem of an absent father. Through his discourse James sought to bridge the gap between his absence and presence, to overcome the silence of that gap.[69]

With James on the road to London, Anne struck, trying yet again to gain custody of Henry. She received encouragement from a letter that the young prince had written her in which he regretted his father's departure and asked Anne to supply that lack by her presence, which, Henry wrote, "I have . . . the more just causse to crave, that I have wanted it so lang to my great greif and displeasure." Possibly misinterpreting this child's expression as being more important than it was, Anne swung into action. Her hysterical reactions, when rebuffed by the earl of Mar, produced a miscarriage. Eventually James gave in, allowing Anne and Henry to travel together to England. He also wrote her a rather stern letter, analyzing with some insight the nature of their marriage:

> And therefore I say over again, leave these womanly apprehensions, for I thank God I carry that love and respect unto you which, by the law of God and nature, I ought to do to my wife and mother of my children. . . . For the respect of your honourable birth and descent I married you; but the love and respect I now bear you is for that ye are my married wife and so partaker of my honour, as of all my other fortunes.

No more romantic poems, written in the glow of recent marriage; instead, James, businesslike, professes his love and respect, but all according to what the laws of God and nature dictate. Anne, as one contemporary observed, "had but little Notion of Love; and that small Portion of it, which she had felt for the King, was soon worn out, by their frequent Wrangles: She grew to despise him for his Want of Spirit, and took so little Care to conceal her mean Opinion of him." Husband and wife had reached an understanding of one another. We certainly cannot call it romantic; at best we can note a sense of accommodation that begins to govern their relationship. In England additional problems would further damage the marital relationship and pose threats to the Stuart royal family as family.[70]

For the moment, they left Scotland in states of relative joy and excitement. Much on the political scene could be looked at with pride. As one scholar notes: "Scotland was far more peaceful and prosperous than it had been for generations, the aristocracy under control and the church on the way to being so. He [James] and Maitland between them had brought into being a group of loyal and diligent government servants who had been vital to his success." Jenny Wormald comments: "James VI was an undoubted success as king of Scotland. His high opinion of himself had sufficient grounds for it to be accepted by others."[71]

Having survived childhood without the nurture of parents, having fallen in love as a teenager, having repressed the cries of his mother for help, having benefited politically from her death, having married Anne primarily for the sake of the commonwealth, and having fathered three surviving children, James by 1603 had already garnered a lifetime of experiences. Politically strong, he stood ready for the new adventure as king of England. From the cragged strength of an Edinburgh Castle he moved to the smooth prosperity of London: a father and husband bringing his family to a new life in England.

## Chapter Three

# England (1603–1613)

# A Magnificent Spectacle

No paintings exist of the Stuart royal family during its first decade in England. No picture captures the initial joy that attended this family, reveals lines of anxiety eventually etched in their faces by sorrow, arrests their life at a given moment—not even a fanciful one, such as the one of James and his mother in 1583—that might idealize this special family. But word pictures abound; and from them we can create a portrait of this family in transition from Scotland to England, as the royal children mature, ready to play their roles in international politics. If someone could capture all this on canvas, such a portrait would be multicolored but with abiding shades of gray.

The Venetian ambassadors in February 1610 captured for a moment this Stuart royal family at the apogee of its early life in England, successful and hopeful. Other portraits will have to be superimposed over this one, however, in order to gain a valid picture of their life. In a dispatch sent to the Doge and Senate of Venice, Francesco Contarini and Marc' Antonio Correr wrote of an audience with the king, surrounded by his family. Contarini explained that they arrived at the palace in Whitehall and went to the Great Chamber where the chamberlain met them. The account continues:

> We passed between two rows of the great ladies and gentlemen of the Court, all richly dressed and covered with jewels. When we had drawn near to the King with many bows and mounted the steps of the dais, the King took a step or two forward and embraced us with a joyful countenance and signs of singular courtesy and affection. The Queen stood by him and with her the Princess, who, in common opinion, is held to be of a rare beauty; she is fourteen years old. On the King's right stood

**II**                *Sic pacem habemus .*

To the High and mightie *I A M E S* , King of greate Britaine,

      T WOO Lions ſtout the Diadem vphold ,
           Of famous Britaine, in their armed pawes :
*Scilicet Anglicùs*   The one is Red , the other is of Gold ,
*et Scoticus .*       And one their Prince , their ſea , their land and lawes ;
          Their loue , their league : whereby they ſtill agree ,
         In concord firme , and friendly amitie .

      B E L L O N A henceforth bounde in Iron bandes ,
      Shall kiſſe the foote of mild triumphant P E A C E ,
      Nor Trumpets ſterne, be heard within their landes ;
      Envie ſhall pine , and all old grudges ceaſe :
         Braue Lions , ſince, your quarrell's lai 'd aſide ,
        On common foe., let now your force be tri 'de .

      Vnum ſuſtentant gemini piadema Leones ,        Fœdere iunguntur ſimili, cœloque, ſaloque,
       Concordes vno Principe , mente, ſido ..          Nata quibus Pax hæc inviolanda manet ,

                                                          *Qme*

Emblem devoted to King James as peacemaker in Henry Peacham's
*Minerva Britanna* (1612).

13 ·TO THE THRICE-VERT·VOVS,AND
FAIREST OF QVEENES, ANNE QVEENE
OF GREAT BRITAINE..

Anagramma D:
Gul ; Fouleri.

In ANNA regnantium arbor.

ANNA *Britannorum Regina*..

A N Oliue lo, with braunches faire difpred,·
Whofe top doth reach vnto the azure skie,
Much feeming to difdaine, with loftie head
The Cedar, and thofe Pines of THESSALIE,
Faireft of Queenes, thou art thy felfe the Tree,
The fruite * thy children, hopefull Princes thrée.

Which thus I ghefſe, fhall with their outftretcht armés,
In time o'refpread Europa's continent,
* To fhield and fhade, the innocent from harmes ;·
But overtop the proud and infolent :
Remaining, raigning, in their glories greene,
While man on earth, or Moone in heauen is feene.

\* Non claffes,
non Legiones,
ſ eri :de fi.ma im-
perii munimenta
quam numerum
liberorum. Ta-
citus. 4. Hift :

\* parcere fubiec-
tis. &c.

*Fatum*

Emblem for Queen Anne in her role as mother in Peacham's *Minerva Britanna* (1612).

the Prince of Wales and hard by the Queen the Duke of York, his father's and mother's joy. The officers of the Crown and other leading gentlemen of the Kingdom, who were all present, each in his rank of preeminence and in seemly order, surrounded the dais at the foot of the steps; a magnificent spectacle.

One cannot reasonably disagree with the final assessment, but the vibrant word picture requires additional observation.[1]

Order reigns as the theme of this portrait with everything and everybody in its place. James, Anne, Henry, Elizabeth, and Charles are all present, both supporting and defining the royal family. Something very solid permeates this portrait, an impression reinforced by the presence of royal parents and royal children: the past and future coalesce at this moment. The fourteen-year-old Elizabeth has taken her place at court and charmed everyone; the sixteen-year-old Henry stands on the threshold of a yearlong celebration of his investiture as Prince of Wales; the ten-year-old Charles has only begun to be admitted to formal courtly circles. James and Anne would have many reasons to beam with pride at this moment in 1610. Contarini refers to the occasion as a "magnificent spectacle," which it assuredly is. But "spectacle" calls attention to outward show. Our task will be to explore those unspoken matters that go together also to define this moment or any other such public moment. If the members of this royal family could share with us their silent hearts, what would they say about one another? James was fond of wishing aloud, usually in speeches to Parliament, that his heart were a crystal mirror that all might gaze on it and know him and his motives. From our vantage point we can try to peer into the deeper recesses of this family's life, their own "coffers of perplexity," in order to see beyond and behind the outward show.

As the royal family gradually made its way south to England in 1603, great festivities and celebrations greeted them along the way. James came first, then Anne and Henry, and finally Elizabeth. Charles remained in Scotland until 1604 because of his sickly condition. Hundreds of English citizens, noblemen, members of the Privy Council, and ordinary people made their way to greet James in Berwick, York, Doncaster, and other places along the route. Not only had James peacefully resolved for them the succession issue, but also he had brought a royal family with him. As William McElwee observes: "A virgin queen of Elizabeth's calibre was a phenomenon to be proud of, but in many ways it was a comfort to have a man with a wife and young family and with the ordinary, obvious human weaknesses." Francis Bacon in his fragmentary *History of Great Britain* describes

England's situation with the arrival of James and his family: "A king, in the strength of his years, supported with great alliances abroad, established with royal issue at home, at peace with all the world." For the first time since the reign of Henry VIII, England enjoyed a royal family—parents and children.[2]

Bacon reminded the recipients of a letter of 1612, in which he wrote to collect "aid" for Princess Elizabeth's forthcoming wedding: "Then may you declare the reasons why the like hath not been demanded of late times . . . : which are apparent: for that Queen Elizabeth, Queen Mary, and King Edward had no children, and King Henry 8 died before his son was of the age of 15 or his daughters married." England faced the prospect of marriageable royal children, a situation not confronted in decades. George Marcelline wrote in 1610 that James was "the Common *Father* of all his people" and enumerated the advantages of the royal children. These children made the kingdoms happy "whereon dependeth their peace and freedom from strife . . . which wanting before in that Empires felicity, makes it now an Empire abounding in felicity." Such confidence grew out of the political stability afforded by the royal family's presence.[3]

Greeting James outside of London on May 7, 1603, Richard Martin welcomed him with praise and observed that James's "Princely offspring" might sit "upon the throne of their fathers for evermore." The recorder of Southampton made similar remarks later in 1603, when James visited that city. In Southampton the recorder referred to the "most noble Progenie of your Royall Children." Though such comments focused on the political advantage of the children, they also revealed an enthusiasm in the simple pleasure of there being royal children. The children were to be gazed upon, wondered at, and enjoyed, in addition to the political stability they gave the country.[4]

A year after this initial arrival, James recalled the excitement of the English people in a speech to Parliament in 1604: "Shall it ever bee blotted out of my minde, how at my first entrie into this Kingdome, the people of all sorts rid and ran, nay rather flew to meet mee? their eyes flaming nothing but sparkles of affection, their mouthes and tongues uttering nothing but sounds of joy, their hands, feete, and all the rest of their members in their gestures discovering a passionate longing, and earnestnesse to meete and embrace their new Soveraigne." Even allowing for James's gift of hyperbole, this statement captures the enthusiastic response that greeted him. Ironically, James actually detested crowds, fearful as always for his personal safety. But a year after the event he was able to look back nostalgically; perhaps indeed he longed for that early spontaneous joy, long since diminished. James responded warmly and liberally to the people's excitement: he distributed jewels and knighthoods as if serving up from a bottomless treasure-hoard. He activated the Anglo-Saxon concept of the king as ring-giver with a passion unseen in the parsimonious days of Queen Elizabeth. Responding to increasing complaints about such liberality, James in a 1607 address to Parliament admitted: "My three first yeeres were to me as a Christmas, I could not then be miserable." To the cheers that greeted him, James responded like a child with a chest full of toys, unaccustomed as he was to such experiences in Scotland.[5]

In the midst of all the shouting, however, a silence and chill also existed in the private lives of the royal family, as we have already discerned in the Scottish period. At first glance this family's life seems to follow a comic trajectory in the 1603–1613 period, from the glorious arrival into England in 1603 to the wedding festivities for Princess Elizabeth in February 1613. But this festive comedy also carried with it tragedy, great sorrow, jealousy, and disappointment: the ingredients that burnished this family's life with an ironic sheen. The children dominated the personal and public life of James's family in this period. In Scotland they were not yet of great consequence because they were so young, whereas in England they developed, matured, faced crises, and became the object of marriage negotiations. Additional children were born, and some children died. England's future took shape during this decade in ways that began to look beyond James's reign.

One cannot overstate the importance of these royal children, even though their father ruled the country. Illness or accident could have claimed James's life at any moment. As in Shakespeare's final plays, England began to look to the royal children for redemption, for a future perhaps brighter than the present reality. This first decade in England also defined clearly the relationship of James and Anne; their bitter struggles over the children remain largely a product of the past, but an alternative to struggling is indifference. In 1607, James began a serious involvement with another favorite, Robert Carr, thereby threatening family structure and generating numerous political problems. Finally, in this period James at last assuaged the guilt about his mother. Mary's death had held a firm grip on James's conscience, but he tried to still and silence that particular ghost of the past.

Anne made her own triumphant journey through England in spring 1603, being welcomed, feasted, and celebrated numerous times along the route toward London. She had at least two reasons

Queen Anne (c. 1605) attributed to Marcus Gheeraerts. Reproduced by permission of the Nelson-Atkins Museum of Art, Kansas City, Missouri (Nelson Fund) 47–85.

to feel particularly pleased, if not smug, about her experience. First, she was being received in her own right as queen of a new country without the presence of her husband-sovereign. The adulation and excitement fastened onto her presence. Second, she had Prince Henry with her—surely a victory of sorts. The trip from Edinburgh marked the longest time that mother and son had spent together. After nearly a decade of acrimonious debate with her husband she at last had Henry in her possession. Anne thus had her own special reason for joy and for thinking of England as indeed the Promised Land. The festivities certainly encouraged such a view, as in, for example, Ben Jonson's Althorp entertainment in June at the estate of Sir Robert Spencer. In the midst of a pastoral world of fairies and satyrs, Anne heard great praise of herself as one who might exceed their former Diana (Queen Elizabeth). This entertainment marked the beginning of Jonson's long involvement in royal masques and entertainments. The royal family, including Princess Elizabeth (who traveled most of the way with her mother and brother), finally came together again in late June. James was clearly delighted to see them safely arrived from the long journey. Life for the Stuart royal family in England could now begin.

July 1603 began with the investiture of Prince Henry into the Order of the Garter on July 2, an important ceremony for linking him solidly to English tradition (James had been invested into the order by Elizabeth in 1594 on the occasion of the birth of Henry). The duke of Lennox, son of James's former great love, Esmé Stuart, also became a Knight of the Garter on this occasion. All attention now focused on the coronation. But, because of the outbreak of the plague, ceremonies had to be greatly curtailed and crowds severely limited.

On July 25, St. James Day, King James achieved formal, cere-monial recognition of that for which he had striven assiduously for decades: he was crowned king of England. But on that rainy late July day, the streets were desolate and Westminster Abbey half empty, thereby sapping this occasion of some of its excitement and spectacle. Nevertheless, the ceremony went ahead. Anne became the first crowned consort since Anne Boleyn. In a dazzling robe of crimson velvet Anne proceeded to the cathedral. A contemporary account noted: "She so mildly saluted her new subjects that the women weeping cried out with one voice, 'God bless the royal Queen. Welcome to England. Long to live and continue.' " But inside the Abbey, Anne, despite the entreaties of James and the archbishops, stead-fastly refused to "*take the Sacrament along with him, after the Protestant rite."* The inner court circle doubtless shared the open secret of Anne's Catholicism, but her refusal here at her coronation to follow the Protestant rite must have been rankling. One does not quite know whether to applaud Anne's seeming stand on principle or to accuse her of willful pride.[6]

Apparently Anne became a convert to Catholicism while still in Scotland, sometime in the late 1590s. Brought up a Lutheran, she did not care for the practice of religion that she found in Scotland. David Willson concludes: "Very likely she adopted Catholicism in the half-trifling way in which idle persons sometimes occupy themselves with a new faith. Her conversion did not make her serious or devout, nor did it strengthen her character." Without historical evidence, one can just as fairly allow Anne a serious purpose in her religious choice. Whatever her motivation, Anne's Catholicism must have been a source of some tension in her relationship with James; in fact, he on occasion denied that she was Catholic. As they went their separate ways, a silent gap emerged on what for James had to be a major issue, given his interest in theology and in church matters as a champion of the Protestant faith.[7]

Robert Abercromby, S.J., reported to his superior in Scotland in 1602: "Three years have passed since the Queen sent for one of our fathers and began secretly to tell him how ardently she desired to embrace the Catholic religion and renounce every heresy. After a long conversation with the father, she earnestly entreated him to stay with her three days that he might instruct her fully in the Catholic doctrines and ceremonies, which he did willingly to the great satisfaction of both." On the fourth day Anne received "the most holy sacrament with the utmost spiritual joy in the presence of only a few persons of rank." Knowledgeable English Catholics looked with great hope to Anne's arrival in their kingdom, and evidence suggests that she did work for a lenient policy toward Catholics. Events, however, such as the Gunpowder Plot, overtook policy.[8]

At the end of 1603, Anthony Standen, who had been sent on a diplomatic mission by James, was arrested. The charges included his bringing rosaries and gifts from Pope Clement to Queen Anne. In response to this event, Robert Cecil in a letter to Thomas Parry, English ambassador in Paris, took pains to dissociate Anne from any Catholic beliefs: "Although when she was in Scotland, she misliked many of those precise opinions which were maintained by most of those churches, yet for matters of faith she never was tied to the Romish assertions." Yet, as reported by Hicks, numerous ambassadors had conversations with Anne in which she affirmed her Catholic faith. For example, Montecuccoli reported to the Grand

Duke of Tuscany: "In the third audience I had with the Queen she told and confessed to me in the greatest confidence and under seal of secrecy that she was a Catholic and wished to live and die as such." James, with Cecil's connivance, would create a fiction to displace the reality of Anne's faith. Against such a background one must read her act of defiance at the coronation.[9]

James himself did not entirely behave in an exemplary manner at the coronation. "During the paying of homage . . . Philip Herbert, earl of Montgomery, had the effrontery to kiss King James on the cheek, but what profoundly shocked the congregation was that the King instead of resenting his insolence, merely laughed and lightly tapped him on the cheek." One wonders if the Scots in the congregation would have been only amused, not shocked. Out of these somewhat unorthodox happenings, James nevertheless had what he wanted most: the official coronation as king of England. He had to feel slightly more secure as a result of the ceremony.[10]

Safely on the throne, James then made a move to confront the issue of his long-dead mother. In August 1603, James dispatched a rich pall of velvet to hang over Mary's grave in Peterborough Cathedral. Virtually every modern interpreter has seen this action as the beginning of some kind of expiation. Actually, we might date the process from his public reaction to the 1596 publication of Spenser's *Faerie Queene*, discussed earlier. After a wide-ranging interview with James in 1604, John Harington reported in a letter their many topics, including witchcraft. Harington wrote, "More serious discourse did next ensue, wherein I wantede roome to continue, and sometime roome to escape." Then James broached the subject of Mary: "The Queene his mother was not forgotten, nor Davison neither. His Highnesse tolde me her deathe was visible in Scotlande before it did really happen, being, as he said, spoken of in secrete by those whose power of sighte presentede to them a bloodie heade dancinge in the aire." James took two more steps of confronting his mother's death in the first decade in England. In 1605 he named the newborn royal daughter Mary, in honor of his mother. Thus the first royal child to be born on English soil in over eighty years bore the name of the executed queen of Scotland. Queen Elizabeth's death in 1603 had enabled James to take this action. His first daughter received the name of Elizabeth and the second, Mary's name; surely this reveals something of James's own thinking about the relative importance—political and personal—of these two women. James also ordered the construction of an elaborate tomb for his mother in Westminster Abbey.[11]

In 1612 this tomb stood ready to receive Mary's remains. On

September 28, 1612, James wrote to the Dean and Chapter of Peterborough Cathedral, ordering the exhuming of her body. James offered his rationale: "For that we remember it appertains to the duty we owe to our dearest mother that like honour should be done to her body and like monument be extant of her as to others her and our progenitors have been used to be done." James observed that he had also ordered the construction of a tomb for Elizabeth. James wrote, "We require you . . . to deliver the corpse of our said dearest mother, the same being taken up in as decent and respectful manner as is fitting." In a rare moment of frugality, James remembered the pall that he sent in 1603 and asked that it be returned with Mary's body.[12]

Under cover of darkness, with only a few torches pushing back that darkness, Mary's body moved in solemn procession through London on October 8 to its final resting place in the magnificent tomb, a monument, as Fraser observes, "to James's taste if not to his filial piety." Mary rests in a tomb near to and rivaling in splendor that for Queen Elizabeth. Jonathan Goldberg comments: "The monument in Westminster Abbey effaces—erases—his [James's] part in Mary's death." A Victorian survey of the royal tombs in Westminster revealed that James shared the tomb of Henry VII, first Tudor monarch, while Mary shared a tomb with several, including her grandchildren, Prince Henry and Princess Elizabeth. James had finally put to rest his mother and the guilt that he bore about her fate. His mother became memorialized in a tomb—a tangible sign of James's stilled conscience. This burial in a magnificent tomb also completed James's fiction of himself as dutiful son, a fiction ironically set into motion by her death, as if her death liberated him not only politically but also imaginatively. Interestingly, the carver of Mary's tomb could not have received any help from James concerning her appearance: his visual image of her came from reports and what he imagined on the basis of letters and messages. If history functions in part as a burial rite, as Michel de Certeau suggests, then James completed Mary's history by this entombing. Those grandchildren eventually also buried in her tomb offer a grim image of familial reunion through death.[13]

The first Stuart Christmas in England reached its peak of celebration with the performance on January 8, 1604, of Samuel Daniel's masque *The Vision of the Twelve Goddesses*, presented at Hampton Court. Anne, at the suggestion of the countess of Bedford, hired Daniel to write this indoor entertainment, consisting of speeches, allegorical and mythological characters, music, and dance. This rarefied form of drama became a hallmark of the Stuart court, often with various members of the royal family performing in masques, as Anne did in this one. In fact, Daniel in a dedication of his text to the countess of Bedford claimed that the masque was "very worthily performed, by a most magnificent Queen, whose heroical spirit and bounty only gave it so fair an execution as it had." The masque celebrated peace, which the kingdom now enjoyed, Daniel said, "by the benefit of his most gracious Majesty, by whom we have this glory of peace, with the accession of so great state and power." In the masque Anne represented the goddess Pallas. The figure Iris closes the spectacle with a wish that "these deities will be pleased the rather at their invocation . . . as ever more to grace this glorious monarchy with the real effects of these blessings represented." As Stephen Orgel and others have pointed out, these masques celebrate royal power and contribute to the image of the sovereign's power. "The masque presents the triumph of an aristocratic community; at its center is a belief in the hierarchy and a faith in the power of idealization."[14]

Orgel also observes that as a genre the masque functions as the opposite of satire. Masques thus existed as idealized versions of reality. As such, they proved helpful to James and the royal family in cultivating and promulgating a favorable image of themselves for public consumption, or at least courtly consumption since the audience would be restricted to noblemen and ladies and the ambassadorial corps. Through the Jacobean period these masques became elaborate and costly tools of royal propaganda. Queen Anne devoted much energy to these spectacles. But such insubstantial spectacles finally underscored the gap between their versions of imagined reality and those that the royal family actually experienced at the convergent point of joys and sorrows, hopes raised and hopes dashed, jealousy and indifference, boisterous noise and agonizing silence. The masques attempted to impose a fiction that the Stuart royal family could not sustain. We will examine a few other masques as they impinge on pertinent issues for the royal family.

Another major burst of festivity took place on March 15, 1604, when James made an official royal entry through the streets of London, from the Tower west to Westminster. The plague in 1603 had rendered such an outdoor, civic pageant impossible. This 1604 pageant recalled those of 1579 and 1590 in Edinburgh, except that it was far more elaborate. Nearly a year after he had been proclaimed king of England, James and some members of his family had the chance to enjoy the public adulation of London's citizens. The magnificence of this occasion must have made it worth waiting for. For the first time in English history we can identify major dramatists with the writing of a royal entry pageant, in this case Ben Jonson, Thomas Dekker, and Thomas Middleton (who contributed only the speech of Zeal). Two professional actors, Edward Alleyn and William Bourne, performed. Shakespeare may also have been present because the King's Men acting company as Servants of the Royal Household lined the streets with other groups under royal patronage and with members of London's twelve principal guilds. Seven triumphal arches, located throughout London's streets, constituted part of the expense, for which the City of London and the guilds spent several thousand pounds.[15]

The Venetian ambassador, Nicolo Molin, captured the form of the royal procession on this occasion: "The Prince [Henry] was on horseback, ten paces ahead of the King, who rode under a canopy borne over his head by four-and-twenty gentlemen, splendidly dressed. . . . The Queen followed twenty paces behind; she was seated on a royal throne, drawn by two white mules . . .; in a richly furnished carriage behind her Majesty came the Lady Arbella, with certain maids of honour in attendance." Princess Elizabeth was deemed too young for the entry, and Prince Charles was still in Scotland. Arbella Stuart, James's cousin, took her rightful place with his family. Queen Elizabeth had kept her a virtual prisoner after 1588, primarily because Arbella's presence at court as potential heir to the throne had reminded Elizabeth of her own mortality and eventual replacement. James, on the other hand, gave Arbella—at least for a while—new prominence.[16]

All the pageant devices acclaimed James's rule over England and attested to his transforming power. The pageant became a glorious piece of mythmaking. James's powerful, transforming, and real presence joined fictional representations of him at the tableaux. For example, the triumphal arch located at Gracious Street contained allusions to James's *Basilicon Doron* and to his poem *Lepanto,* written about the sixteenth-century sea battle between Turkish and Christian forces. On the arch a large square depicted Henry VII dressed in imperial robes "to whome King *James* (mounted on horsebacke) approches, and receyves a Scepter." This painting or carving offered James's genealogy, underscoring his claim to the English throne. The founder of the Tudor line gave his blessing and kingdom to James. So the praise went throughout the five-hour-long spectacle as the royal family wound its way through an adoring London.[17]

Gilbert Dugdale in his eyewitness account of this 1604 civic pageant, entitled *The Time Triumphant,* offered much praise of the royal family. Dugdale called Anne "Pierles," "Her Sonne a Prince, / Her Children since / All royall borne, / Whom Crownes addorne." Near Cheapside an apprentice spoke to James in words not included in any of the printed texts of this pageant. Dugdale recorded the apprentice's praise of the family, including the children: "Thy sonnes and daughters, princely all compleat, / Royall in bloud, children of high Renowne." Dugdale also described the Queen and Prince Henry in the procession: "Our gratious *Queene Ann,* milde and curteous plaste in a Chariot, of exceeding beauty, did all the way so humbly and with mildenes, salute her subjects, . . . that women and men in my sight wept with joy." The "young hopeful *Henry Fredericke*" smiled "as over-joyde to the peoples eternall comfort" and acknowledged the crowd's cheers. James, according to some accounts, seemed less friendly. Indeed, he had nothing to say.[18]

But, given the symbolism of power, the pageant said everything that it needed to say. It confirmed James's legitimacy as ruler, even though no doubt existed on this issue; it ratified his kingship, even though he had already been crowned. The presence of the royal family further solidified James's claim to the crown, and the pageant and the adoring crowds reinforced that claim. Without James and his family the pageant would have been an empty show; without the crowds the Stuart royal family would have remained incomplete. Like the court masque, the civic pageant also functioned as an idealization of power. But at least in London's streets thousands of citizens could see the sovereign and, in his family, evidence of a peaceful succession and promise of a secure future. For the first time in decades Englishmen could celebrate the presence in their kingdom of a royal family—parents and children. Ceremonial trappings; symbolic costume; triumphal arches; mythological, historical, and allegorical characters; and dramatic speeches kept the pageant moving along a fascinating axis of real event and fictional representation. The assent of shouting crowds helped blend James and his family into both the reality and the fiction of this event, reinforcing the dominant ideas of both theater and patriarchy. These two distinctive ideas coalesced in this pageant; in fact, the royal family on display made this spectacle possible. Other days and other occasions would soon reveal how the royal family actually lived and how the government indeed functioned. For the moment, the civic pageant of March 1604 offered a glorious illusion.

Important political events of another sort also took place in 1604. The year began in fact with the Hampton Court Conference, James's effort to bring together and reconcile the competing forces in the Church of England, particularly the high-church Anglicans and the Puritans. James indulged himself in one of his favorite pastimes: theological disputation. Unfortunately, this conference did not resolve the issues, although it helped mask them for a while; the Puritans lived to fight another day. The longest-lasting achievement of the conference was the establishment of a process for beginning a new English translation of the Bible, leading eventually in 1611 to the publication of the Authorized Version, familiarly known as the "King James version." In October 1604, James proclaimed himself as "King of Great Britain," acknowledging a tacit union of the kingdoms by virtue of his being both king of Scotland and king of England. Not everyone greeted this new title with enthusiasm, but the concept of "Great Britain" has certainly prevailed. In another political action, James signed a peace treaty with Spain in August, an agreement not universally applauded. But James probably took the wiser course by seeking peace with Spain. This treaty became the first step in a process by which James sought to be known as a peacemaker king; indeed, *"Beati Pacifici"* (blessed are the peacemakers) became his motto.[19]

James's family life took on a new dimension in 1605 with the birth of a daughter, Mary. Not only did she carry the name of James's mother, but also she had the distinction of being the first royal child born in England since Jane Seymour gave birth to the child who became Edward VI. Obviously, much excitement attended this event; probably no one in England could remember such a royal birth. Samuel Calvert wrote to Ralph Winwood about the preparation for Mary's birth: "The Queen expects her Delivery every Hour, and Prayers are dayly said every where for her Safety. There is great Preparation for the christening Chamber, and costly Furniture provided for Performance of other Ceremonies." Several of the prayers used in churches called attention to the royal family. One, for example, referred to Anne as "a Queene of a fruitfull wombe and an happie ofspring, and preserved . . . heretofore in the prosperous birth of all royall issue, which we with comfort and joy daily behold." With such an anticipated birth, "so shall the King rejoyce, and thy people be glad therof, and we all with thankefull hearts shall praise thy glorious Name for such an increase of the Kings royall issue." Finally the birth came: "The Lady Mary, borne at Greenewitch upon the eight of Aprill about 11 or 12 of the clock at night; for joy whereof, the next day after, the Cittizens of London made bonefiers throughout London, and the bells continued ringing all the whole day."[20]

Such bell ringing, puncturing the silence of watchful expectation, must have been gratifying to James: he now had an English child. James wrote a letter full of joy to his brother-in-law Christian IV of Denmark on the day after Mary's birth:

> Therefore, as soon as our dearest wife had born a most delightful offspring for us; and since we think that an account of this child which has been so happily conceived and born, an even greater cause for happiness and congratulations equal to ours has befallen Your Serene Highness because although this is not our first child, it may nevertheless seem to be the first since it is the first to have occurred for us after the most happy union of our kingdoms; we thus wrote this letter . . . so that Your Serene Highness may learn that a most beautiful daughter has been born to us; that our wife is safe and sound and (as from a recent birth) enjoying a not disagreeable health.

This rather moving letter seems to grow out of James's unvarnished delight in the birth of a child. Without detracting from the sincerity of this letter, one also notes that James always showed his best side to his brother-in-law. This refreshing letter of paternal pride demonstrates James's genuine concern about the well-being of his family. Unfortunately, he did not remain consistent on that issue.[21]

Mary's baptism took place on May 5, 1605, amid much pomp and display at Greenwich. There had been much scurrying about and perusing of historical records in order to recall how a royal child should be baptized. A contemporary description reveals the attention that focused on this the first royal baptism in England since 1537 and the first to follow the Protestant rites of the firmly established Church of England:

> First, the three Courts at Greenwich were rayled in and hung about with broad cloth, where the proceeding should passe. The Childe was brought from the Queene's lodgings through both the Great chambers, once through the Presence, and downe the winding stayres into the Conduit-court. At the foote whereof attended a canapy borne by eight Barons, before which went the Officers of Armes, and divers Bishoppes, Barons, and Earles.

One cushion held many jewels "of inestimable price." Arbella Stuart served as one of the godmothers; the countess of Northumberland, the other. In the chapel "stoode a very rich and stately font of silver and gilt, most curiously wrought with figures of beastes, serpents, and other antycke workes." Not so much attention and splendor had governed a royal baptism since Prince Henry's at Stirling Castle in 1594. In the chapel at Greenwich stood the royal family, parents and children, encircling this new child with their joy. As P. M. Handover suggests, "A christening marked more comfortably than any other ceremony the security with which the family of James the First held the throne of England." His Scottish children had an English sister.[22]

But the security of the royal family had every chance to come apart with the blasts of the Gunpowder Plot, fortunately discovered and aborted on November 5, 1605. Disgruntled Catholics—among them Guy Fawkes, whose name has ever since been associated with the day—intended to blow up James, Anne, Henry, and members of Parliament at its opening on that day. The conspirators also intended to capture Princess Elizabeth and set her up as queen, a child presumably easy to control. Harington reported her reaction when she learned of the scheme: "Her Highness doth often say, What a Queen should I have been by this means? I had rather have been with my royal father in the Parliament-House, than wear this crown on such condition." Enormous relief greeted news of the discovery of the conspiracy, and interpreters saw God's hand of deliverance at work.[23]

Certainly James fastened onto the idea of providential deliverance in an eloquent and politically skillful speech that he delivered in Parliament on November 9. James offered thanksgiving to God "for the great and miraculous Delivery he hath at this time granted to me, and to you all, and consequently to the whole body of this Estate." The occasion gave him an opportunity to reiterate his idea of the divine right of the king. He also took note of the dangers that he had confronted throughout his life, remembering even his prenatal danger: "I amongst all other Kings have ever bene subject unto them [dangers], not onely ever since my birth, but even as I may justly say, before my birth: and while I was yet in my mothers belly," a reference to the murder of Riccio. He also alluded to the Gowrie Conspiracy of 1600. He noted that the intended destruction would have included "not onely . . . the destruction of my Person, nor of my Wife and posteritie onely, but of the whole body of the State in generall." James, careful to give God the credit for the miraculous discovery, did not hesitate to boast of his skill in uncovering the plot. When shown a letter about the plot, James "did upon the instant interpret and apprehend some darke phrases therein, contrary to the ordinary Grammer construction of them." Because of his interpretive skills, he ordered a thorough search of Parliament, and the searchers found the gunpowder. He even wished, "There were a Christall window in my brest, wherein all my people might see the secretest thoughts" of his heart. James's familiar metaphor may be attributed to the enthusiasm of the moment, for he had little intention that anyone should discern his secret thoughts. And, of course, he assuredly did not have a crystal heart. He, like his predecessor, knew much about the political and personal advantages of cultivating "coffers of perplexity." For the moment the country rejoiced in the security of the royal family and would henceforth commemorate November 5. The birth of Mary and the deliverance in November suggested for the moment a comic plot unfolding in the royal family's life: second chances and new hopes.[24]

Once again excitement filled the air about a royal birth in 1606. Anne withdrew to Greenwich to await the birth of her seventh child. Finally, on June 22, Anne gave birth to another daughter, this one named Sophia in honor of Anne's mother. Unfortunately, the child lived only a few hours and died on the day of her birth. Three days later a barge carried Sophia along the Thames to Westminster Abbey for burial. Her monument in the Abbey showed her asleep in an alabaster cradle. The Latin inscription says, "Sophia, a royal rosebud, untimely plucked to death; . . . Torn from her parents to bloom afresh in the rose garden of Christ." After seven births and three miscarriages, there would be no more children. Anne did not try to console James or herself, as she had after the death of Robert, that they would soon have another child. A gulf of silence that already existed between husband and wife would widen. After Sophia's birth and death, Anne sank into a desperate depression.[25]

Only her brother's visit in mid-July 1606 succeeded in lifting Anne's spirits. In 1604 her brother Ulric, duke of Holstein, had visited for several months, and in 1606 her brother Christian IV, king of Denmark, came for a visit. Anne had not seen him for sixteen years, since she sailed away to her life in Scotland. But in July, Christian finally arrived in London, welcomed nobly by James and Henry. He went to Greenwich to find Anne and surprised her with his sudden appearance in her room. She was thrilled to see him, and his zest buoyed her spirits and increased her will to live.

On July 31, all of London celebrated the royal visit with a civic pageant as Christian IV, James, and Henry moved in procession through the streets, starting at the Tower. Though the entertainment was hurriedly put together, it did not lack the essential devices of welcome. The conduit in Cheapside, for example, took the form of a garden, adorned with fruit of all kinds. Nearby stood a triumphal arch covered with sea scenes, including a representation of Neptune dressed in blue and mounted on a seahorse. Atop the arch Concord presided; by a "quaint device" she descended the arch, addressed the kings, and revealed a model of the City of London (reminiscent of the 1604 pageant). The speeches, all in Latin, praised

Christian's visit. In Fleet Street a summer arbor contained a shepherd and his coy mistress who would not love him until she could behold two suns of equal brightness, two majesties of like splendor, or two kings in one state. The presence of James and Christian obviously satisfied these requirements. Throughout, this pageant emphasized concord and harmony. The simple presence of these two royal families underscored dynastic relationships, how one royal family extended into another through marriage. The pageant made clear the Stuart royal family's links to ruling houses of western Europe.[26]

The entertainment that took place at Theobalds under the aegis of Cecil had less salutary results. The famous letter from Harington re-counted a disastrous evening of entertainment with James and Christian present. The notorious indulgence in alcohol by the Danes seems to have affected the whole event. The person representing the queen of Sheba fell into the Danish king's lap; then James arose to dance with this queen, but he fell down and was carried out. The Theolog-ical Virtues, Hope, Faith, and Charity, appeared. "Hope did assay to speak, but wine rendered her endeavours so feeble that she with-drew"; Faith "left the Court in a staggering condition." Charity re-turned to Hope and Faith, "who were both sick and spewing in the lower hall. Next came Victory, in bright armour, and presented a rich sword to the King, who did not accept it." And so the evening went. Instead of a masque a parody occurred, albeit an unintentional one. James apparently did his best to match his brother-in-law drink for drink. Almost a month after he had arrived, Christian IV departed for Denmark on August 11. Anne and Henry especially enjoyed and benefited from the visit: Anne renewed in spirit and Henry finding a king whom he could admire and imitate (except for the drinking). Such festivity helped shove into the background the sad death of Sophia.[27]

Two events in 1607 helped shape the royal family's life from this point on, thereby making 1607 one of those crucial, pivotal years: the death of the daughter Mary in September and the beginning of James's long involvement with Robert Carr. These events also de-fined the future relationship of Anne and James. As their relation-ship began to wane, the importance of the royal children and of Carr began to emerge. In late summer 1607, Mary became ill; she had, according to a letter from Rowland Whyte to the earl of Shrewsbury, "a burning fever for 23 daies, and a continuall rhewme fell to her lunges, and putrified there, which she had not strength to voyd." On September 16 the two-year-old princess died. Shortly before her death, the Venetian ambassador reported: "The King is at Theobalds; the Queen at Hampton Court, very sorry about the indisposition of her daughter, to whom the King is devotedly attached, and it is thought he will give up the chace to go to her." Since Mary died at Lord Knyvett's house at Stanwell, we recognize that neither parent attended the dying child. James allowed himself to contemplate giving up his hunting. Whyte wrote in his letter that the "King takes her death as a wise Prince should doe." The little princess was buried on September 18 without solemnity or a funeral, placed in her final resting place near her sister Sophia, who had died the previous year. After Mary's death, James sent the earl of Salisbury (Cecil) to console the queen, as indicated in a letter from Sir Roger Aston to Salisbury, dated September 17 (?): "[James] desires you to bend all your force to persuade her Majesty that this burial may not be a second grief: it is not for charge, but only for removing of the grievous present and the griefs to come. He is going this morning to Chesson [Cheshunt] Park to hunt."[28]

However we interpret James's reaction to Mary's death—an example of the "psychic numbing" defined by Lawrence Stone or of James's incapacity for confronting death—the episode is disturbing. It also contrasts with the earlier response to the death of Robert in 1602. An obvious insensitivity on the part of both Anne and James strongly suggests that something had been happening to parental and familial sensibilities: an indifference that diminished human feelings had begun to take hold. James's hunting and continuing to live his indulgent life in the immediate aftermath of Mary's death, her almost anonymous burial, and Anne's remoteness speak tellingly about the royal family, one no longer held tightly together by emotional bonds. In the pounding of hooves, the barking of dogs, the scurrying of pursued animals in the chase, we may hear a silent disregard of parental demands.

The Venetian ambassador, Molin, offered in 1607 an excellent analysis of several members of the royal family. He wrote of James:

> His Majesty is by nature placid, averse from cruelty, a lover of justice. . . . He loves quiet and repose, has no inclination to war, . . . a fact that little pleases many of his subjects, though it pleases them still less that he leaves all government to his Council and will think of nothing but the chase. He does not caress the people nor make them that good cheer the late Queen did, . . . they like their King to show pleasure at their devotion, as the late Queen knew well how to do; but this King manifests no taste for them but rather contempt and dislike. The result is he is despised and almost hated. In fact his Majesty is more inclined to live retired with eight or ten of his favourites than openly, as is the custom of the country and the desire of the people.

A French diplomat, Count Harley de Beaumont, had anticipated Molin's analysis as early as 1603: "It appears to them [the people] strange that this king should despise them and live in so complete retirement. They exclaim aloud, the residence at Theobald's will spoil him." Beaumont elsewhere reports James's extreme anger when the public pressed in upon him while he was hunting: "He cursed every one he met, and swore that if they would not let him follow the chase at his pleasure, he would leave England." Such outbursts, Beaumont suggests, "draw upon him great contempt and inextinguishable hate from the people."[29]

Dating from September 1603, barely six months after James came to the English throne, Beaumont's diplomatic report demonstrated James's conflict with the public, a tension that persisted throughout his reign. The word *hatred* crops up with frightening regularity in numerous reports. James seems to have forgotten many of the precepts that permeate his *Basilicon Doron,* such as his concept of the king as set on a stage "whose smallest actions and gestures, all the people gazinglie doe beholde." To his great cost, James chose to play out in the theater of state a role that ignored the people, often more content with hunting than even with responding to the needs of his own family. He made a mockery of the wish that his heart were a crystal that all might gaze on and know his pure intents: he did not truly want anyone to come that close. One recalls that trenchant assessment made by the Frenchman Fontenay in 1584, after an extensive interview with James. Surely James's virtues, as Fontenay perceived them, had not noticeably increased; and his three principal faults or weaknesses remained firmly intact. James continued to live prodigally, love inadvisedly, and remain thoughtless over his affairs by indulging in hunting.

At moments, however, James could be thoughtful, spontaneous, and generous with his family and others. He wrote his brother-in-law in Denmark in early June 1603 as he anticipated the arrival from Scotland of his family, telling Christian about the proposed coronation: "We shall make your sister our choicest and most sweet wife share the crown and diadem." He noted that Anne was bringing Henry with her and "our sweetest little daughter" and that Christian could "easily appreciate how much our enjoyment of this pleasure will be augmented." Sometime shortly after Anne's arrival in England, James took note of her looks and, calling some nobles around him, asked them "if they did not think his *Anny* (as he generally called her) looked passing-well; and my little *Bessy* too (added he, taking his Daughter up in his Arms, and kissing her) is not an ill-faur'd [ill-favored] Wench, and may out-shine her Mother one of these Days." In December 1603, James wrote Christian again, recounting the summer's coronation: "We saw to it that she [Anne] was adorned equally with us by a crown and the insignia of the royal office; thus we have now allotted and prepared a most ample dower for her, which corresponds to our love for her." James claimed that Anne would have a dower larger "than any of our royal ancestors in this kingdom ever bestowed on a wife." Lord Harington, Princess Elizabeth's guardian, wrote to Salisbury in early 1607, reporting a gift that James had sent his daughter: "I have received your letter and therewith the jewel of a diamond, a ruby and a pendant pearl, the diamond set about with little diamonds; which was delivered to the Lady Elizabeth from the King, which she received with great joy as an assured testimony of his favour." The extravagance of this gift aside, James had responded to his daughter in a way that he understood.[30]

When James decided to give material gifts, he gave liberally. The old and sick archbishop of York wrote to Salisbury in 1604, complaining of James's gift-giving: "His Majesty's subjects hear and fear that his excellent and heroical nature is too much inclined to giving, which in short time will exhaust the treasure of this kingdom and bring many inconveniences." The archbishop's fears correspond to those expressed by Fontenay twenty years earlier in Scotland. James remained consistent in some matters. Financial records of the period reinforced the image of a profligate court. James gave generously, and he spent lavishly on himself. For example, he spent up to £37,000 per year for jewels. The nearly empty coffer of James's treasury marred his reign throughout, leading to some embarrassing searches for money. The land of milk and honey to which James came in 1603 from the bleak northern latitudes of Scotland did not have limitless resources for a squandering monarch.[31]

Jealousy and insensitivity also defined some of James's actions. Gervase Holles recalled asking why the earl of Clare had never attained prominence in James's court; the answer came from Sir Francis Nedham: "For (sayes he) two sortes of men K. James had never kindness for: those whose hawkes and dogges flew and run as well as his owne, and those who were able to speake as much reason as himselfe." Within a month of James's arrival in England a special representative of the French government had numerous private conversations with him and thereby reached some conclusions about James. No one, M. Sully noted, could come into the king's presence dressed in mourning black in memory of Queen Elizabeth. Indeed, "so strong an affectation prevailed [at court] to obliterate the memory of that great princess, that she was never spoke of, and even the mention of her name industriously avoided." Sully detected other evidence of James's contempt for Elizabeth, as James insisted that he had actually ruled England in Elizabeth's last years. Surely part of this attitude grew out of James's jealous response to his revered predecessor. So James indulged in a kind of reverse fiction about Elizabeth: that is, she and Mary seem to have exchanged positions in James's mind, diminishing the role of Elizabeth and elevating that of his mother.[32]

On one occasion, Sully recorded, James drank a toast to the royal family of France; Sully responded by drinking to him and his children. James then "inclined himself to my ear when he heard me name them [the royal children], and told me softly, that the next health he would drink should be, to the double union which he meditated between the royal houses." Since James had not before broached the subject of dynastic marriages between the royal children of England and France, Sully said: "I thought the opportunity which he had thus taken for it was not extremely well chosen." At the least, Sully found this conversation a breach of decorum. To raise the question of marriage on this occasion when the oldest child was but nine years old may be understandable if not overly eager. Certainly the French ambassador found the occasion inappropriate.[33]

Having observed James closely and having had many conversations with him, the Frenchman Sully reached some conclusions about the character of this new king of England. Sully wrote in 1603:

> Let me add, that he [James] meant well, was conscientious, eloquent, and had some erudition; though less of the latter, than of penetration and a disposition to learning. He loved to hear discourses on state-affairs, and to be entertained with great designs, . . . but he never thought of carrying them farther, for he naturally hated war. . . . He was indolent in his actions, except in hunting, and wanted application in his affairs; all which were signs of an easy and timid disposition, that made it highly probable he would be governed by others.

Fontenay, Molin, and Sully reached surprisingly similar conclusions about James, perhaps from their vantage point as foreigners. Sully's last point about James's weak disposition implied James's vulnerability: he could easily be governed by others, although not by members of his family. In this regard James remained susceptible to attractive young men.[34]

Enter Robert Carr in 1607. Carr, a Scot, had actually come to England with James in 1603 as a lowly page in the royal household. Eventually he was dismissed from this service and went to France, where he gained some level of sophistication; he then returned to England. Courtiers had seen James's attraction to Philip Herbert, earl of Montgomery, and angled to find some young man to replace him and thereby gain power at court. A single accident brought Carr to James's attention: he fell from his horse during the Accession Day Tilt, attended by James. James wanted to determine if the young man had been seriously injured, took one look at Carr, and apparently became immediately smitten with him. He had his own physicians take care of Carr, visited him daily, and began trying to teach this handsome young man Latin—James ever the pedant. The English had not yet seen in 1607 much of James's vulnerability to attractive men; but surely the Scots might have recalled Esmé Stuart, Arran, and Huntly.

By December 1607, John Chamberlain wrote his friend Dudley Carleton: "Sir Robert Carre a younge Scot and new favorite is lately sworne gentleman of the bed-chamber." As we know from James's earlier experience, he had a tendency to shower favorites with gifts and titles with alacrity. A contemporary described Carr as "rather well compacted than tall, his features comely and handsome rather than beautiful; the hair of his head flaxen, that of his face tinctured with yellow." James's physical attraction to Carr cannot be denied. Thomas Howard wrote to Harington that Carr was "straight-limbed, well-favoured, strong-shouldered, and smooth-faced, with some sort of cunning and show of modesty." In this 1611 letter, Howard also described James's reaction to Carr: "The Prince leaneth on his arm, pinches his cheeks, smoothes his ruffled garment, and, when he looketh at Carr, directeth discourse to divers others." Other sources bear out Francis Osborne's conclusion about James's treatment of his favorites: "Nor was his [James's] love . . . carried on with a discretion sufficient to cover a lesse scandalous behaviour; for the kings kissing them after so lascivious a mode in publick, and upon the theatre, as it were, of the world, prompted many to imagine some things done in the tyring-house, that exceed my expressions no lesse then they do my experience." Sexual attraction aside, James wanted to shape this young man in his own image and at the same time to use him. Someone like Carr could become not merely a fulfillment of pleasure but an increasing force in the government. In fact, Carr was the first favorite since Esmé Stuart to be of much political importance. As we shall see, by 1611 Carr had become viscount Rochester and by 1613 earl of Somerset. James's response to Carr clearly affected his familial relationships; indeed, James lavished attention and affection on Carr in ways that his own family seldom experienced from him. Carr's prominence continued to dominate the next period of James's life in England until his downfall.[35]

Surely Anne saw the danger in Carr's rise to power and the way in which James's fixation moved family members a little farther out of his view, to the outer edges of a growing silence. Molin offered this evaluation of Anne in 1607: "The Queen is very gracious, moderately good looking. . . . She likes enjoyment and is very fond of dancing and of fêtes. She is intelligent and prudent; and knows the disorders of the government, in which she has no part. . . . All she ever does is to beg a favour for some one. She is full of kindness for those who support her, but on the other hand she is terrible, proud, and unendurable to those she dislikes." On the final point many people, such as the earl of Mar, could testify. The Frenchman Sully saw her as the opposite of James: "She was naturally bold and enterprizing; she loved pomp and grandeur, tumult and intrigue." We recall that some evidence pointed to her possible involvement in the Gowrie Conspiracy in 1600. Generally, she seems not to have functioned much in national politics, preferring to set her sights a bit lower. But she struggled bitterly to win control of Prince Henry back in Scotland.[36]

Anne still had designs for Henry after they arrived in England. Imprudently, Anne informed the French diplomat Beaumont in 1604: "It is time that I should have possession of the Prince and gain his affection, for the King drinks so much, and conducts himself so ill in every respect, that I expect an early and evil result." Beaumont captured the essence of Anne's strategy "to corrupt the spirit and disposition of the Prince . . . by flattering his little passions, by diverting him from his lessons and exercises, and (to the vexation of his father) representing the sciences to him as unworthy of a great commander and conqueror." On another occasion, she even told Beaumont, to his dismay, that she hoped "her son will one day overrun France as well as his ancestor Henry V." The struggle for Henry appears often to have been a striking out against James and may have represented a frustration that Anne felt in her relationship with James. Or the child merely became the battleground on which the parents acted out their conflict with one another. In any event, the struggle for parental power affected the political world as well, especially given that Henry was heir apparent. Domestic family life inevitably intersected state politics.[37]

Yet Anne wrote her brother of James's increasing affection toward her; she claimed: "There is nothing fit for us in honour and contentation wherein we shall need any other means than the merit of our own love and due observation of his princely and just desires." A letter from Anne to James in the British Library collection implies genuine concern:

> Sir, as nothing is more wellcom to me then your letters (for which I thank you) so can they bring me no better tidings then of your good health (of me much desired) for I cease not to praye for the encrease and continuance of your good both of mynd and bodie, and thereof rest assured, so kissing your handes I remaine she that will ever love you best
> Anna. R.

Responding to James's recent illness, Anne wrote: "I was glayde to have the occasion of this bearer that thereby I might knowe of your good healthe nowe after your last so unpleasant removeing day, and I have commanded him to bring me bak certane word therof from your selfe." In other letters she and James shared a joke between them. In private conversation with her friend and James's kinswoman Arbella Stuart, Anne could reflect a rather more cynical view of love. A contemporary reported a conversation between the two women. Anne said to Arbella: " 'Oh! I ask no more,' interrupted the Queen, 'and I have no Fear of your Success, for Love is nothing but a Fancy, which soon goes off, if not indulged.' " Arbella could not respond because James entered the room. Anne no longer had any patience with romantic notions about love, though she remained capable of love for her family and at least genuine concern about James's welfare.[38]

What can one make of the relationship of husband and wife, James and Anne, in 1607 after nearly twenty years of marriage? The "revisionist" writer William Sanderson commented in 1656: "A matchless pair, drawing evenly in all courses of honour, and both blessed with fair issue, because never loose from eithers Bed." Osborne noted an outward display of affection presumably shortly after the arrival in England: "He [James] that evening parted with his queene, and to shew himselfe more uxorious before the people . . . than in private he was, he did at her coach side take his leave, by kissing her sufficiently to the middle of the shoulders." In Jonson's entertainment devised for their visit to Theobalds in May 1607, the speaker Clotho says:

> When underneath thy roof is seen
> The greatest King, the fairest Queen;
> With Princes an unmatched pair;
> One, hope of all the earth, their heir.

At such a moment all seems well in the royal family; but masques present versions of reality that may not square with the facts.[39]

Just a month before Queen Elizabeth's death, Chamberlain wrote to Carleton: "New troubles arise dayly in Scotland, but the worst of all is the domesticall daungers and hartbreaking that the Kinge findes in his owne house." One wonders precisely what Chamberlain referred to in February 1603; it could have been the ongoing struggle over Prince Henry. Regardless, the observation says much about what many contemporaries understood of the climate in the royal household. Chamberlain reported in 1607 of a feast at the Merchant-Taylors hall at which James and Henry became "free" of the guild; he added, "The Quene was not there though she were assuredly looked for"—another example of Anne's habit or strategy of being absent. This event in and of itself was relatively unimportant; but it did underscore a growing chasm in the royal family as each member sought his or her own place, leaving a void of silence where union and harmony might have existed.[40]

Bishop Godfrey Goodman, writing about 1650 in reaction to Anthony Weldon's unfavorable account of James, tried to make the best possible case for James and Anne, observing that at least they did have children. He wrote: "It is true that some years after they did not much keep company together. The King of himself was a very chaste man, and there was little in the Queen to make him uxorious; yet they did love as well as man and wife could do, not conversing together." By "not conversing together" the good bishop presumably meant not having sexual intercourse, a now obscure meaning of "converse." Clearly Edward Peyton implied this idea when he reported: "Now King James, more addicted to love males then females, though for complement he visited Queen Anne, yet never lodged with her a night for many yeers." Only a tortuous kind of logic could lead Sanderson to claim that they were never "loose from eithers Bed." Weldon noted that James "was ever best, when furthest from his Queene, and that was thought to be the first grounds of his often removes, which afterwards proved habituall." Not conversing together—habitual absences—indifference: these seem to be the qualities that defined much of the married life of James and Anne.[41]

One can safely assume that after 1607 little remained of a husband-wife relationship—only personal accommodation and separate little kingdoms within the kingdom. Only the rosiest-colored spectacles would allow one to see James and Anne as a "matchless pair." McElwee suggests that the death of Sophia in 1606, followed by the death of Mary in 1607, "seems to have damaged the relation-ship between James and Anne irreparably." McElwee also argues that James had lost the affections of Henry and Elizabeth by 1607 and that Charles was still too young to fill James's need to spoil and pamper his children. With the members of his family in some state of disaffection, James's attention turned in 1607 to Robert Carr; and the involvement with him would be a source of continuing tension within the royal family, especially with Anne and Henry. Not only a question of personal behavior, Carr's rise to power had dangerous political implications. The James who wrote love poems to Anne, who sailed across dangerous seas to fetch his bride home to Scot-land, who had her crowned queen of Scotland and later queen of England, had lost all interest in her as his wife; she remained a con-venient political symbol of a family. James, after all, made clear that he had married for political reasons; the first blush of love for Anne lasted about as long as morning dew.[42]

At the same time a growing chorus of talk focused on the royal children, especially Henry and Elizabeth, who by 1608 and there-after had taken their full places at court. The remainder of this first decade of life in England for the Stuart royal family would center on these children. We recall the portrait by the Venetian ambassador in 1610, with which this chapter began, with each member of the family in place at court, offering an image of solidarity, though tensions clearly existed in the royal household. But a gap occurs between the one-dimensional portrait of an ambassador and the cumulative ev-idence that provides us a much fuller picture. The ambassador's verbal portrait remains incomplete, concerned as it is only with the outward image, the theatrical appearance ("magnificent specta-cle"). Behind this picture lies another reality. The Stuart royal family offered a fiction to the public, a spectacle that may or may not have coincided with the truth. Apart from the task of governing, the royal family has, simply stated, a twofold function: offer a magnificent spectacle and provide for an orderly political succession. James stood there to receive the ambassador, full of frustrated hopes about getting from Parliament an Act of Union that would legally join Scotland and England, desperate to find new revenues to finance the royal indulgence, perhaps wary of the rising importance of the children, enamored of Carr, and eager to get out on the hunt. Anne, dis-abused of love, cognizant of her political irrelevance, disturbed by James's governing, uneasy about the future of her children, and de-termined to foster more court masques and festivities, went through her paces as royal consort. The children, as yet unburdened with all these problems and uncertainties, basked in the excitement of Henry's investiture as Prince of Wales.

The paradox of royal children manifests itself repeatedly, especially in the person of Henry and his father's reaction to him. Osborne, writing later in the century, aptly stated the nature of the problem: "Kings may be concluded farre more unhappy then ordinary men: for though, whilest children are young, they may afford them safety, yet when arrived at that age, which useth to bring comfort to other parents, they produce only jealousies and feares." These children disturb instead of offering felicity. Osborne's assessment, borne out many times, proves that royal families resemble other aristocratic families, except that problems assume greater importance. James Welwood notes: "King *James* was equally happy and unhappy in every one of his Children. Prince *Henry* . . . the Darling of Mankind . . . was too soon Man, to be long-liv'd." Roger Coke notes that Henry's court "was more frequented than the King's, and by another sort of Men; so the King was heard to say, *will he bury me alive*?" James apparently found even the presence of a separate and orderly household an implicit threat.[43]

James in 1603 stated his awareness of Henry's obvious function: "He was not ours only, as a child of a natural father; but as an heir apparent to our body politic, in whom our estate and kingdoms are especially interested." The child, like his father, had two bodies: his natural body and his body politic. Henry belonged to the country as well as to his family. James had offered a reliable summary of the nature of family politics. Charles Cornwallis, the treasurer of Henry's household, wrote to him from Madrid in March 1609, observing that James was particularly blessed by a son "in whom he may hope to be succeeded not only in his Kingdoms but in his knoledge, wisedome and other vertues." The more people talked about Henry as James's successor, the more jealous James became.[44]

Having commented on James and Anne, the Venetian ambassador, Molin, in 1607 also had observations about Henry. Molin wrote: "Henry is about twelve years old, of a noble wit and great promise. His every action is marked by a gravity most certainly beyond his years. He studies, but not with much delight, and chiefly under his father's spur." The young man became increasingly involved in political matters. Roy Strong notes: "From as early as 1607, when Henry was only thirteen, he [Cecil] had kept the Prince and his tutor, Adam Newton, abreast of political events. Ambassadorial dispatches were even sent for his perusal." Ironically, James himself did little to encourage Henry's political education. Having written *Basilicon Doron,* James apparently concluded that he had done his duty of instructing his son in the art of government. Presumably James understood the paradox of this royal child whose ultimate function was to replace him; not offering political instruction might forestall, at least in the mind, that seeming inevitability. On March 21, 1610, in an address to Parliament, James referred to Henry as "that posteritie and issue which it hath pleased God to send me for your use." Then he turned to the question of Henry's investiture as Prince of Wales, planned for 1610: "As for him [Henry] I say no more; the sight of himselfe here speakes for him." Apparently James does not intend to speak for Henry: "I say no more"—silence. This revealing statement to Parliament says more than James probably intended. Its brevity astounds: what remains unspoken? The verbose James has nothing to say about his son and heir apparent. Such an image fits well the irony, paradox, and tragedy that would govern Henry's life from 1610 to his death in November 1612.[45]

At the beginning of 1611 Henry appeared in the masque *Oberon,* written by Jonson, as the title character. Given this mythological character's link to Shakespeare's play, Henry indeed for a while seemed Oberon in a midsummer night's dream; by November 1612, however, that dream had transformed into a winter's tale—one of tragedy and woe. Writing in the late nineteenth century, the historian Samuel Gardiner offered this self-congratulatory, glowing assessment of Prince Henry: "In his bright face old men saw a prospect of a return to the Elizabethan glories of their youth. His mind was open to all noble influences, and, if he had lived, he would have been able to rule Engla•d, because he would have sympathised . . . with all that was good and great in the English character." Gardiner further suggested that in time Henry would have acquired the qualities of prudence and circumspection that he lacked. Gardiner's Victorian excesses aside, this view of Henry squared with much that his contemporaries said. Francis Bacon, for example, wrote: "The goodness of his disposition had awakened manifold hopes among members of all ranks, nor had he lived long enough to disappoint them." E. C. Wilson, J. W. Williamson, and more recently Strong have provided modern book-length studies that do much to put Henry in proper perspective.[46]

The year 1610 marked Henry's full arrival on the public stage, culminating in his investiture as Prince of Wales in June. On Twelfth Night *Prince Henry's Barriers,* written by Jonson and designed by Inigo Jones, took place at the Banqueting House in Whitehall. In this indoor tournament set in Arthurian England, Henry, designated as "Meliadus," awakened the spirit of Chivalry. Chivalry cried out:

> Break, you rusty doors
> That have so long been shut, and from the shores
> Of all the world come knighthood like a flood
> Upon these lists to make the field here good.

These *Barriers* idealized Henry, at some cost to James. Strong notes: "The *Barriers* presented the Prince as the exponent of a policy diametrically opposed to the royal one. We see the young Prince present the new court of St. James's as the thinly veiled focus for a revival of the Elizabethan war party, fiercely Protestant and anti-Habsburg." Chamberlain wrote to Winwood that the *Barriers* "were well performed, and the Prince behaved himself every way very well and gracefully." The next day, Chamberlain reported, the Prince "with his assistants all in a liverie, and the defendants in theyre best braverie rode in great pompe to convoy the King to St. James whether he had invited him and all the court to supper (the Quene only beeing absent)." Anne's odd absence from such festivity, Chamberlain explained, was due to her melancholy: "She hath ben somwhat melancolike of late about her joynter that was not fully to her liking." The realities of finances crept in to counter the festive mood, leading the queen at least to refuse to join in. Melancholy undercut all Twelfth Night festivities.[47]

Henry experienced his own melancholy, the result of the assassination of Henry IV of France on May 4, 1610. Strong reports: "On hearing of the news of the French king's murder he [Henry] is said to have taken to his bed for several days repeating the words, 'My second father is dead.'" Henry IV thus had functioned as a substitute father for Henry, but one he could know only at a distance and through discourse. Some of the prince's letters to the French king survive. What Henry never spelled out—possibly because he could not—is why he needed a "second father." Henry had idolized the French king and may have been involved in some of the king's secret plans to reshape western European politics. The French king had carefully cultivated Henry's good will, as Strong notes, sending him presents, such as horses and armor. The prince's enthusiasm for Henry IV far exceeded that expressed by King James. Henry had developed a strong case of hero worship. Henry recovered from his grief in time for all the festivities associated with his investiture.[48]

On May 31, Henry received the City of London's adulation in a water pageant on the Thames written by Anthony Munday and entitled *Londons Love to the Royall Prince Henrie.* The figure Corinea, riding on a whale, addressed Henry, calling attention to the province of Cornwall and also acknowledging the "Royall Soveraigne your Father, his Queene your peerlesse Mother, your sacred selfe, and the rest of their illustrious race." Amphion on a dolphin, a role performed by Richard Burbage, represented Wales and said to Henry, "The Sunne of true-borne Majestie shines in your bright eye." This hurriedly put together pageant suitably launched the official investiture, if in a somewhat diminished form.[49]

The investiture ceremony took place on June 4 amid much pomp and extraordinary color. The young boy baptized at Stirling Castle in 1594 now had gained the title of Prince of Wales, a clear sign of his status as heir apparent. The royal patent document, preserved in the British Library, that proclaims Henry as Prince of Wales contains a beautiful illuminated portrait in its upper left-hand corner. This picture shows Henry kneeling before his father, who presents him with a scroll, presumably the very patent for his creation. This may well be the only picture of father and son together: typically members of this Stuart royal family were portrayed alone. Therefore, the patent itself simultaneously anticipates and depicts the moment at which Henry would become Prince of Wales. This rare portrait of James and Henry underscores the importance of this event in the political and personal life of the Stuart royal family.[50]

On June 5 at Whitehall, a masque, arranged by Queen Anne, written by Daniel, and designed by Jones, entitled *Tethys' Festival,* took place with all the royal family involved. Anne performed the role of Tethys, queen of the ocean and wife to Neptune; Princess Elizabeth represented the nymph of Thames; Arbella Stuart, the nymph of Trent; and Prince Charles, Zephyrus. Strong says that the masque "attempted to restage the investiture in allegorical form." In the opening speech Triton linked together the Stuart family, with Henry retaining his fictional name from the *Barriers.* The tritons sang:

> Bear Tethys' message to the ocean King,
> Say how she joys to bring
> Delight unto his islands and his seas,
> And tell Meliades [i.e., Henry],
> The offspring of his blood,
> How she applauds his good.

Triton then presented James with a trident and Henry with a "rich sword and scarf." Anne and Charles were especially busy in the masque. In many ways one may see this masque as Anne's triumph,

Prince Henry kneeling before his father King James (1610), accepting the patent that created him Prince of Wales. The portrait appears on the patent itself, British Library Add. MS. 36932. Courtesy of the British Library.

too; that is, the son that she had fought over and desired to control had at last received royal sanction as the king's successor. She and the masque "applaud good."[51]

The conclusion to this year of celebration and spectacle came with the performance on January 1, 1611, of the masque *Oberon, the Fairy Prince*, prepared by Jonson and Jones, with Henry performing the role of Oberon. As Orgel aptly observes: "Spenserian romance joins with classical myth to create a Britain that unites the traditions of chivalry with classical order." The design for Henry's costume suggested both a medieval knight and a Roman emperor. Strong writes: "In the masque, the Prince is presented as the heir to the Elizabethan world of fairy." But, as Strong argues, the ideology and mythology of James and Henry conflicted with one another in *Oberon*. Therefore, Jonson found it difficult to present an apotheosis of the prince while in the presence of the king. Oberon made a spectacular entry in a chariot drawn by two white bears; the song that greeted him welcomed him to Arthur's chair. Sylvan and Silenus gave long speeches that outlined the fairy land to be presided over by Oberon, a world now governed by his majesty and "his great empress." Sylvan concluded:

> That all that shall tonight behold the rites
> Perform'd by princely Ob'ron and these Knights
> May, without stop, point out the proper heir
> Design'd so long to Arthur's crowns and chair.

Dancing and singing continued until "*Phosphorus the day-star appeared and called them away.*" A new day dawned in England as a young fairy prince readied himself to rule the kingdom. This fairy prince Henry became the mythical inheritor of the former world of the fairy queen Elizabeth. One can understand if James did not entirely approve the fiction or the obvious reality of a shifting tide of enthusiasm and allegiance toward his sixteen-year-old son. The yearlong spectacle that gripped the courtly world and caught the public's attention enunciated a view of the royal family and of royal power that honors and flatters. But such pageants fade.[52]

Despite the praise and adulation heaped on Henry then and later, an occasional voice spoke of the dangers inherent in such expectations. Osborne in his *Memoirs* described Henry as one "whom they [people] ingaged by so much expectation, as it may be doubted, whether it ever lay in the power of any prince meerly humane, to bring so much felicity into a nation." Those disgruntled with James, those yearning for a Protestant union of Europe, those itching for war—all rallied to the cause and hope of Henry. Surely some who looked on him with adulation did so through nostalgic eyes, a view rather encouraged by the masques. As a growing political force, Henry stood out among the royal children. Assessing his own designs is difficult, but we know that he did little to dissuade those who wanted to use him for a political cause. The crucial years from his arrival in England to his death marked an ever-enlarging role for Henry in politics, as the festivities of 1610 make clear. His death dashed all expectations.[53]

Sanderson in his *Compleat History* offers a physical description of Henry, indebted to Cornwallis: "Hee was comely tall, five foot eight Inches high, strong and well made, broad shouldred, a small wast, amiable with Majesty, Aborn Hair, long-faced, broad forehead, a peircing grave Eye, a gracious smile, but with a frown, daunting." This description corresponds with the pictures of Henry, such as the militant one in Michael Drayton's *Poly-Olbion*. Francis Bacon adds: "In body he was strong and erect, of middle height, his limbs gracefully put together, his gait kinglike, his face long and somewhat lean, his habit rather full, his countenance composed, and the motion of his eyes rather sedate than powerful." Bacon also says that "his mouth had a touch of pride." His speech was slow "as it were embarrassed." But "his slow and seldom speaking," Bacon says, "seemed to come rather from suspense and solicitude than weakness or dulness of judgment." Henry's speech pattern certainly contrasts with the garrulous nature of his father. These accounts hint of something slightly mysterious about Henry: the sedate yet piercing eye, the smile that carries with it a frown, the severe forehead—daunting, to use Sanderson's term.[54]

Praise of Henry as a warrior governs a number of contemporary accounts. Marcelline, for example, in *The Triumphs of King James* (1610), says boldly: "This young Prince is a warrior alreadie, both in gesture and countenance, so that in looking on him, he seemeth unto us, that in him we do yet see *Ajax* before *Troy*, crowding among the armed Troops, calling unto them, that he may joyne body to body with *Hector*, who standes trembling with chill-cold feare." Marcelline speaks darkly of Henry's waiting for the right opportunity to spring into action, "Yet let it not be immagined, that the execution of great desseignes, are utterly lost by deferrence and delay." Portraying his ultimate image of Henry, Marcelline offers a veritable emblem of him "as one figured Caesar, aloft, deposing or treading a Globe under him, holding a book in one hand, and a sword in the other: so that it may be saide of you, *That for the one & other you are a*

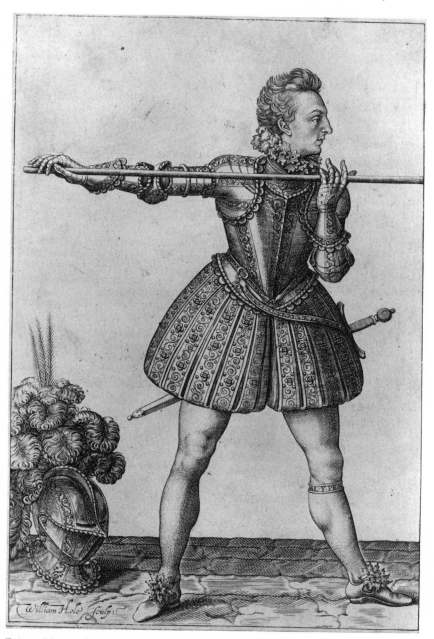

Prince Henry, from Michael Drayton's *Poly-Olbion* (1612) an engraving perhaps inspired by the Oliver miniature. Courtesy of the Folger Shakespeare Library.

**17** **TO THE MOST RENOWNED, AND**
Hopefull, ʜᴇɴʀɪᴇ Prince of ᴠᴠᴀʟᴇꜱ, &c.

Anagramma Au-
thor.s.

Βρεῖῖαννίκὲ ᾖ γαρεῖ.

ʜᴇɴʀɪᴄᴠꜱ Walliæ Princeps.
*Par Achillis, Puer vne vinces.*

Tʜᴠꜱ, thus young ʜᴇɴʀʏ, like Macedo's ſonne,
    Ought'ſt thou in armes before thy people ſhine.
A prodigie for foes to gaze vpon,
But ſtill a glorious Load-ſtarre vnto thine:
    Or ſecond ᴘʜᴏᴇʙᴠꜱ whoſe all piercing ray,
    Shall cheare our heartes, and chaſe our ſeares away.

That (once as * ᴘʜɪʟʟɪᴘ) ɪᴀᴍᴇꜱ may ſay of thee,
Thy ʙʀɪᴛᴀɪɴᴇ ſcarcely ſhall thy courage hold,
That whether ᴛᴠʀᴋᴇ, ꜱᴘᴀɪɴᴇ, ꜰʀᴀᴠɴᴄᴇ, or ɪᴛᴀʟɪᴇ,

* . Plutarch in A-
lexandro.

The ʀᴇᴅ-ꜱʜᴀɴᴋᴇ, or the ɪʀɪꜱʜ Rebell bold,
    Shall rouze thee vp, thy Trophees may be more,
    Then all the ʜᴇɴʀɪᴇꜱ euer liu'd before.

Baſil: Doron.

Maſte tua virtute decus, ſpes alma ʙʀɪᴛᴀɴɴᴇᴍ Provocet Hiſj anus, ſeu Turea, rebellis Hibernus
    Alter ᴀʟᴇxᴀɴᴅᴇʀ conſpiciende tuis : Herulus a tergo ſive laceſſat inops.
                                        E corpore.

Emblem for Prince Henry which emphasizes his potential role as warrior
in Peacham's *Minerva Britanna* (1612), a book dedicated to the prince.

Caesar." The implications frighten; this is no Oberon. Two years later, in 1612, Henry Peacham depicted Henry, in full armor astride a rearing horse, suggesting in the verses that whatever enemy confronts Henry, his "Trophees may be more, / Then all the HENRIES ever liv'd before." Unintentionally, this view echoes Anne's imprudent threat to the French diplomat. Clearly, some who rallied about Henry did so precisely because of his militaristic tendencies, which stand in great contrast to his father's pacifist policies.[55]

But this same Peacham saw another side of the prince: his generous interest in and support of the arts. Peacham, in fact, dedicated his emblem book to Henry, making him titular patron of the volume. Peacham wrote in the dedication: "Having by more then ordinarie signes, tasted heeretofore of your gratious favour . . . I am emboldened once againe, to offer up at the Altar of your gratious acceptance these mine *Emblemes.*" In addition to Peacham, Henry served as patron for George Chapman, Jonson, Drayton, and Jones. Henry also began to build an impressive collection of paintings that eventually passed to Prince Charles. Henry's interests extended to architecture and music. He also served as patron for one of the London adult acting companies, which bore his name; but a contemporary account by "W. H." says that Henry was not carried "away with any affection to stage-plays." Nor did Henry's interests extend to serious study and scholarship. James, Molin reports, admonished Henry for not studying more, threatening that the crown would be left to his brother Charles, "who was far quicker at learning and studied more earnestly." Henry held his tongue until later, when his tutor carried on in the same vein, he snapped: "I know what becomes a Prince. It is not necessary for me to be a professor, but a soldier and a man of the world. If my brother is as learned as they say, we'll make him Archbishop of Canterbury"—a witty if insolent response, even daunting.[56]

With those who worked for him Henry could be exceptionally kind; the case of Phineas Pett, the builder of a royal ship for Henry, illustrates the point. Pett had accusations of corruption made against him, culminating in a "trial" in 1609 with James and Henry present. Henry had great faith in Pett and made a public display of it. As Pett reported, Henry summoned him to St. James, "where his Highness vouchsafing to lead me in his hand through the park to Whitehall, in the public view and hearing of many people there attending to see him pass to the King, . . . did in such loving manner counsel me with such comfortable, wise, and grave advice touching my carriage and resolution in my trial." Exonerated in the trial, Pett went on to complete the ship. Pett recalled his last meeting with Henry in August 1612: Henry "gave me a farewell in these words 'Go on cheerfully' saith he 'in that which I entrust you with, and let not the care for your posterity incumber you any ways, for you shall leave the care both of yourself and others to me.'" Moved to tears, Pett parted from Henry, "though I little thought . . . that had been the last time I should have seen him alive." Pett's account of Henry's unaffected, sincere, and generous nature counters the severe and militaristic image that we find elsewhere, the "warlike spirit" that Bacon perceived.[57]

Strong, the latest to write of Henry's household, which came into existence in 1609, describes it: "In the first place the contrast in atmosphere with James's court can hardly be overestimated. . . . Henry's was to be a model of order." Henry excluded Catholics and surrounded himself with "men of action, practising soldiers, or, at the least, those adept at martial sports in the tiltyard." Henry, in radical contrast to his father, even severely fined those around him who indulged in swearing. Henry's household, in a word, seemed an ideal of circumspection and efficiency. But in our eagerness to be sympathetic to Henry, we must not overlook some negative evidence: his household succeeded no better than his father's at being frugal.[58]

As Pauline Croft observes, "The prince's new household, in scale and organization, was modeled on the king's." Ironically, its expenditures tracked those of James's household. Croft points out: "In the only complete year of its existence the total costs of Henry's household were £33,765, and by May 1612 his yearly disbursements had risen to £51,296. Even more worrying was the fact that the prince was proving as cheerfully cavalier as his father in money matters." By March 1613, "£42,000 was still unpaid to his creditors." In light of this extravagance, Croft suggests that "Henry's premature death in 1612, although a political blow, was nevertheless a financial relief to the crown." Cecil had been every bit as worried about the financial affairs of Henry's household as he was about James's. This information about Henry, not included in the modern biographies of him, offers a dash of realism in what is often an idealized portrait of Henry. Therefore, before we assume that all would have been well in the kingdom if only Henry had lived to succeed his father, we might pause to remember his apparent inability to manage household expenditures—like father, like son.[59]

As we turn to investigate Henry's relationship to his family, we can start with Bacon's summary assessment: "He was a wonderfully obedient son to the King his father, very attentive also to the Queen, kind to his brother; but his sister he especially loved." With James, Henry could be both dutiful and obstinate. Isaac Casaubon, writing to friends, said that Henry was remarkable "for his piety and unaffected reverence for his Royal Father and Mother." Thomas Birch noted that Henry sometimes opposed his father but that "filial piety" mainly governed Henry's actions. One must take with suitable caution James Maxwell's enthusiastic verse about Henry: "That from his Cradle to his mournfull end, / He never did his father once offend." Small wonder that this stanza closes by referring to Henry as a "Saint"; one could easily write Henry's hagiography, given such effusive praise. Sending his father a New Year's gift in 1608, Henry said that he "did not despair of having it received as a testimony of his piety and obedience, especially by a most loving and most benign Father." He closes a letter in February 1608 to James: "For whose fatherly affection I have great cause ever to prayse God and crave the continuance whereof and of a long and happy lyfe." Beneath such apparent dutifulness lies a tension that both father and son recognized even if they did not acknowledge it.[60]

Writing from Thetford in early December 1608, Henry seized the opportunity to convey greetings to his mother, "though the countrey where now I remaine doe afford no new thing either Worthy of yo$^r$ Ma$^{ties}$ knawledge, or of my Wryting." Nevertheless, Henry offered Anne his "most humble service and best devoted affection," as well as his hearty prayers for her happiness. But occasionally Henry had to function as intermediary between his father and mother. In a puzzling letter of December 1609, Henry was obviously trying to mediate between quarreling parents. He wrote to James: "I durst not reply, that your Majesty was afraid, lest she [Anne] should return to her old biass; for fear that such a word might have set her in the way, and made me a peace-breaker, which I would eschew." Probably because he was the eldest child, it fell Henry's lot to be caught in the middle between his parents—sometimes the cause of their battle, at times the mediator or arbiter.[61]

One of William Haydon's anecdotes captures a fusion of Henry's concern for James as father with a political concern for him as king. Coming out of his house at St. James in order to walk in the park, Henry was accompanied by a large number of people. But seeing James approaching "with a verie small companie, he was ashamed, and looking about him commanded his followers to depart and goe no further with him." This action enabled Henry to meet his father "not having past three or foure to attend and waite on him."

Such modesty and sensitivity, reflected in this episode, redound to Henry's credit. Henry clearly understood his political function and remained sensitive to his father's position.[62]

On the other hand, considerable evidence demonstrates that father and son often annoyed each other: Henry by poking into things his father deemed not his business, and James by presiding over a profligate and unruly court. In 1609, Henry wrote to his friend John Harington, baron of Exton: "I have sente you certain matters of ancient sorte, which I gained by searche in a musty vellome booke in my fathers closet." Why was Henry rummaging around in his father's private chamber: was it childish curiosity or evidence of the prince's obscure nature (as Bacon terms it)? Bishop Goodman admitted: "I confess that the prince did sometimes pry into the King's actions and a little dislike them." Prying into kingly closets and peering into secretive kingly actions asks for trouble.[63]

The word *jealousy* crops up with regularity as a way to describe James's attitude toward his son. Molin noted in 1607 that James was not "overpleased to see his son so beloved and of such promise that his subjects place all their hopes in him; and it would almost seem, to speak quite frankly, that the King was growing jealous." Surely James understood some of the problems in his court; and if indeed Henry set up a rival household, then it became the foil to James's decadence. Even in the elaborate festivities for Henry's investiture, James tried to manipulate the public's perception of his son. The Venetian ambassador Correr reported: "The King would not allow him [Henry] on this occasion, nor yet on his going to Parliament, to be seen on horseback. *The reason is the question of expense or, as some say, because they did not desire to exalt him too high.*" A week later on June 23, Correr wrote: "*It seems that the King has some reasonable jealousy of the rising sun; and indeed the vivacity of this Prince grows apace, and every day he gives proof of wisdom and lofty thoughts far in advance of his years.*" This jealousy may account for the late notification of the City of London about an expected pageant for Henry's investiture and therefore led to its truncated nature. In the midst of the masques, pageants, and investiture ceremonies of 1610, we apparently find a father jealous of all the attention being lavished on his son. Henry's very presence, which should be a source of joy, reminded James that he can be supplanted, as was already happening in the public affection.[64]

As Strong observes: "During the years 1610–12 the division between the Prince's and King's courts was aggravated, owing to the increasing influence of James's new favourite Robert Carr." Henry opposed Carr's rise to prominence and power and resented his father's devotion to the favorite. In 1611 Carr became Viscount Rochester and in April became a Knight of the Garter. Cecil's death in May 1612 removed a major obstacle to Carr's further advancement, and in that year James made Carr a member of the Privy Council, to the chagrin of Henry. "In June 1612 Thomas, Viscount Fenton, wrote that Rochester was 'exceeding great with his Majestie' but he had 'not find the rycht waye to pleis ather the Quein or the Prince.'" With his friend Thomas Overbury as his intelligence, Carr became increasingly powerful and began to affect the functioning of government, serving as James's private secretary. The seventeenth-century writer Arthur Wilson offered his commentary on the opposition of Henry to Carr:

> Thus was he [Carr] drawn up by the Beams of Majesty, to shine in the highest Glory, grapling often with the *Prince* himself in his own *Sphear,* in divers *Contestations.* For the *Prince* being a high born *Spirit,* and meeting a young *Competitor* in his Fathers Affections, that was a *Mushrom* of yesterday, thought the *venom* would grow too near him, and therefore he gave no *countenance,* but *opposition* to it.

Henry, just about seven years younger than Carr, naturally resented the attention and affection given to Carr, as he opposed his father's dubious judgment. James bestowed on Carr the love and attention that might have been given to his family.[65]

Bacon, writing of Henry's passions, said: "For of love matters there was wonderfully little talk, considering his age: insomuch that he passed that extremely slippery time of his early manhood . . . without being particularly noted for any affairs of that kind." The years 1610–1612 witnessed, however, considerable activity on James's part to secure a marriage partner for Henry—and also for Elizabeth. On the question of marriage Cornwallis reported that Henry "shewed no vehement desire, yet he demonstrated a good inclination." Like his father, Henry saw marriage as a political duty. Haydon observed that Henry, in response to the marriages of some of his young gentlemen, said: "I would not be so soone maried, and yet I wish to see my Father a grandfather." As a royal child, Henry deferred to James's judgment on the issue of marriage.[66]

Various potential matches—Spanish, Italian, French—rose and fell in their prospects. A letter from Rochester to Henry, on behalf of James, in 1611 referred to the proposed marriage to the French princess Christine, the nine-year-old second daughter of Marie de' Medici. Much of the letter concerned money matters, a point uppermost in James's mind as l.. arranged to marry off his children. Rochester did acknowledge the age difference: "Only that Incongruety betwixt your highnes age and hers, is one Inconvenience W^ch ney-ther syde can helpe." Sir Walter Ralegh argued that Henry should not marry at all, at least not now. But by 1612, Henry seemed des-tined for a marriage to Catholic Maria, third daughter of the duke of Savoy. In late October 1612, the council approved the idea of such a marriage on the same day, the twenty-sixth, that Henry took ill to his bed. In a letter to James written from Richmond, October 5, 1612, just a month before his death, Henry wished his father to re-solve the marriage issue, to determine "my part to play, w^ch is to be in love w^th any of them." The names of the potential bride changed, but Henry remained willing to fulfill his princely duty, to play his part.[67]

A pawn in the hands of his father with regard to marriage and often at odds with his parents, Henry nevertheless had strong emo-tional bonds with his brother and especially his sister. Cornwallis said that Henry did "entirely" love Elizabeth and Charles. Haydon noted that Henry "did send often to inquire of her [Elizabeth's] health, with divers unfallible signes and tokens of his great love & affection towards them both." But the expected childlike struggles occurred, too. Cornwallis reported: "Yet must I confess that sometimes by a kinde of rough play and dalliance with the one, and a semblance of contradicting the other, in what he discerned her to desire, he tooke a pleasure in giving both to the one and to the other, some cause in those their so tender yeares to make proofe of their patiences." This sounds all very human and much to be preferred to the growing indifference that governed much of the royal family.[68]

The absence that defined Henry and Elizabeth's relationship came from physical separation, not a distance of souls. Henry wrote his sister several times about the matter of absence. (She was living in the Harington household in Warwickshire.) In one letter Henry beseeched Elizabeth to accept his written lines "as witnesses of my duetiful/tender affection towards you being persuaded that by our absence no part shallbe diminished but rather with our yeeres shalbe increased." The strong bonds remained intact despite absence. Re-sponding to a letter from Elizabeth in which she desired their re-union, Henry assured her of his similar desire, "There is nothing I wish more then that we might be in one companie." Alas, parental considerations prevailed over their desires. "In the mean tyme," Henry wrote, "I shall entreate both their Mat^ies to that effect"—that is, that they be brought together. After Elizabeth arrived perma-nently at court, brother and sister doubtless saw more of each other. Their obvious mutual love, despite obstacles of distance and the inadequacy of letter writing, offers refreshing testimony to the possibility of such love within this royal family. As Camillo says of Leontes and Polixenes in *The Winter's Tale:* "Their encounters . . . have been royally attorneyed with interchange of gifts, letters, loving embassies, that they have seemed to be together, though absent."[69]

For what was to be the last time, Henry entertained his family in late August 1612 at Woodstock—a most pleasant occasion for the royal family. James, impressed by the order and excellence of everything at this feast, "was forced to say, that he had never seen the like before all his lifetime, and that he could never doe so much in his owne house." On the latter point James was surely right. But by late October, illness, possibly typhoid fever, afflicted Henry. Despite the best and often gruesome efforts of the physicians, Henry died on November 6 at the age of eighteen. The account found in *The Life and Death of Prince Henry* offers day-to-day details of the last two weeks of Henry's life.[70]

Shock, dismay, and a profound sense of loss gripped the country in reaction to his death. The failure of either James or Anne to be at the bedside of their dying son causes some difficulty in interpretation. We know that each parent visited Henry during his illness; but as the fateful time drew near, James went to Theobalds and Anne to Somerset House. James's well-known aversion to death could explain his absence; but on earlier occasions—the death of Mary, for example—the parents also were not present. Perhaps the grief of seeing their dying son rendered it impossible for them to be present. Evidence certainly suggests that they felt Henry's loss keenly.

The Venetian ambassador, Foscarini, summed up the grief of the royal family:

> The King received the news of the Prince's death at Theobalds; it affected him greatly and made of the happiest the saddest father in the world. . . . The Queen's life has been in the greatest danger owing to her grief. She will receive no visits nor allow anyone in her room, from which she does not stir, nor does she cease crying. The Princess has gone two days without food and cries incessantly. . . . The Duke of York . . . shows a grief beyond his years.

The ambassador added poignantly that the "Elector Palatine does not know what to do," having arrived for his betrothal and wedding to Elizabeth and now having to face this severe loss in the royal family. "And so the nuptial festivities of this house are turned to mournful trappings." Chamberlain wrote to Carleton specifically about the loss that Elizabeth felt: "The Lady Elizabeth is much afflicted with this losse, and not without goode cause, for he did extraor-

Prince Henry, a miniature painted by Isaac Oliver, probably in 1612, the year of his death. Copyright reserved to Her Majesty Queen Elizabeth II.

dinarilie affect her, and during his sicknes inquired still after her, and the last wordes he spake in good sense, (they say) were, Where is my deare sister?"[71]

In the throes of obvious pain, James wrote his brother-in-law Christian IV to tell him the dreadful news. The letter dates from November 7:

> The grief which we can scarcely express outloud, but on behalf of our greatest trust and love we must nevertheless report the death of our dearest first-born, which happened yesterday. . . . We cannot fully express our immense grief in a longer letter, so let this suffice for you; we are still so confused by the distress and sorrow from this most serious and unexpected misfortune that we could scarcely collect our thoughts.

James remained at Theobalds; he did not go to console Anne. Neither parent went to Henry's funeral in early December. In January 1613, Foscarini reported that James still experienced grief: "For many a time it will come over him suddenly and even in the midst of the most important discussions he will burst out with 'Henry is dead, Henry is dead.'" The same ambassador said that in April he could not offer condolences to Anne "because she cannot bear to hear it mentioned; nor does she ever recall it without abundant tears and sighs." Uncertainty clouded the future for the kingdom and the royal family.[72]

The outpouring of grief just in terms of written and published accounts surpassed anything that England had experienced in decades. The dashed hope that Henry represented for so many people permeates Weldon's comment: "He was only shewed to this Nation, as the Land of *Canaan* was to *Moses*, to look on, not to enjoy: wee did indeed joy in that happinesse we expected in him." The central fact of death, which Stone has emphasized in his history of the English family, also touched the royal family: two infant daughters and now the teenage son—all dead within six years. Mystery surrounds Henry's death because we cannot be certain of the precise nature of his illness. One can note that several contemporaries thought that he had been poisoned—a view apparently shared by Anne. The dreams of a fairy prince, an Oberon, had been shattered; and darkness gripped a family and a country.[73]

Princess Elizabeth remained the other great star in the Stuart firmament; the period 1610–1613 witnessed her increasing importance. When the family came to England, Elizabeth was placed in the care of Lord and Lady Harington at Combe Abbey in Warwickshire, where she remained until 1608, when she arrived at

Princess Elizabeth, an engraving by Crispin van de Passe (1613) the year of her wedding. Courtesy of the Folger Shakespeare Library.

court, although still under the care of the Haringtons. Lord Harington spoke of Elizabeth in glowing terms, referring to her in May
1604 as the king's "jewel": "Her Grace is very healthful and every
way a child of such hope that when the King shall be an eye-witness
it will be much to his comfort." Maxwell in his *Laudable Life*, pro-
claiming Henry's love for his sister, said that she was one of the
Graces, "whose happie breeding, worthy inclination, / Makes her
admir'd, desir'd of every Nation." Thomas Ross, in a Latin tribute
to Elizabeth, described her thus:

> A princess of lovely beauty, in whom, at the first glance, majesty shines
> out, though hidden by courtesy. Although she has not yet passed her
> 12th year, yet all behold in her lively proofs of most excellent and noble
> disposition. . . . her manners are gentle; and she shows no common
> skill in those liberal exercises of mind and body which become a royal
> maiden. In fine, whatever was excellent or lofty in Queen Elizabeth, is
> all compressed in the tender age of this virgin princess, and if God
> spare her to us, will be found there accumulated.

Few could resist linking the princess to her namesake. Ross's assessment epitomized the general view of Elizabeth when she arrived at
court in 1608. Thus, both Elizabeth and Henry evoked memories of
the earlier reign of Queen Elizabeth: the future inextricably linked
to the past.[74]

A strong bond existed between this brother and sister, as noted
above. Harington, writing to Henry's tutor, encouraged the deep-
ening of their relationship: "For my part, I wish with all my heart
his highness might see her grace every day, to increase the comfort
they receive in each other's company. I will be ready to further all
occasions that may draw them together." Frances Erskine recorded
a scene of their departing from each other, early in their time in England: "Her Separation from her Brother was what afflicted her
most, she hung about his Neck, crying and repeating a hundred
Times, I cannot leave my *Henry*, he was also much moved, but com-
forted his Sister as well as he could, with Assurances of his coming
to see her." The theme of shared time and love runs through many
of Elizabeth's letters to Henry; the following, though undated, is
typical:

> I will ever endeavor to equall you, esteeming that time happiest when I
> enjoyed your company, and desiring nothing more then the fruition of
> it again: that as nature hath made us neerest in our love together, so
> accident might not separate us from living together. Neither do I ac-
> count yt yᵉ leste part of my present comfort that though I am deprived

of your happy presence yet I can make these lines deliver this true message that I will ever bee during my lyfe

Yo<sup>r</sup> most kinde and loving syster
Elizabeth.

Nature brought them close in age, but they created the love that
bound them. How often must they have taken refuge in each other
against the disagreements of their parents and the disarray of the
court about them.[75]

Other letters pursued the theme of absence and the function of
letters in sustaining the relationship. The return of one of Henry's
servants, Elizabeth wrote, "ministered the occation of this ill penned
object to yo<sup>r</sup> princely vew w<sup>c</sup> only tells you that I had rather be messenger my self then to substitute any other to let you knowe how
much I desire to see you." Several of the letters written in French
also call attention to these issues. In one, Elizabeth wrote: "Rom-
pons je vous supplie ce silence qui a fait si longtemps sejour avec
nous, & estans separez voyons nous en noz lettres." (Let us break
this silence, I beg you, that has remained so long with us; and having been separated, let us see ourselves in our letters.) The letters
became the essential link. Elizabeth wrote elsewhere to Henry: "Mon
esprit me representant continuessement voz rares perfections, se
plonge tersement en la contemplation imaginaire d'icesses, que si
ma plume pouvoit exprimer ce qui est en l'interieur de mon coeur."
(My spirit, continually representing to me your rare perfection,
plunges directly into their imaginative contemplation, as if my pen
were able to express what is within my heart.) The pen and letter
writing became the instrument of expressing the heart, albeit a poor
substitute for actual presence. One perceives a tension, frustration
perhaps, in these letters, born of absence and the inadequacy of the
pen truly to represent the heart. But at least Henry and Elizabeth
continued to try to bridge the gaps of their existence, to reach across
the chasm to express their mutual love. Such a love puts into sharp
relief the absences, silences, and frustrations felt by other members
of the Stuart royal family.[76]

The princess, whom Peacham in *Minerva Britanna* described in
an emblem as "great, religious, modest, wise, / By birth, by zeale,
behaviour, judgment sound," became the focus of news by the summer of 1612 when marriage negotiations for her entered the final
stage. Henry, supporting his father, favored the choice of Frederick,
Elector Palatine of Germany, a solidly Protestant prince. As early as
September 1611, in fact, John Holles wrote to Sir John Digby, "Yet
have I good grounds to believe that the Palsgrave will get the golden

fleece." Elizabeth would obviously be a fortunate match for any eligible suitor. As Foscarini noted on August 9, 1612: "If the King of Spain is to marry, he could find no better match, as the Princess is eligible for the succession to these realms if her two brothers died childless; besides which she is very beautiful, of the noblest blood, gentle manners, speaking several languages and of singular goodness." When Frederick arrived in England in October 1612, the royal family received him graciously, and Elizabeth clearly fell in love with her sixteen-year-old future husband. They spent much time together at Denmark House. Chamberlain noted in a letter of October 22, to Carleton: "[Frederick] is every day at court, and plies his mistresse hard and takes no delight in running at ring, nor tennis, nor riding with the Prince, . . . but only in her conversation."[77]

But the choice of Frederick annoyed Anne; perhaps she did not like the Protestant arrangement, given her work in behalf of a Catholic choice. In any event, despite Henry's recent death, the betrothal ceremony went ahead on December 27, 1612, but without Anne's presence. The Frenchman Spifame reported: "The Queene was not present, either on account of an inflammation in her foot, as she pretended, or for another reason, as others believe." Chamberlain wrote to Winwood on January 9, 1613: "The Quene is noted to have geven no great grace nor favor to this match, and there is doubt will do lesse hereafter." For the sake of the young couple, however, Anne mellowed by the time of the wedding and even abandoned her contempt for the choice of Frederick. Therefore, Chamberlain could write Winwood on February 23: "The Quene that seemed not to taste yt so well at first, is since so come about that she doth all she can to grace yt, and takes special comfort in him [Frederick]." In the long run history has probably vindicated Anne's reservations about Elizabeth's husband. But for the moment excitement reigned about the February 1613 wedding. Interestingly, James had cut short the official mourning period for Henry in order to get on with the wedding.[78]

Elizabeth and perhaps the country itself had begun to transfer some of the affection formerly felt for Henry to Frederick, who in his name echoed one of Henry's names. Amid the elaborate preparations for the wedding, Chamberlain wrote of his perceptions to Alice Carleton: "On Tewsday I tooke occasion to go to court because I had never seen the Palsgrave, nor the Lady Elizabeth (neere hand) of a long time: I had my full view of them both, but will not tell you all I thincke, but only this, that he owes his mistres nothing yf he were a Kings sonne as she is a Kings daughter. The worst is mee thincks he is much too young and small timbred to undertake such a taske." Cautionary notes about Frederick, about the youth of the couple, lost out in a swelling tide of excitement about the wedding.[79]

The Jacobean court was *en fête* for days before and after Elizabeth's wedding on Sunday, February 14: masques, plays, fireworks displays, and mock sea battles on the Thames made their contribution to the celebration. Actors performed numerous plays, such as Shakespeare's *The Winter's Tale* and *The Tempest*, during the time immediately before the wedding. The royal entry pageant of 1604, the investiture ceremonies for Henry in 1610, and now the wedding celebration demonstrate the importance of spectacle in creating and sustaining the image of the Stuart royal family. Accounts of the 1613 festivities alone occupy nearly one hundred pages in the second volume of Nichols's *Progresses of James*. After all, England had not experienced a royal wedding for decades. Surely some of the impetus behind such an elaborate display came from the desire to transmute the tragedy of Henry's death into a romantic comedy of festivity and marriage, to create a fiction to displace difficult reality.

An anonymous report captured the splendor of the royal family at the wedding. Elizabeth proceeded to the chapel, walking between her brother Charles and the earl of Northampton. She made a stunning appearance:

> Upon her head a crown of refined golde, made Imperiall by the pearles and diamonds thereupon placed, which were so thicke beset that they stood like shining pinnacles upon her amber-coloured haire, dependantly hanging playted downe over her shoulders to her waste; between every plaight a roll or liste of gold-spangles, pearles, rich stones, and diamonds; and, withall, many diamonds of inestimable value, embrothered upon her sleeves, which even dazzled and amazed the eies of the beholders.

James wore a "sumptuous blacke suit, with a diamond in his hatte of a wonderfull great value; close unto him came the Queen, attired in white satin, beautified with much embrothery and many diamonds." Such dazzling and opulent display belied the state of the royal treasury.[80]

In the center of the royal chapel at Whitehall a "stage," some five feet high and twenty feet in length, stood waiting for its occupants, the royal family:

> On the stage, in the chair upon the right hand sate the King, most richly arraied, his jewells being esteemed not to be less worth than six hundred thousand pounds, the Earl of Arundell, bearing the Sword, stood

close by the chair. Next below the Sword sate the Bridegroom upon a stool; and after him Prince Charles upon another stool. . . . On the other opposite side sate the Queen in a chair most gloriously attired; her jewels were valued at four hundred thousand pounds. Near unto her sate the Bride on a stool; the Lady Harington her Governesse stood by her, bearing up her train; and no others ascended this place.

Upon a stage for all to see sat the royal performers. This moment in 1613 literalized James's metaphor in the *Basilicon Doron* that a "King is as one set on a stage" whom people gazingly behold. The archbishop of Canterbury performed the service according to the Book of Common Prayer in the first royal wedding in England that followed the rites of the Church of England. Frederick had learned enough English to get him through the ceremony. Through marriage James had extended his family into another royal lineage.[81]

With perhaps a case of overdeveloped sexual curiosity, James went the next morning, according to Chamberlain, "to visit these young turtles that were coupled on St. Valentines day, and did strictly examine him [Frederick] whether he were his true sonne in law, and was sufficiently assured." James's interest may strike modern sensibilities as peculiar, although such checking on sexual consummation was not unknown. But, then, James could be counted on for unusual behavior. For example, at the end of the masque on February 15, "the King made the maskers kisse his hand at parting, and gave them many thanckes, sayeng he never saw so many proper men together, and himself accompanied them at the banket, . . . and speakes much of them behind their backes, and strokes the master of the rolles [Edward Phelips] and Dick Martin who were the cheife dooers and undertakers."[82]

Wedding festivities included the presentation of three masques: *The Lords' Masque* by Thomas Campion (February 14), *Masque of the Middle Temple and Lincoln's Inn* by George Chapman (February 15), and *Masque of the Inner Temple and Gray's Inn* by Francis Beaumont (February 20), the latter two organized and financed by the respective Inns of Court. In Campion's masque the figure Orpheus motivates the action, other mythological figures participate, statues transform into women, and statues "of the Bridegroom and Bride, all of gold," stand in gracious postures. Entheus wishes for Elizabeth and Frederick: "Live you long to see your joys / In fair nymphs and princely boys." Chapman's masque celebrates the marriage through the allegorical figure of Honour, who refers to "the sacred nuptials / Of Love and Beauty, celebrated here." The masquers eventually retreat to the Temple of Honour, who offers this benediction: "Now may the blessings of the golden age / Swim in these nuptials, even to holy rage." The last masque explores the theme of the marriage of the rivers Thames and Rhine with Mercury and Iris as the presenters. Iris says early in the masque: "I only come / To celebrate the long-wish'd nuptials." As Knights dance the parting measure, Priests sing a final song:

> Peace and silence be the guide
> To the man, and to the bride!
> If there be a joy yet new
> In marriage, let it fall on you.

These masques sweep Frederick and Elizabeth into their mythology and idealization; life appears for the moment to be beautiful and new.[83]

The winter of 1612–1613 became another turning point in the life of the royal family: Henry died in November, and Elizabeth married in the following February. Two great hopes for the kingdom were in a way lost: one by death, the other by a marriage which, although desired, nevertheless separated parents from child. The royal family in this winter resembled a paradigm of tragicomedy, as it risked dissolution. No poet documented the changing moods better than John Donne, who first responded to Henry's death with an "Elegie on Prince Henry." In Henry's death the poet found the center shaken and a dying that all had experienced; for Henry, "whose reputation was an extasie / On neighbour States," had the potential to create a "general peace." But death rendered such faith in him a "heresie." Donne's "Epithalamion, or Mariage Song on the Lady Elizabeth, and Count Palatine" sings quite a different song—one of joy and expectation as the poet followed them through the cycle of their experience on the wedding day. The poet urges the bride to fashion herself in her jewels and

> make
> Thy selfe a constellation, . . .
> Bee thou a new starre, that to us portends
> Ends of much wonder. . . .

Frederick and Elizabeth would again restore nature, thereby healing the rift felt by Henry's death.[84]

Elizabeth's inevitable departure from her family and England countered all that dazzling glory of mid-February. Certainly the letter that Elizabeth sent to James, April 16, 1613, as she readied herself to leave England, put into perspective the long-term effects of those glittering masques, fireworks displays, and play performances that surrounded the opulent wedding itself. Elizabeth wrote:

> Sire, I now feel the sad effects of separation and distance from your majesty. My heart, which was pressed and astounded at my departure, now permits my eyes to weep their privation of the sight of the most precious object, which they could have beheld in this world. I shall perhaps, never see again the flower of princes, the king of fathers, the best and most amiable father, that the sun will ever see. But the very humble respect and devotion, with which I ceaselessly honour him, your majesty can never efface from the memory of her, who awaits in this place a favourable wind, and who would return again to kiss the hands of your majesty, if the state of affairs, or her condition would allow it, to show to your majesty with what ardent affection she is and will be, even to death.

This remarkable letter, as effusive and affectionate as any that James received from his children, underscores a separation that Elizabeth began to experience. She would never write quite so warm a letter to her father again. She would never see her father or any other member of her immediate family again. Writing from Canterbury, Elizabeth had unwittingly prophesied her future. Happy with her new husband but saddened at leaving England, the youthful Elizabeth went to face the unknown in a strange land: more than an ocean would separate her from her parents and brother Charles.[85]

When the royal family had moved to England in 1603, Charles, born in 1600 and in unstable health, remained behind in Scotland. Illness marred his first few years, and he did not come to England until late in 1604. Assessing Charles's condition, Dr. Henry Atkins, who attended him, wrote in a letter to the queen on June 3, 1604: "His Highness now walketh many times in a day all the length of the great chamber at Damfermelinge like a gallant soldier all alone. He often talketh of going to London and desireth to see his gracious Queen mother." Atkins promised the queen that when next she saw Charles, she would "behold a most sweet picture and 'vive' image of his most royal father. Then shall you behold wit and beauty striving for superiority, his body and mind contending which of the two nature hath most adorned."[86]

The doctor's enthusiasm may have been a bit ahead of the facts, at least regarding Charles's health. Anne, apparently exercising her own will, chose the family of Sir Robert Carey in which to place Charles, already in his fourth year, when he arrived in England. Carey's *Memoirs* contains information about the care of the young prince. In it Carey noted, rather bluntly, the risk involved in taking

Prince Charles, from Robert Dallington's *Aphorismes Civill and Militarie* (1613). Courtesy of the Folger Shakespeare Library.

care of a sick royal child: "Those who wished me no good were glad of it [the choice of his family], thinking that if the Duke should die in our charge . . . then it would not be thought fit that we should remain in court after." When Charles moved to their household, he was, according to Carey, "not able to go, nor scant to stand alone, he was so weak in his joints, and especially his ankles, insomuch as many feared they were out of joint." Fortunately, for the sake of the Careys and Charles, he got better.[87]

But James occasionally attempted to interfere in Charles's care. "The King was desirous that the string under his [Charles's] tongue should be cut, for he was so long beginning to speak as he thought he would never have spoke." James also suggested that iron boots should be put on Charles's feet in order to strengthen them. Lady Carey, however, won the battle on both of these issues. Carey pointed out: "My wife had charge of him from a little past four, till he was almost eleven year old." When Charles left their household, Lady Carey "with great grief took leave of her dear master, the Duke." Charles had reached the stage at which male tutors would govern him: "the Duke to have none but men to attend upon him." The schedule of Charles's nurturing ran several years behind Henry's, probably because of his illness. Henry had moved into the male world at about six years of age.[88]

The studious, intellectual quality of the young prince, encouraged by his illness and enforced inactivity, attracted James to Charles. The Venetian ambassador, Giustinian, revealed something of James's delight in Charles in a report of February 1608: "While talking on this point the young Duke of York, the King's second son, came in; he is the joy of the King, the Queen and all the Court. His Majesty began to laugh and play with him. In the course of his jokes he took up the Duke and said, 'My Lord Ambassador, you must make my son a Patrician of Venice.'" Bishop Goodman insisted that "the Queen did ever love Charles better than Prince Henry"; but little support exists for such a judgment, except that Anne may have realized that she could not control Henry and therefore turned her attention to Charles.[89]

Bravely Marcelline wrote in 1610 that God "will very quickly raise and exalt Great *Brittain,* in the *Apogaeum* of his [Charles's] Greatnesse." Further, Marcelline compared the ten-year-old Charles to other famous rulers also named Charles. In keeping with the militaristic image that Marcelline had painted of Henry, he said of Charles: "Methinkes I see a Sword in your hand, and you upon the walles of *Nicomedia, Nicea, Antioche,* and *Tripoli,* ayming at the fairest through all perilles"—a farfetched image. Hard pressed in his emblem of Charles, Peacham emphasized that Charles "bear'st thy Fathers Image right / Aswell in bodie, as thy towardly mind." In Charles's cheeks the red and white roses "yet againe conjoind." His virtues "shall make us love thee more, / Then all thy state we outwardly adore." Literary license operates here. Lamenting the death of Henry and indulging in some wishful thinking, Maxwell in his *Laudable Life* suggested that Charles was "another / Great-hearted HENRY, borne by starrie fate, / This Ilands honour to perpetuate." The mythmakers strained to make much of Charles; he was simply too young for these high-flown images. He took Henry's place in succession, but he never replaced him.[90]

Charles's innocent letters to his father and brother reveal a child-like devotion but not much else. He wrote James at an early time in England: "Sweete Father i learne to decline substantives and adjectives / give me your blessing." Having apparently been punished in some way by James, Charles wrote to him on March 11, 1612: "I cannot expresse the thankes I owe to so good a Father, first in showing my fault so vivelie, and then in forgiving my fault so frilie: Albeit I cannot love and honnor youre M[tie] more then I did, Yet this shall leave me heerafter not to be so foulish."[91]

The same James who wrote a poignant letter to Christian IV about Henry's death could write scarcely a month later (December 14) to his ambassador to France, Thomas Edmondes, urging him to pursue marriage negotiations for Charles. Apparently some sort of dispatch had even preceded the December letter. James wrote:

> And first, whereas you excuse yourself of not fulfilling the direction of our last despatch, in renewing again the motion of the match betwixt our dearest son Charles and Madame Christine, we do very well allow of your carriage therein. . . . For it had been a very blunt thing in us that you, our minister, should so soon after such an irreparable loss received by us have begun to talk of marriage, the most contrary thing that could be to death and funerals. But because we doubted not that that motion would be renewed again unto you, . . . our meaning was therefore that you should entertain the motion and that with so much the greater hope that that great and irremediable inequality of years is now taken away.

James added further some discussion about the terms of the marriage, noting the obvious extreme youth of Charles and Christine. Clearly, such a marriage could not be imminent. James tellingly referred to "our power of disposing of our children." James moved to solidify and stabilize the future by arranging a possible marriage for Charles. So far so good. But to substitute Charles for the dead Henry so soon after Henry's death betrayed needless haste and perhaps insensitivity. This negotiation, which fell through, nevertheless underscores the pawnlike existence royal children had when the subject was marriage. Statecraft says that Charles and Henry are essentially interchangeable: the point is to have a royal son to offer as a potential marriage partner.[92]

Writing to his brother, Charles thanked him for a letter and offered his possessions: "I will send my pistolles by Maister Newton. I will give anie thing I have to you, both horss and my bookes, and my pieces and my cross bowes, or anie thing that you would haive. Good Brother, loove me, and I shall ever loove and serve you." In March 1611, Charles wrote, longing to see Henry: "Most loving Brother I long to see you & hope that you will returne shortly therfore I have presumed to wreat [*sic*] these few lynes to you that I may rest in your favour." Out of Henry's growing art collection Charles had apparently been given a small bronze horse sculpted by Giovanni Bologna. In a moment of poignant affection Charles pressed into the hands of the dying Henry this bronze horse. A few weeks later Charles had the honor and responsibility of leading the mourners at his brother's funeral. The twelve-year-old Charles was moving painfully out of the world of childhood pleasures into the adult world of responsibility as a royal son and heir apparent.[93]

A few words should be said about Arbella Stuart, James's cousin. She participated in the 1604 royal entry pageant and served as godmother to James's daughter Mary. James had in fact incorporated Arbella into his family, to some extent. She became a favorite of the royal children and a companion to Queen Anne. Having, at Anne's request, sent one of her servants to the court of the king of Denmark, Arbella wrote to Prince Henry in March 1608, suggesting that her action revealed "the humble respect" that she owes him and his mother. It indicated also "the readinesse of my disposition to be conformed to your good pleasures, whearin I have placed a great parte of the satisfaction which my heart can receive." The Venetian ambassador, Molin, who in 1607 had described and analyzed the royal family, also included Arbella. "She is twenty-eight; not very beautiful, but highly accomplished, for besides being of most refined manners she speaks fluently Latin, Italian, French, Spanish, reads Greek and Hebrew, and is always studying." Her studious quality should have endeared her to James; yet he seems to have paid little attention to her. The ambassador added: "The King professes to love her and to hold her in high esteem. She is allowed to come to Court, and the king promised, when he ascended the throne, that he would restore her property, but he has not done so yet." James put her off, saying that she would receive her property when she married. But as Molin observed, nothing had happened yet on that issue: "She remains without a mate and without estate."[94]

James moved from benign neglect of Arbella to direct confrontation when she in 1610 fell in love and attempted to marry William Seymour, the future earl of Hertford. James summoned Arbella and

William before the Privy Council and ordered them to give up all negotiations for marriage. Despite Arbella's impassioned plea, James remained adamant. The following year, 1611, the situation grew worse because the couple defied James by getting married. James's objection rested on a narrow and jealous understanding about his control of kingship and likely heirs to the throne. Bishop Goodman explained the issue: "She did match with one of the blood royal who was descended from Henry the Seventh, so that by this match there was a combination of titles, which princes have ever been jealous of." James's action is puzzling. After all, he had three healthy children in 1611, who could presumably succeed to the throne. Arbella offered no threat at all; she simply wanted to be married. Even Bishop Goodman conceded that the marriage was a "fit and a convenient match" and that James had acted perversely. Yet, ironically, his behavior squares with how he treated family members.[95]

James eventually had the couple imprisoned. When they escaped, James had them rounded up. Captured and brought to the Tower, Arbella was to spend the remainder of her life in prison there. In despair, Arbella, signing her name as "Arabella Seymoure," had written to her friend Queen Anne on July 23, 1610, in the midst of her troubles: "Since I am debarred the happinesse of attending your Ma:$^{ty}$ or so much as to kisse your Royall handes to pardon my presumption, . . . my most humble thanckes for your Ma:$^{ts}$ gratious favour and mediation to his Ma:$^{ty}$ for me. Which your Ma:$^{ts}$ goodnesse (my greatest comfort and hope in this affliction) I most humbly beseech your Ma:$^{ty}$ to continue." Whatever efforts of intervention Queen Anne made in behalf of Arbella came to nought. As Handover says, "Indifferent to his cousin's suffering, absorbed in his hunting and favourites, James was well content to let her pay the penalties of disobedience." The public, apparently moved by the romance of Arbella's escape, took a dim view of James's action.[96]

Rather like James's mother, Arbella persisted in believing that James would relent and release her. One particularly poignant action during her final years was the purchase of four new and expensive gowns for Princess Elizabeth's wedding, but James did not let her attend. Arbella's mind increasingly filled with illusions, and she went mad in the Tower, eventually dying there in 1615. The peacemaker king did not make the effort to reconcile himself with his cousin. The residue of tragedy and irony overwhelms these events as family feeling and ties count for little. Arbella's sad story adds another chapter to our understanding of how James chose to respond to family issues: jealousy and neglect characterize his behavior repeatedly.

The shining moments in the Stuart royal family's life in the pe-riod 1603–1613 glitter like so many masques and spectacles: the arrival from Scotland, the deliverance from the Gunpowder Plot, the births of daughters, the investiture of Prince Henry as Prince of Wales, the wedding of Princess Elizabeth. But as the daystar rises and the light of a harsher reality dims the masque, we see the family in another, sometimes ironic, perspective: deaths of two daughters, death of heir apparent, departure of a daughter, the rise of a new favorite, a disturbing silence in a husband-wife relationship. "Do-mestical dangers and heartbreaking" noted in Scotland in early 1603 remain evident in the private lives of this family.

In the very month that Henry contracted his fatal illness, Octo-ber 1612, the body of Mary Queen of Scots moved under cover of darkness through the streets of London in order to be reinterred in a magnificent tomb in Westminster Abbey: "The Tapers placed by the Tomb and the Altar, in the *Cathedral*, smoaking with them like an *Offertory.*" The crooked smoke from the tapers reached the cathe-dral's ceiling, a kind of smoldering sacrifice for James's conscience. Fires of passion, enthusiasm, hope, and anger burned brightly in this Stuart family; the ice of isolation, loneliness, despair, uncon-cern, and silence banked and sometimes extinguished the flame. Physical separation, distance, and fragmentation characterized much of the private life of James's family. When husband and wife became that in name only, when children were disaffected from par-ents, when the father presided over a court of dubious political morality, then the family could only sustain a tenuous bond. Hopes flashed momentarily in the lives of the royal children, only to be frustrated.[97]

*Chapter Four*

# England (1613–1625)

## Nothing but Silence

*W*hen George Villiers, duke of Buckingham, late in James's life tried to think of a way to respond to the king's astounding love and generosity, he dared not speak. In a letter full of gratitude, Buckingham acknowledged that he had received from James "more tendernes then fathers have of children of more friendship then betweene equalls of more affection then betweene lovers in the best kinde man and wife, what can I returne[?] nothinge but silence." Silence not born of jealousy, indifference, or tension, but instead a silence growing out of satisfaction and happiness. Words fail to express such contentment.[1]

Ironically, no member of James's family could have written such a letter. Buckingham, who dominated the last ten years of James's life, moved into the center of the royal family, a beloved member of that family, as far as James was concerned. Terms, relationships, and familial structure changed in this last period of James's life—a period not dominated by achievement or fruition of careful efforts, but rather a time of sadness and disappointment, mixed with a residue of tragedy.

Obviously, this period ended with James's death, but that event does not truly account for its sadness. Few things went well in the politics and life of James's family. Frustrated desires and irreconcilable differences define a plot that could not be called comic, nor fully tragic. It seems more like the vanity of human wishes. Elizabeth's wedding, that high note of expense and expectation in early 1613, left doubt and frustration in its wake rather than certainty and fulfillment. This only daughter found herself trapped in the beginning of the Thirty Years War and isolated from her family in England. For one brief dazzling moment she was queen, but even that particular dream shattered. The sole surviving son and heir apparent struggled for recognition from his father. Queen Anne, long separated from the emotional and spiritual bonds of her husband, died in isolation; only Charles provided her a link to her family.

In contrast with the Venetian ambassador's 1610 positive and hopeful account of the royal family, the two reports that appeared in 1617 and 1618 in the foreign dispatches of the Venetian State Papers offer a less glowing assessment. These accounts survive as the last such dispatches before Anne's death. In 1617, Horatio Busino had separate audiences with the royal family and recorded his observations. He described James as "a man of ordinary stature with red face. He is now beginning to turn white. . . . It is said that he eats little or no bread and a great deal of meat, and that he drinks the strongest wines he can get." Busino also contrasted James's appearance at court and at the chase: "Sometimes when he walks he likes, for display, to be supported under the arms by his chief favorites, but in riding he cares for nothing, never holding his reins in his hand." The image of James being physically supported by his favorites reveals much about his dependence on them, a dependence more emotional than physical. Busino noted that Charles resided in a separate palace "very far from the king's"; in this he resembled Prince Henry. "The prince is a youth of about sixteen, very grave and polite, of good constitution so far as can be judged from his appearance. His hair is light and he much more closely resembles his royal mother." In yet another place the queen resided. Busino recorded a rather amusing portrait of Anne: "Her Majesty's costume was pink and gold with so expansive a farthingale that I do not exaggerate when I say it was four feet wide in the hips. Her bosom was bare down to the pit of the stomach, forming as it were, an oval." Diamonds and other jewels sparkled in her hair, which also contained "such a quantity of false hair dressed in rays (*sparsi in giro*) that she looked exactly like a sun flower." James walking about supported under the arms by favorites and Anne looking like a sunflower appear more than slightly comical. The magnificent spectacle of their appearance in 1610 had become almost an unconscious parody of itself, in the brief space of only seven years.[2]

A year later in December 1618 the Venetian ambassador, Antonio Foscarini, gave another assessment of the royal family. He noted, for example, James's intellectual powers and his facility with languages and commented on James's excessive liberality, saying that James had "reduced the treasury from wealth to poverty." James treated those who served him with kindness and familiarity, and yet he typically preferred a single favorite. Foscarini said that James spent at least ten months a year in the country hunting and on progresses. Such constant exercise, the doctors said, was his salvation. James called himself, Foscarini reported, "an old negotiator." Something frivolous runs through the character of the king, as analyzed by the ambassador. James's constant movement from place to place not only impeded the functioning of the government but also suggests a puzzling restlessness in James—as if he could make forward progress only through constant motion.[3]

Foscarini attributed to Anne "the utmost kindness and affability." His dispatch reminds us that she "is daughter, sister and wife of a king, which cannot to-day be said of any other." Anne took great pride in her beauty—recall the 1617 report. She had strong attachments to her brother the king of Denmark "and to the prince above all her other children, calling him her little servant." Of course, in 1618, Charles remained the only royal child left within the queen's sway. Foscarini observed Charles's "gentle and amiable character," his love of hunting and of study. "He is tenderly loved by his father and mother." Even his health had much improved. A simple statement of fact revealed much about Charles's situation: "He is now eighteen, and he is the only son." In a word, Charles was the only hope, in contrast to the optimistic portraits of the royal family earlier, say in 1610. Diminution and disintegration had begun to characterize James's family: deaths and separation accelerated the process. In fact, within a few months of Foscarini's report Anne died.[4]

Gazing at a composite portrait of James's family in the period 1613 to 1625, one can see faces largely etched with failure: the fall of Somerset, the death of Anne, the fall of Bohemia and expulsion of Frederick and Elizabeth, the failure of the Spanish Match, and finally the death of James. But a few shimmers of light penetrate the darkness, and the future can be perceived: the birth of James's grandchildren starting in 1614, the rise of Buckingham, and the maturation of Charles. Whatever may have happened afterward, in 1625 at least, Charles and Buckingham offered political stability. The progeny of James's grandchildren control the English throne today. Using James as the center of the royal family, we will see different spheres of importance and influence in a kind of descending order of significance: Buckingham, Charles, Elizabeth, Anne, and Carr (Somerset).

### Robert Carr, earl of Somerset

In the same April 1613 letter in which John Chamberlain reported the departure of Frederick and Elizabeth for their new home in Germany, he also noted the confinement of Sir Thomas Overbury to the Tower. Chamberlain wrote: "The King hath long had a desire to remove him from about the Lord of Rochester [Carr], as thincking yt a dishonor to him that the world shold have an opinion that Rochester ruled him and Overburie ruled Rochester wheras he wold make yt appeare that neither Overburie nor Rochester had such a stroke with him." James, easily led as the Venetian ambassador had noted, wanted from time to time to assert authority, to remind even favorites that he had the ultimate power. Chamberlain explained that Overbury, when offered an ambassadorial position abroad, refused it and gave "a peremptorie answer." For such a sin he went to the Tower. Overbury was, as several historians have noted, the favorite's favorite, the precise nature of their relationship being a little difficult to determine. In the summary drawn up by Francis Bacon in preparation for the eventual trial of Somerset, Bacon quoted from some of Overbury's letters in a search for motive: "Is this the fruit of nine years' love, common secrets, and common dangers?" In another letter: "Do not drive me to extremity to do that which you and I shall be sorry for." In another letter: "Can you forget him, between whom such secrets of all kinds have passed?" These letters and other documents reveal a close relationship between Carr and Overbury. Overbury had responded jealously to Somerset's marriage. At the least, Overbury had the intelligence that Carr needed in his vaulting ambition. But Overbury crossed swords with Carr when Carr decided to marry the treacherous and wily Frances Howard, at the time married to the earl of Essex.[5]

This inconvenience vanished in the divorce proceedings of the summer of 1613. Frances Howard insisted that her youthful husband was impotent and that the marriage had never been consummated. James, as usual, took great interest in such matters, and he arranged for a commission to rule on the divorce. When it seemed reluctant to rule in favor of divorce, James simply added two more bishops to the panel, being assured that they would vote the right way. By a vote of seven to five the commission reached a favorable decision on September 25. Whatever one may think about James's method of securing justice, justice ironically prevailed because the earl of Essex and his wife both genuinely wanted a divorce, just not on each other's terms. Equally important, this episode and the imprisonment of Overbury demonstrated the power that Robert Carr still exercised over the king, whose relationship with him dated from 1607.

The year 1613 that began with festivities associated with Princess Elizabeth's wedding closed with another wedding: Carr and Frances Howard married on December 26. James, in typical fashion, decided to pay all the costs—of course, from money that he did not have. On November 4, James had named Carr to be earl of Somerset. From a mere page arriving from Scotland in 1603, Carr had truly come a long way: he was the king's favorite and an earl. In December he married into the powerful Howard family. Both James and Anne attended the wedding, according to Chamberlain, who also noted that the bride "was maried in her haire," meaning that her hair hung down over her shoulders, symbolizing her virginity— a minor fiction that compounded with several others. The wedding gifts, Chamberlain reported, "were more in number and value, then ever I thincke were geven to any subject in this land." Thomas Campion's *The Description of a Maske* closed the day's celebration. Its fourth song touched on the subject of love in a slightly uncomfortable way, given the audience:

1. Let us now sing of Love's delight,
   For he alone is Lord to-night;
2. Some friendship between man and man prefer,
   But I th' affection between man and wife.
3. What good can be in life,
   Whereof no fruites appeare?

One wonders if James sensed any special topicality in the song. The Chorus closed: "That pleasure is of all most bountiful and kinde, / That fades not straight, but leaves a living joy behinde." James would soon have reason to ponder what kind of living joy derived from his relationship to Somerset. Meanwhile, as Akrigg observes, "Somerset reached the peak of his fortunes in 1614." He continued to serve as secretary of state; and in July, he became Lord Chamberlain, James declaring "that no man shold marvayle that he bestowed a place so neere himself upon his frend, whom he loved above all men living." But Somerset's arrogance, petulance, and insolence eventually caught up with him. Court intriguers scurried about devising means to topple him and to put George Villiers in his place, and James simply grew weary of him. Then Somerset committed the unpardonable sin: he began to ignore James and to assume certain prerogatives. Out of a jealous and wounded heart James wrote Somerset a long letter early in 1615, one of the king's most exceptional personal letters. Its great length prevents quotation in full. The control that James exhibited in this letter surprises because the letter grew out of great passion. But James the writer worked to give shape to his grief and to articulate his emotion. Clearly James took the initiative in trying to repair a fractured relationship.[6]

James began the letter by accusing Somerset of misleading him about court factions and court opinion, while he never credited unflattering stories about Somerset. In fact, James had climbed out on several limbs in Somerset's behalf, including accepting Somerset's nephew in his bedchamber, "the fashion thereof being done in needless bravery [defiance] of the Queen." James had risked the displeasure of Anne, but then his whole relationship with Somerset displeased Anne greatly. James noted the changes in Somerset's recent behavior, "especially of late since this strange frenzy took you, . . . strange streams of unquietness, passion, fury, and insolent pride, and (which is worst of all) with a settled kind of induced obstinacy as it chokes and obscures all these excellent and good parts." James found offensive the "new art of railing" that Somerset had invented and used on him. In the past James had apparently borne these outrages: "I bore (God Almighty knows) with these passions of yours of old, dissembling my grief thereat."[7]

Much of the letter focused on Somerset's faults, "this little mirror," which James hoped would bring reformation. James enumerated four major sins: first, Somerset's interruptions, "being uttered at unseasonable hours and so bereaving me of my rest," had been especially vexing. "Next, your fiery boutades [sudden outbursts] were coupled with a continual dogged sullen behaviour toward me." James continued:

> Thirdly, in all your dealing with me ye have many times uttered a kind of distrust of the honesty of my friendship towards you. And fourthly, which is worst of all and worse than any other thing that can be imagined, ye have in many of your mad fits done what you can [to?] persuade me that ye mean not so much to hold me by love hereafter as by awe, and that ye have me so far in your reverence as that I dare not offend you or resist your appetites.

With breathtaking rhetorical craftiness and force James added: "I leave out of this reckoning your long creeping back and withdrawing yourself from lying in my chamber, notwithstanding my many hundred times earnest soliciting you to the contrary, accounting that but as a point of unkindness." Clearly James alluded to sexual favors being denied him. Something slightly desperate and poignant pervades James's comment; he felt tyrannized by Somerset's "appetites" (desires or inclinations) while his own appetites apparently had been ignored or gone unfulfilled.[8]

James put into perspective all the sorrow that he had experienced in his lifetime when he said that "the infinite grief of a deeply wounded heart" he then experienced exceeded any other: "never grief since my birth seized so heavily upon me." He warned Somerset: "Be not the occasion of the hastening of his death, through grief, who was not only your creator under God but hath many a time prayed for you, which I never did for no subject alive but for you." James as "creator" had sought to fashion Somerset's life, a practice consistent with James's desire to impose his fiction on the world. James's arsenal of rhetorical and persuasive devices overflowed. Having held the mirror up to nature, James now moved to recommend change in behavior: "All I crave is that in all the words and actions of your life ye may ever make it appear to me that ye never think to hold grip of me but out of my mere [entire] love, and not one hair by fear." There must be, James insisted, "exterior signs of the amendment" of behavior—or at least a change in appearance—"make it appear to me." Somerset may presumably have indulged his own self-fashioning, his improvisation in the role that James had created for him.[9]

Throughout, James made clear that his feeling for Somerset had been unusual if not unique. "For I am," James wrote, "far from thinking of any possibility of any man ever to come within many degrees of your trust to me." "God is my judge my love hath been infinite towards you." If infinite towards Somerset, where does that leave the members of James's family? Allowing for James's hyperbole, one nevertheless understands where Somerset stands in James's affection: a place nearer to his heart than that occupied by any other—wife, son, or daughter. James made one essential demand of Somerset: "Let me be met then with your entire heart, but softened with humility."[10]

James concluded this powerful letter by summing up his position and the options available to Somerset: "It lies in your hand to make of me what you please, either the best master and truest friend or, if you force me once to call you ingrate, . . . no so great earthly plague can light upon you. In a word, ye may procure me to delight to give daily more and more demonstrations of my favours towards you, if the fault be not in yourself." Sweet reasonableness gave way to veiled threat. James sensed that the relationship had reached a crucial point. His unstinting love had been sorely tried by an insolent and ungrateful young man. The controlled passion of this letter indicates much thought and much care in the crafting of it. However we consider this document, it represents a testament of a love that had been injured and unrequited. Another, briefer letter, possibly written in June 1615, continued in a similar vein. But as James wrote these letters, he did not know a shocking fact about Somerset: his complicity in Overbury's murder.[11]

"In mid-October [1615] London was electrified by the news that Sir Thomas Overbury's death in the Tower had been due to poisoning, and that the Earl and Countess of Somerset were under house arrest for complicity in the crime." Over the course of the summer of 1615 evidence came to light, primarily by confessions, that the countess had arranged to have Overbury poisoned, this having been successfully carried out on September 15, 1613, just a few months after he had been committed to the Tower. Thus as Frances Howard went to her wedding that December, she knew of her guilt. The exact nature of Somerset's involvement was less clear, but he surely knew something about what had happened. James was profoundly shocked. In October 1615, he appointed Lord Chancellor Ellesmere, the duke of Lennox, and Lord Zouche as a commission to investigate the charges against Somerset and his wife. These startling events dispelled whatever remaining hopes James had for repairing his relationship with Somerset. He now sought to put a safe distance between himself and his favorite, having correctly sensed the potential danger.[12]

Sober and pointed, James wrote to Somerset in October 1615, denying Somerset's plea that the investigation be called off. The king defined his position: "In a business of this nature I have nothing to look unto but first my conscience before God, and next my reputation in the eyes of the world." James took the high road of conscience and yet hoped, "If the delation prove false, God so deal with my soul as no man among you shall so much rejoice at it as I." But the king could not afford such a murder "to be suppressed and plastered over." He urged Somerset and his father-in-law to read over this letter at least twice to be certain of its contents. What a contrast this October letter made to the passionate one from earlier in the year.[13]

To James's great credit, he did let the investigation go forward, although he managed to meddle in its procedures. One wonders if James may have felt some perverse sense of relief at the turn of events; that is, if Somerset would not change his behavior toward the king, this criminal activity gave James the perfect excuse to turn his back on a favorite. In any event, the story unfolded that way. Several contemporary accounts tell of a final scene of leave-taking between James and Somerset, presumably late October 1615 as Somerset left to go answer the official commission of inquiry. One of the more restrained versions of the story recorded that "when he [Somerset] came to take his leave of the King, he [James] embraced and kist him often, wisht him to make haste back, shewed an extreme *passion* to be without him; and his back was no sooner turned, but he said with a *smile, I shall never see thy face more.*" The chronicles referred to James's dissimulation, and that cannot be denied. But one would need to know more about the tone of James's comment: it could have been poignant, or it could have been cynical. Given James's awkward position, he could have intended either response, or both.[14]

Realizing that James had, for all practical purposes, abandoned him to the working out of justice, Somerset got ugly, made threats, and generally cast aspersions on James. James confronted the problem head-on in a secret May 1616 letter to George More, then keeper of the Tower: "But it is easy to be seen that he [Somerset] would threaten me with laying an aspersion upon me of being, in some sort, accessory to his crime." A few of James's letters to Somerset would have proved embarrassing for the king. James had become convinced of Somerset's guilt, at least as an accessory after the fact, and steadfastly refused to save him. In May 1616 both Somerset and his wife faced trial; she pleaded guilty. On May 25 the assembled lords, after a daylong trial, found Somerset guilty. Both husband and wife received sentences of death, which James commuted. They continued their residence in the Tower; Somerset even found money to remodel his quarters in the prison to suit his taste. The relationship between Somerset and his wife had soured badly; it had not withstood the scandal well. "Perhaps the most distasteful thing about life in the Tower for the Somersets was that they had to endure each other's company." In 1622, they gained release from prison and moved to the country, and on October 7, 1624, James granted Somerset a pardon. But in 1615, James had watched an essential part of his world crumble when he encountered the disaffection of the man whom he had loved for eight years, the man who, James wrote, had enjoyed his "own infinite privacy" with James. The king had much time to contemplate and remember, to feel the frustrated desires and lack of reconciliation, to endure the silence that spanned the distance between the palace and the Tower.[15]

### Scotland

In 1616, the year in which Somerset fell and in which James published his *Workes*, a handsome folio collection of his writings, the Venetian ambassador offered an assessment of the causes of James's

King James, an engraving by Simon van de Passe included in *The Workes of James*, published in 1616. Courtesy of the Department of Special Collections, Spencer Research Library, University of Kansas.

political failures and unwittingly repeated evaluations spanning back to the Scottish period. Giovanni Lionella wrote on October 7:

> The chief [causes] are the daily increasing abhorrence which he feels for the toils and cares involved in government. In order to escape them he lives almost entirely in the country, accompanied by a few of his favorites. . . . Another reason is His Majesty's powerlessness to incur any considerable expense unless he receives the material from parliament. . . . In proportion as his reputation continues to diminish abroad the dissatisfaction of his subjects keeps increasing.

The character *Fant'sy* in Jonson's court masque *The Vision of Delight* (January 1617) says,

> Behold a king
> Whose presence maketh this perpetual spring,
> The glories of which spring grow in that bower,
> And are the marks and beauties of his power.

Clearly, we confront the illusion of power. The real world offers an ironic commentary on James's political acumen.[16]

A vision of delight sent James to Scotland in 1617. The enormous expense and arduous nature of the proposed journey left only James enthusiastic for this experience. Most of the Scots serving in the English court in fact chose to remain in London. In a letter to the Scottish Privy Council, James offered his reasons for the visit:

> First, wee ar not achamed to confesse that we have had theise many yeiris a great and naturall longing to see our native soyle and place of our birth and breeding, and this salmonlyke instinct of ours hes restleslie, both when wee wer awake and manie tymes in our sleip, so stirred up our thoghtis and bended our desyris to make a Jornay thither that wee can never rest satisfied till it sall pleas God that wee may accomplish it.

Leaving London on March 15, James set out with an entourage to visit his homeland for the last time. The reasons for his going surely were personal and psychological, not primarily political. The English did not want to go, and the Scots did not want them to come. As Chamberlain wrote to his friend Dudley Carleton, ambassador in Holland: "I never knew a journy so generally misliked both here and there."[17]

Many of the courtiers who began the journey with James dropped off along the way. Buckingham made the entire seven-month excursion. The trip buoyed James's spirits; he did indeed seem to be revived by being on his native soil, as he moved restlessly from city to

city in Scotland. On May 16, James made his official entry into Edinburgh, received a gift from the city, heard a sermon, moved through
the streets, and heard soothing words of welcome. The speaker,
John Hay, praised James for uniting the kingdoms and for his kingly
bearing: "During the whole time of your Majestie's most happie
reigne hath so in publicke carried your selfe towards us your subjects
. . . that no man could lay any imputation to your unspotted life;
yee never more desiring to bee above us than for us." Hay closed by
singling out James's piety and zeal. James nostalgically celebrated
his fifty-first birthday in Edinburgh, his native city. He visited Stirling, Falkland, St. Andrews, and many other places associated with
his childhood and youth.[18]

James went through the motions of calling the Scottish Parliament and tried to impose Anglican worship rituals on the reluctant
Scots, but mainly he enjoyed being a royal tourist. One witty observer, Anthony Weldon, saw irony and satire where James saw
obeisance and adulation. In an amusing piece Weldon mercilessly
satirized the Scots. James was not amused. Weldon summed up the
mood: "They protested, if Christ came from heaven hee could not
have bene better welcome and I beleive it, for, his majestie came but
to summon them to a Parliament, and Christ would have summoned
them to a Judgment, which they love not." But James saw the Scottish trip through royal-colored glasses. In many ways the journey
may have been his last relatively peaceful time.[19]

### Anne

With James in Scotland, Anne remained in England to contemplate her status. She had, for example, shed no tears at Somerset's
fall. Anne disliked him intensely, a view she had shared with Prince
Henry. She saw Somerset as a political and personal threat. With
Somerset the center of James's life, she and other family members
moved to the outer limits of James's affection. Arthur Wilson, in out-
lining several possibilities for Anne's animosity, included "an apprehension that the Kings love and company was alienated from
her, by this *Masculine conversation* and intimacy." Such a reason may
have been operating in Anne's resistance to Somerset. Anne also
feared his political power, in part as another sign of James's weakness in governing.[20]

Anne's position as queen, wife, and mother did not greatly differ
in this final period from what we have seen earlier. She had already
lost James to his favorites and the hunt, lost Henry to death, and lost
Elizabeth to marriage and a distant home in Germany. Anne's former

delight in court masques and other such activities waned as a deep melancholy began to settle into her soul. Accumulating illnesses, such as dropsy, gout, and poor circulation, compounded her difficulties. Having participated in the Carr-Howard wedding in late December 1613, an event that she found distasteful, she celebrated the wedding of Lord Roxburgh and Jane Drummond, her friend, at her residence of Somerset House, February 3, 1614. Samuel Daniel's *Hymen's Triumph,* performed on that occasion, began with unstinting praise for Anne. (She had, after all, first employed Daniel for the masque in 1604.) Daniel says that "never yet was Queene / That more a people's love hath merited / By all good graces." Daniel defines her as "the meanes our State stands fast established, / And blest by your blest wombe." Because of Anne, England experienced no quarrels or factions. The poet praises her: "Renowned Denmarke! that hast furnished / The world with Princes!" But Daniel does not acknowledge what had happened to those "princes" by 1614; he indulged a fiction. His praise would have fit more appropriately the situation in 1604 than that of 1614. Anne could be forgiven if she savored this praise; she would not hear many more such words in the years to come.[21]

Chamberlain's letters documented not only Anne's increasing illnesses but also her absence from many occasions at which one might reasonably expect her to be present, only some of which could be attributed to sickness. Writing to Carleton on March 16, 1615, Chamberlain reported the visit of James to Cambridge University: "The Prince came along with him, but not the Quene by reason (as yt is saide) that she was not invited." Anne receded farther into the background of court life: forgotten but not gone. A month later Chamberlain noted that Anne had been ill: "The Quene continues crased and in phisicke, not without daunger (yf yt be not presently prevented) to fall into a dropsie." After the springtime trials of the Somersets in 1616, the court looked eagerly to the formal investiture of Prince Charles as Prince of Wales in early November. Chamberlain observed James's presence at this occasion: the king "stoode on the gallerie staires at Whithall to see the Prince come along from Richmond attended by the Lord Mayor and all the companies of London in theyre barges in very goode order and made a goodly shew." But Chamberlain added, "The Quene wold not be present at the creation, lest she shold renew her griefe by the memorie of the last Prince who runs still so much in some mens mind." Anne's absence here contrasts with the excitement that attended Henry's 1610 investiture in which the whole family participated. Diminution and disintegration in the royal family seem evident.[22]

Chamberlain wrote to Carleton in January 1617: "The Quene removed yesterday to Whitehall from Somerset House where she hath lien this fortnight sicke of the gowte or somewhat els, yt beeing suspected that she dreames and aims at a Regencie during the Kings absence in Scotland." If Anne truly wanted to be named regent of England while James went on his trip to Scotland in 1617, she once again was disappointed. In fact, James named Francis Bacon to be regent. Anne accompanied James as far as Ware in March 1617 but then returned to London, doubtless to nurse her hurt at not being either named regent or invited to make the trip. Chamberlain noted in January 1618: "In the mean time the Quene is not well, but they say languisheth whether with melancolie or sicknes, and continues at White-hall beeing scant able to remove." A constant thread runs through the reports: Anne's illnesses were as much emotional as physical. On March 27, 1618, Chamberlain reported to Carleton: "The Quene wold not appeare nor shew herself that day, whether yt were that she was not well, or whatsoever els was the cause: the King sent divers and some of his bed-chamber, and lastly the Marquis Buckingham to perswade and entreat her comming but all wold not prevayle." James went to visit her the next day at Denmark House (formerly Somerset House). In what turned out to be her last opportunity, Anne refused to participate in the festivities that annually celebrated James's accession to the English throne on March 24. Illness became a convenient excuse. Her actions assured her isolation and alienation. Anne suffered a serious psychological struggle during the last decade of her life, which resulted in or from the physical reality of her illnesses. Her melancholy grew from a profound loneliness that dominated her relationship with her family. Apparently Anne wrote no letters to her daughter, or her daughter to her. She received nourishing affection only from Charles.[23]

Anne, trapped in a world that she could not control, ironically got involved in the process of pushing Villiers as James's new favorite. The courtiers who wanted to supplant Somerset thought that they needed a replacement; the dashing, handsome Villiers made the obvious candidate. Roger Coke reported that James would receive no one into his favor if not first recommended by the queen—a fiction perpetrated by James for reasons best known to him. Thus, George Abbot, archbishop of Canterbury, whom Anne respected greatly, came to ask her help in advancing Villiers's cause. Coke noted that when the archbishop proposed the idea, "She was utterly averse from it, having before been stung with Favourites; but by her Observation of *Villiers*, she told the Archbishop, she saw that in him, that if he became a Favourite, he would become more intolerable than any that were before him." At last Anne relented, "but withal told *Abbot*, he among the rest would live to repent it." She later warned the archbishop: "*If this young Man be once brought in, the first Persons that he will plague must be you that labour for him; yea, I shall have my part also, the King will teach him to despise and hardly intreat us all.*"[24]

On April 23, 1615, the queen entered James's bedchamber and asked him to make Villiers a groom of the bedchamber. With Prince Charles's sword, James conferred this new honor. Somerset took this event for what it represented: a shifting tide of James's favor. Knowing what the new favorite's prominence would mean to her, Anne nevertheless occupied the unusual position of furthering his cause, thereby sealing the enlarging gap that existed between royal husband and wife. Some sense of hopelessness must have governed Anne's action, a recognition that she had lost James's genuine interest years ago. Anne may have seen herself as merely playing a role, participating in James's fiction while fully understanding the reality. Perhaps she held some small vestige of hope that her action would endear her to James, a hope nevertheless unsupported by facts. By seeming to be instrumental in Villiers's advancement, Anne temporarily exercised a kind of political power. Any or all of these ideas might have prompted her action.

She came, perhaps grudgingly, to a kind of toleration of Buckingham; in fact, every member of the Stuart royal family would eventually need this man's help. In an undated letter, Anne informed James about her health; and she added: "My dog dothe well, for I did Command him, that he should make your eare hang lyke a sows lugge [ear] When he comes home I will treete him better then anie other dog." Her letter to Buckingham clarified to whom she referred:

> My kind dog, I have receaved your letter which is verie wellcom to me yow doe verie well in lugging [pulling] the sowes eare, and I thank yow for it, and would have yow doe so still upon condition that yow continue a watchfull dog to him and be alwaies true to him, so wishing you all happines
>
> Anna R.

Her affectionate term "kind dog" referred to Buckingham, and the "sow" was James. Her letter to Buckingham seems quite genuine in its hope that he would watch after and take care of James. Anne tacitly acknowledged the favorite's control over James and tried to turn that to a good purpose. In a letter presumably written in 1618, Anne even sought Buckingham's intervention with the king in sparing Sir Walter Ralegh's life. If Buckingham tried to dissuade James from this execution, he did not succeed: Ralegh died on the executioner's block on October 29, 1618. Having helped raise Villiers to prominence, Anne on occasion tried to use him to serve her purposes. He became an intermediary between the king and the members of the royal family, as we shall see later.[25]

The question of a Spanish marriage for Charles occupied Anne's attention in 1618, the last major political and familial issue in which she became involved. Piero Contarini reported that the Danish ambassador told James that he would be sacrificing Charles in marrying him to the Infanta. Outraged, James announced that "he chose to dispose of his children according to his own fancy." Anne confessed to the Venetian ambassador that the king "was not aware of her being acquainted with these particulars and would be much annoyed if he thought she were, so that she pretended to know nothing about them and requested me not to mention the circumstance to any one." As seen earlier, James considered it his kingly and fatherly prerogative to "dispose" of his children as he saw fit. Anne had little voice in such matters. To the same ambassador Anne later expressed her apprehension about the Spanish matter: "She herself did not see the necessity for such haste, the Infanta being so young and the Prince in a state to wait four or five years. She added that these precocious marriages were generally failures." Since Anne herself was not quite fifteen years old when she married James, did she perceive her own "precocious" marriage as a failure?[26]

Given Anne's melancholic state in the last years of her life, one would not be surprised if she viewed her marriage as a failure; indeed, one would be surprised if she did not. Contarini analyzed the queen's position in 1618: "She is unhappy because the king rarely sees her and many years have passed since he saw much of her. She possesses little authority in the court and cannot influence the king's favour." Less than a month before her death, Antonio Donato reported, "But the estrangement between their Majesties has by now become public and the separated lives they lead only encouraged this." During her illness in January 1619, Chamberlain observed that James did not visit her at Hampton Court where she lay. But the estrangement to which Donato referred we have seen for a long time: the distance, separate residences, and alienation.[27]

The end for Anne finally came on March 2, 1619. A manuscript account in the National Library of Scotland reveals something about Charles's attendance on his mother in her dying days. At one point the prince entered her chamber, "Then sche baid him go home, No he sayed I will wayt upon you$^r$ M$^{tie}$. Sche answered, I am a prettie piece to Wayte upone Servand (for sche ever called him so)." Later, "sche layd her hand upone the prince his head and gaif him her blessing." But Anne had difficulty accepting the possibility that death was near, despite the urgings of various bishops and the arch-bishop of Canterbury. Finally, "her sight fayled her, wherupon the Prince and the rest were called up to be present at her departing and she had her speach to the last gaspe."[28]

Anne had, the Venetian ambassador said, "released herself from the prison of a perpetual death." Donato's account back to Venice contained a sympathetic analysis well worth noting carefully. The ambassador reported:

> Her Majesty died three days ago in the palace at Hampton Court, . . . without seeing the king, who was at Newmarket. She breathed her last amid a few attendants in a country place, without the help of those remedies which might have lengthened her days even if they did not cure her. However, before dying, she had time to embrace the prince, her son, and had this satisfaction as mother of the succeeding king.

Donato referred to the beauty and popularity that Anne had enjoyed; but that had changed: "But of late her Majesty had to bear a change of fortune, suffering countless bitter things and great pain. She lost her health and fell out of favour with the king. . . . Thus at the end of her days, at the age of 44, she had nothing but to lament her sins and to show herself . . . very religious and sincere in the worship of the true God." This poignant account hits on an essential fact: Anne died alone, cut off from familial support, except for Charles. Chamberlain added this note: "The King continues still at New-market, and so is saide will do till the funerall be past." James had his own illness to contend with; but illness or no, he remained consistent in avoiding scenes of death, no matter that the person might be a wife or a son. He could not provide emotional support in such circumstances.[29]

On the day of Anne's death, James wrote to Christian IV of Denmark, informing him of his sister's death: "She who was a most excellent wife to us and a most dear sister to you has now died, and our common loss has apportioned grief to both of us." James described Anne's religious piety as she confronted death: "She eagerly entered upon that heavenly journey for which her entire being yearned." Her death, James wrote, "Was indeed premature if her age is regarded, but because of her previous ill health not unexpected." James praised Anne's "felicity of departure" and hoped that he might "conclude the brief drama of this life" in such a spirit. He added, "Many pledges of both love and virtue remain after her life, whence she has left us a great longing for her." This statement, if nothing else does, reveals that James wrote for public consumption: we have good reason to question the "great longing" that James felt for his wife. The editor of James's letters characterizes this letter as "thoroughly mendacious." Certainly James's assertion of Anne's saintlike departure did not square with the facts; only under pressure of the bishops did she prepare herself for death. As in other letters that James wrote to his brother-in-law, he did not hesitate to create a fiction of familial love, to put the best face on events.[30]

The daughter Elizabeth wrote to her father when she learned of her mother's death: "Sire, J'ay receu la lettre de V.M. ou il me mende a mon extreme regrette la morte de la Regne, ce m'est un affliction si grande que je n'ay de parolles pour exprimer, je prie a Dieu de consoler V. M. et pour moy je suis bien assuré que je regretteray ceste morte toute ma vie." (Sire, I have received the letter of your Majesty in which was sent to my extreme sorrow news of the death of the Queen; it is to me so great an affliction that I have not words to express it. I pray to God to console Your Majesty, and as for me I am assured that I will lament this death all my life.) Since we know of no communication between mother and daughter after 1613 when Elizabeth left England, one must tentatively accept Elizabeth's assurance that she will regret Anne's death all her life. We understand with unintended irony Elizabeth's lack of words to express her sorrow: speechlessness the result of truly having nothing to say. With considerable poetic license, James Maxwell wrote an elegy for Anne's death, including the following among its 543 lines:

> ELIZA so laments, her mother ANNE,
> That languishing she lyes, black, pale and wanne. . . .
> But most of all, Prince CHARLES her hopefull Sonne,
> Bemoanes his Mothers death; as though undone
> He were by this great losse; me thinkes of Teares,
> A Christall Tombe he to his Mother reeres.

Fictions threaten to displace reality.[31]

James also wrote a poem in response to Anne's death. One of many versions of this poem follows:

Thee to invite to heaven god sent his starr
Whose nearest freinds and kinn good princes are
Soe though they runn the race of men & dye
Death serves but to refine their Majestie
Soe did my Queene from hence her Court remove
And left the earth to be inthron'd above
Thus shee is chaynged, not deade: noe good prince dies
But like the day-starr only setts to rise.

This poem strikes one as more honest than, say, James's letter to Christian, though it scarcely bristles with deep-felt emotion. In a sense the poem reveals James merely trying to rationalize the problem of death—any prince's death, including his own. We may, however, recall James's *Phoenix*, the allegorical poem that responded to the death of Esmé Stuart, a poem whose emotional depth cannot be doubted. Anne, safely enthroned above, an idea consonant with Christian theology, became mythic and less human. Ironically, her new idealized location only underscored the distance between the king-husband and queen-wife.[32]

Chamberlain's letters tell the sad story of trying to set a date for Anne's funeral. Typically, funerals of royalty took place about a month after death. Chamberlain wrote on March 27, 1619 (twenty-five days after Anne's death): "The Quenes funerall is put of till the 29th of Aprill, and perhaps longer unles they can find out monie faster, for the master of the ward-robe is loth to weare his owne credit thread-bare." Chamberlain added an ironic note: "In the meane time the Ladies grow wearie of watching at Denmarke House, though all day long there is more concourse then when she was living." On April 24, Chamberlain again wrote to Carleton: "The day of the Quenes funerall is not yet set downe; . . . they are driven to shifts for monie, and talke of melting the Quenes golden plate and putting yt into coine: besides that the commissioners for her jewells and other moveables make offer to sell or pawne divers of them to goode value." Therefore, the king and court engaged in an unseemly hunt for money. Finally, on May 13, about ten weeks after her death, Anne's funeral took place, a funeral that Chamberlain described as "a drawling tedious sight, more remarqueable for number then for any other singularitie." Prince Charles attended, but James did not. In the early evening the funeral service at Westminster Abbey concluded; darkness and silence claimed Queen Anne.[33]

Wilson offered a contemporary and decidedly masculine assessment of Anne, calling her a "good Woman, not tempted from that height she stood on, to embroyl her spirit much with things below her." She indulged in "*Recreations* as might not make *Time* tedious to her," a reference to Anne's delight in masques and other kinds of entertainments. Wilson concluded: "And though great Persons Actions are often pried into, and made *Envies* mark, yet nothing could be fixt upon her, that left any great impression, but that she may have engraven upon her Monument a *Character* of *Virtue*." Anne's patronage of the arts encouraged the flourishing of certain dramatic forms in the Jacobean era. But as a political force, Anne had a negligible impact; as a mother she endured much frustration and incompleteness, and as a wife she suffered neglect and disregard. Donato, the Venetian ambassador, commented: "Her Majesty's death does not make the slightest difference in the government of these Kingdoms." We have some reason to think that it did not by 1619 make a great difference in the lives of the surviving members of the Stuart royal family. Perhaps the Venetian ambassador had the correct perspective: Anne in death had been released "from the prison of a perpetual death."[34]

In early June 1619, less than a month after Anne's funeral, James made an entry into London, dressed festively in pale blue satin with silver lace and a blue and white feather—resembling more a "wooer then a mourner," Chamberlain noted. No funeral blacks for James; no mourning. One can scarcely resist the temptation to see such action as strange; at the least, we find here additional evidence that James could be insensitive. James also displayed an unseemly eagerness to get his hands on his wife's legacy, most of which she had verbally committed to Prince Charles. Thomas Lorkin wrote to a friend in March: "The king is impatient to hear of the notion [her testament], and means to seize upon all for himself." In fact, James gave a sizable portion of the legacy to Buckingham. Could James have possibly understood the hollowness of the metaphor that he used in a speech to Parliament in February 1624: "As it is the husband's part to cherish his wife, to entreat her kindly, to reconcile himself towards her, and procure her love by all means, so it is my part to do the like to my people." These nice-sounding words serve finally to indict James's relationship with Anne. They also echo the kind of fiction making that we have seen in James's reaction to his mother and to some extent to Queen Elizabeth. Especially after their deaths, James moved to create a favorable image of himself in relationship to these women: he rewrote history from a masculine, self-centered perspective.[35]

### The Children

The focus now shifts to James's relationship with Elizabeth, Charles, and Buckingham, whose lives all intertwined. James's responses ranged from delightful joy in his children and Buckingham to jealousy and annoyance. He could rejoice at the birth of another grandchild as he did in 1620. The Venetian ambassador reported James's reaction: he "joyfully asked for a large beaker of wine and drank to the health of the new born prince in Bohemia. . . . He then took his purse and gave it with all that it contained to this gentleman, saying to him, Run and tell the good news to the prince." Or James could be petty: "The king says that the Palatine, his son-in-law, is very cold, and sometimes allows two months to go by without writing to him, and such like things." Of course, reading some of the letters from James to Frederick, housed in the State Papers at the Public Record Office, one understands why the son-in-law might have been a reluctant correspondent as these letters often contained admonitions and unsolicited advice.[36]

Two foreign political problems dominated the last years of James's life: the Bohemian issue and the Spanish Match. Each involved one of the royal children and to a large degree Buckingham. Like the daughter of Leontes in *The Winter's Tale,* James's daughter also went to Bohemia, in this case to become queen; her husband became king. Their tenure as sovereigns lasted briefly—they became known as the "Winter Queen" and "Winter King"—a real-life winter's tale. The Elizabeth who wrote so movingly to her father in April 1613 from Canterbury as she made ready to depart England would come to resent him when he failed to rescue her and her husband. She and Frederick ignited one of the sparks that began the Thirty Years War in Europe. Weldon has analyzed the predicament astutely: "He [James] was unfortunate in the marriage of his Daughter, and so was all Christendome besides; but sure the Daughter was more unfortunate in a Father, then he in a Daughter."[37]

Elizabeth and Frederick had settled into a comfortable life in his principality the Palatinate and lived in Heidelberg. Elizabeth gave birth to their first child in January 1614. The correspondence with her father between 1613 and 1618 revolved mainly around routine matters. She asked his guidance and responded dutifully, but James could inquire about the smallest matters. Some of Elizabeth's letters from 1615 contain, for example, an explanation of how one of her servants possessed some ruby buttons that James had apparently heard about. Elizabeth wrote to Sir Ralph Winwood in January 1615: "They were given me by the Queene at Yorke for a faire Chayne of pearle that his Matie [Majesty] sent me, and her Matie changed with me and gave me the Rubies for the Chayne this, that you lett the King understand, is truth." James had disapproved of Elizabeth's giving the jewels to a servant; and she eventually sought his forgiveness in yet another letter from Heidelberg: "I shall ever be in pain and unquiet till it please your M: [Majesty] to write me word you have pardoned this fault which if it please God shall be the last I will ever ofend your M."[38]

In June 1615, in one of her many French letters, Elizabeth wrote to her father: "Je remercie tres humblement V.M. et la supplie de me continuer ainsy sa Royal paternelle affection et monstrant avoir tel soing de moy on me negligera aussy taunt moins icy." (I thank your Majesty very humbly and request that you continue thus to me your such paternal royal affection and, showing such regard for me, I will be that much less neglected here.) At the end of the year, Elizabeth informed her father about her husband and child: "The Elector and my little black baby are very well, thank God"—"black baby" apparently being Elizabeth's affectionate term for her child.[39]

In April 1616, Elizabeth wrote James trying to clarify what ought to be the order of precedence in her husband's court. James had insisted that Elizabeth should be first among equals among the spouses of the German princes, but Frederick's mother had claimed precedence. James wrote to Frederick in June that "no father is more desirous than he is that his daughter should be humbly faithful to her husband; but she would be unworthy to live if she gave up her place without her father's consent." James wanted to control.[40]

Sir Henry Wotton visited the court of Heidelberg in April 1616 and reported, for example, that "it is a Court of great sobriety." He said, "I do not find the Count Palatine, in the judgement of my eye, much grown since your Majesty saw him, either in height or breadth." Wotton commented on Frederick's "malincolique," his apparent depressive tendency. Of Elizabeth, Wotton claimed: "My Lady, your gracious daughter, retaineth still her former virginal verdure in her complexion and features, though she be now the mother of one of the sweetest children that I think the world can yield." Outwardly, Frederick and Elizabeth exhibited kind rather "than amorous demonstrations." Wotton explored in some detail the precedence issue, emphasizing to Frederick that "my Lady was not to be considered only as the daughter of a King, like the daughters of Fraunce, but did carry in her person the possibility of succession to three crowns." Even though Wotton could not convince Frederick to give Elizabeth a preferential position, he did conclude that the court at Heidelberg seemed stable and peaceful. Such peace would soon surrender to new challenges and accompanying turmoil.[41]

In Bohemia events began in May 1618 that affected James's rule until his death. In that month Bohemian nobles revolted against Ferdinand, the ruler imposed on them, and deposed him, throwing his possessions into the streets. The Protestant nobles of Bohemia took control, but the Catholic Hapsburgs throughout Europe saw the danger of this action. By August, the deposed Ferdinand had been named emperor of the Holy Roman Empire. Philip of Spain informally asked King James to mediate between the emperor and the Bohemians.

Flattered, James began a series of diplomatic moves that would have been simply ludicrous if they had not been so serious. He understood almost nothing about the Bohemian situation. To complicate matters, James's son-in-law encouraged the Bohemians in their rebellion. Indeed, in late summer 1619, the Bohemians elected Frederick as their new king; he hesitated for a moment, then accepted, arriving in Prague in October. In December, Frederick and Elizabeth were crowned king and queen of Bohemia—another reason 1619 became such a crucial year in the Stuart royal family's life.

James rightly saw the danger of Frederick's action: namely, that it would rouse the Hapsburg forces. He faced enormous pressure from the Spanish in the person of their shrewd ambassador to England, the count of Gondomar. The Spanish, with whom James wanted to remain friends, insisted that Frederick should renounce the crown of Bohemia. James felt pulled in several competing directions. He thought that Frederick should not have accepted the crown because the people had deposed their ruler and because Frederick had not adequately consulted with James before taking such precipitate action. According to the historian Lee: "Of all the crosses James had to bear in his declining years, the greatest was his foolish and obstinate son-in-law. The unreality of Frederick's political ambition was matched only by the fatuity of his tactics." On the other hand, James rather enjoyed the idea that his daughter had become a queen—only fitting, he thought, for a daughter of his. James told Gondomar: "The Palatine [Frederick] is a godless man and a usurper. I will give him no help. It is much more reasonable that he, young as he is, should listen to an old man like me, and do what is right by surrendering Bohemia, than that I should be involved in a bad cause." As storm clouds arose, James sank into irresolution, a hallmark of his foreign policy in the waning years. He alternately vowed support of Frederick and the German states and denounced them. Truth to tell, James had no money with which to establish and outfit an army. Also, he continued to relish his reputation as a peacemaker.[42]

Barely had Frederick and Elizabeth had a chance to enjoy their new status as rulers and their new child before serious problems arose. In August 1620, Spanish forces invaded the Palatinate, Frederick's homeland, while at the same time the emperor's forces invaded Bohemia. The Spanish captured the Palatinate, and Frederick found himself cut off from his own principality. And in November 1620, Frederick and the Bohemian forces suffered a major defeat at the battle of White Mountain. As a consequence, fearing for their very lives, Frederick and Elizabeth fled from Prague, literally burning the bridges behind them in order to slow the advancing enemy. As they looked back at Prague, the rising smoke they saw did not ascend as a sacrifice to the gods but rather curled its way defiantly skyward in the cold November air as a sign of what had happened to their dreams. Their nightmare had been realized.

Outraged at the duplicity of the Spanish, even James became eager for war. Whatever he thought about Frederick's claim to Bohemia, he knew that the claim on the Palatinate could not be doubted. As war fever in England grew, James called a parliament in early 1621 and got from them woefully inadequate funds for a military endeavor. The Spanish then played their trump card: they reopened the prospect of a Spanish marriage for Charles. How, then, could James go to war against his potential relatives? Suddenly the Bohemian-Palatinate-Spanish Match questions became hopelessly intertwined. Tying James in diplomatic knots rendered him negligible as a military or even diplomatic force. He would spend his remaining days futilely trying to untie these knots. A contemporary noted: "And he [James] knew the loose Honour with all the Potentates of *Europe* . . . if nothing were done for re-possessing the *Palatinate*. Yet in fine, he sate down, and it cleaft his Heart." Meanwhile, Frederick and Elizabeth had found safe refuge in The Hague. From there they could anxiously wait for rescue, for the restoration of Bohemia and the Palatinate. Each passing year diminished whatever prospects they had: they would not look on Bohemia or the Palatinate again. James wrung his hands, and they wept bitter tears of frustration and resentment.[43]

With this sketch of the basic events of this sad, possibly tragic story, we can fill in the details of Elizabeth's relationship to her father during this agonizing period. In late August 1619, Elizabeth wrote to Buckingham explaining that the Bohemians desired Frederick for their king, "which he will not resolve of till he knowe his Majesties [James's] opinion in it." Elizabeth couched the issue in terms of an opportunity for James: "The King hath now a good occasion to manifest to the world the love he hath ever professed to the Prince heere. I earnestlie entreat you to use your best meanes in perswading his Majestie to shew himself now, in his helping of the Prince heere, a true loving father to us both." Helping Elizabeth and Frederick became in her view a means for James to verify his paternal love. Elizabeth had raised the stakes very high: their subsequent difficulties became not only political and military problems for James but also a test of his familial love.[44]

In October 1619, Chamberlain wrote to Carleton that James had summarily dismissed Baron Donha, Frederick's emissary. Furthermore, James "did not allow of the Palatines election, but esteemed yt rather a faction, which he wold in no wise favor nor further, and that his subjects were as deere to him as his children, and therfore wold not embarke them in an unjust and needlesse quarrell." The Venetian ambassador reported on November 22, 1619, the paradox of James's displeasure at Frederick's acceptance of the Bohemian crown and yet "his delight at this new royal title for his son-in-law and daughter." Despite the advice of some of the German electors and James's reluctance, Frederick had accepted the crown, "at last seduced by hopes and amibition to despise their counsels," as one contemporary noted. As the new year of 1620 began, Chamberlain wrote: "I know not what we shall say to the busines of Bohemia, but that we are like to be ydle spectators." He observed that the bells did not ring when word reached London of the birth of Elizabeth's latest child. Chamberlain concluded ominously and correctly: "He is a straunge father that will neither fight for his children or pray for them."[45]

Early in 1620, Elizabeth wrote her father with the usual request for aid and for continuation of his good graces: "C'est un des choses que je desire le plus en ce monde." (It is one of the things that I desire most in the world.) Thomas Rowe, faithful follower of Elizabeth, wrote to her from England on June 7, 1620, praising her and Frederick. By his tacit support, James "hath shown him selfe a wise and wary Prince & yet at last, an affectionat & good father" ready to assist then in their "just & glorious cause." In late summer Elizabeth, Frederick, and others began to become apprehensive about the security of Bohemia. On August 5, Frederick wrote his father-in-law, thanking him for "son amitié" (his friendship) and his "affection paternelle" (fatherly affection) and hoped that James would help conserve his country and maintain religion. James saw the struggle in Europe as a religious one between Catholics and Protestants, as he noted in 1620: "For all the causes of Religion are involved in it; for they will alter Religion where they conquer, and so perhaps my grand-child may suffer." Even Frederick's mother wrote James an urgent letter on August 17, 1620. She wanted to show

James "the sympathy I feel for the misfortunes which will overwhelm [Frederick and Elizabeth], if God and your majesty do not shew your paternal love towards them." She added, "Your majesty will know also in what pain is the queen your daughter, and that she is about to be entirely surrounded with enemies." By supporting them, James could "shew himself a good father." Surely part of this increased pressure grew out of a recognition that James tended to get bogged down in legal details or philosophical disputation. Appealing to him as a father whose daughter and son-in-law were in danger cut through the issues and made his response a measure of his love.[46]

The fall of 1620 became the crucial time in Bohemia and in the Palatinate. On September 15, Elizabeth wrote to Buckingham, urging that James now "shew himself a loving father to us, and not suffer his children's inheritance to be taken away. You see how little they regard his Ambassadours and what they say." Knowing her father well, Elizabeth added a postscript: "I pray tell the King that the enemie will more regard his blowes then his wordes." While this topic remained uppermost on her mind, Elizabeth wrote Charles on the same day, raising many of the issues that she had in Buckingham's letter. She added to Charles: "Dear brother, be most earnest with him; for, to speak freely to you, his slackness to assist us doth make the Princes of the Union [German princes] slack too, who do nothing with their army." Elizabeth documented in these letters the failure of James's policies and his inability to settle on all-out support, including military. Elizabeth had now written the two people most likely to have had significant influence with her father: the favorite and her brother. (Interestingly, Elizabeth could not have known Buckingham, having left England before he became known even to James; however, she clearly understood his position.)[47]

Escaping Bohemia, Elizabeth wrote on November 27, 1620, a letter, possibly to Carleton, sketching their fate:

> I am sure by this tyme you had the unwelcome newes of our armies defeat w<sup>ch</sup> forced the king & me to leave Prague not w<sup>th</sup>out danger to have bene taken by the ennemies yf they had followed us w<sup>ch</sup> they did not. I have left the king at Breslau in Silesia. . . . The good news you write of the king my fathers declaring himself for the Palatinat, I pray God they may be seconded w<sup>th</sup> the same for Bohemia.

On November 29, Elizabeth wrote her friend the Duchess de la Tremoille, assuming that she has heard the bad news ("entendu le malheur que nous avons eu"). Elizabeth consoled herself that the war had not ended and that God had done this only to test or improve them ("que Dieu aura seulement fait cecy pour nous esprouver"); in the end things would turn out better for the love of his church ("il nous donnera le meilleur, pour l'amour de son eglise"). Elizabeth valiantly tried to make sense of what had happened. How could the year 1620 have begun with their being crowned king and queen of Bohemia and then ended with their being driven out of the kingdom, wandering about the landscape looking for a place to land?[48]

By early April 1621, the Winter King and Queen had safely reached The Hague, where, according to the Venetian ambassador, Elizabeth "enjoys more popularity among the people, with her husband, than she has ever experienced anywhere else, and where she will stay a while, seeing she cannot come where she ought." On May 21, Elizabeth wrote Thomas Rowe: "I hope it will be the better for us, though I confess to you that I doe not look for anie good change of fortune for us, if my father doe no otherwise then he hath done."[49]

But James, who complained that Frederick did not listen to him, remained intransigent, having accepted the Bohemian debacle, and powerless to do much about restoring the Palatinate to Frederick. In a letter, dated March 14, 1621, James broached the question of marriage between Charles and the Infanta, at the urging of the Spanish ambassador. He added to Philip IV: "We wish likewise, that your Serenity, out of your goodness, would ease our other care, touching the *Palatinate*, which concerns our Daughter and Son in Law, and their innocent Children, banished from their Ancestor's Inheritance." Thus, while Elizabeth sat in The Hague eagerly awaiting her father's help, James wrote the Spanish king asking for his mercy. To expect "goodness" from Philip IV emphasized the bankrupt nature of James's policy. Small wonder that Elizabeth anticipated little from her father. He meanwhile had walked into the Spanish trap.[50]

Logically, one might have assumed that Elizabeth and her family, having lost their kingdoms, would have taken refuge in England with her royal father and brother. But Elizabeth's failure to come to England did not derive from her lack of desire or even particularly from a lack of money. Rather, she did not return to her homeland because her father would not allow it. James conveyed his rather shocking position in a letter to Carleton: "If our daughter also do come into those parts, with any intention to transport herself hither, you do use all possible means at this time to divert her; and rather than fail, to charge her, in our name and upon our blessing, that she do not come, without our good liking and pleasure first signified unto her." The French ambassador tried in May 1621 to explain

James's resistance to Elizabeth's return. James feared, said the ambassador, that Elizabeth would stir the passions of the people, rousing the Puritans and others opposed to Spain. Second, "the sight of her would be a continual reproach to him for having deserted her, and her demands for aid might involve him with Spain." Aside from the political issues, James's resistance to his daughter can be explained in part by jealousy. Her presence would have deflected attention from his reign, and James did not like royal competition for attention—as was obvious in his dealings with his family. He remained therefore perversely consistent: unlike Leontes in Shakespeare's play, James did not welcome back his daughter from Bohemia. Instead, he closed the door.[51]

As if one more letter might bring the desired result, Elizabeth continued to write to James throughout the spring of 1621, desperately seeking his aid. In early April, she told of their safe arrival to The Hague and asked for his paternal affection, else all would be lost ("je crains que tout sera perdu"). She complained in a letter of April 12 that the princes of the Union had abandoned them and put the fault on James, which angered Elizabeth above everything ("ce que me fasche plus que nul autre chose"). Through his actions, Elizabeth suggested, James could demonstrate that he would not abandon them. While James wrote to Carleton blocking any hope that Elizabeth had of returning to England, he also wrote to his son-in-law on May 13, telling him, among other things, that, God helping, they would survive if Frederick listened to James's counsel ("car a la fin, Dieu aydant, si vous continuer a escouter nos conseils"). James insisted that everything that he had done had come from his heart, proceeding out of solicitude and affection ("N'y ayant rien que nous ayons plus a coeur, et a quoy nous travaillons avec plus de solicitude et d'affection")—all for the reestablishment of Frederick in his homeland. Frederick might be forgiven if he took all this with a huge grain of salt. Part of James's heart stayed closed to the plight of his daughter and son-in-law or at least unable to reconcile their demands with his policies. James's heart remained that "coffer of perplexity" that he had so accurately described decades earlier.[52]

Three images from late summer and early fall 1621 reveal precisely the feelings and responses to Elizabeth's predicament. On July 23, Elizabeth thanked James for a portrait of himself that he had sent her, a simple portrait that she had always esteemed above all the rings in the world ("le simple pourtrait je l'eusse tousjours estime pardesus toutes les bagues du monde"). Elizabeth, at least in the letter, interpreted the gesture as a sign that she continued in her father's good graces ("ce m'est une extreme contentement de voir par cela que je continue tousjours aux bonnes graces de V. M."). Frederick had received admonition from James that he should listen to James's counsel, and Elizabeth received a portrait of the king. Perhaps indeed James intended the picture as a sign of his love, but the daughter had vainly looked for other signs.[53]

Writing Buckingham in late July, Elizabeth again pleaded for help and added a poignant postscript: "The King [Frederick] is much troubled at the newes more then ever I saw him. I ernestlie intreat you therefore to get his Majestie to send him soe effectuall comfortable answere that may a little ease his melancholie, for I confess it troubles me to see him soe. I pray lett none know this but his Majestie and my Brother." Sir Henry Wotton in 1616 had detected Frederick's melancholy, and, clearly, Elizabeth had understandable fears about her husband. When Frederick asked James's personal representative to them, Edward Villiers, about James's promises of military aid, Villiers responded, "We are in different times." Such casual indifference exacerbated Frederick's depression. And the Venetian secretary added in his report of October 11, 1621, "The queen has been observed weeping bitterly in a dark room," though she tried to keep up outward appearances.[54]

James's simple portrait, esteemed as it might be, nevertheless stands in the context of the portraits of a depressed king and a daughter weeping bitterly in a dark room. Frederick and Elizabeth had reached the nadir of their experience. Never had one of the royal children had more reason to feel alienated from the father. Elizabeth had terribly misjudged James when she wrote to him in April 1613, praising him as "the best and most amiable father, that the sun will ever see." James had given the lie to Elizabeth's assertion, "Your majesty can never efface from the memory of her." Heading into the winter of 1621–1622, Elizabeth felt not only the chill of the weather but also the ice of isolation and betrayal.

Three letters from Frederick to Elizabeth, written while he was away from her in late summer 1622, seeking support wherever he could find it, reveal the depth of their joint despair. On August 4, Frederick reported his dealings with the French king and reminded his wife ("mon cher coeur") of the afflictions that they had endured. "Je baise la chere bouche un million de fois en imagination," Frederick wrote (I kiss your dear mouth a million times in my imagination). Desiring a peaceful existence with his wife, secure from the problems of the world, Frederick on August 20 lamented:

Croyez, mon cher coeur, que je me souhaite bien auprès de vous. Je
vous ai déjà mandé ce qui m'en retient: plut à Dieu qu'eussions un
petit coin au monde pour y vivre contents ensemble, c'est tout le bon-
heur que je me souhaite.
(Believe, my dear heart, that I desire to be near you. I have already sent
to you that which keeps me: may it please God that there be a little
corner of the world for to live content together; that is all the happiness
that I wish.)

A month later Frederick wrote of the partition of the Palatinate,
adding, "Voilà mon pauvre Heidelberg pris!" (Behold my poor Heidelberg taken). Out of such despair Elizabeth wrote her friend Rowe
on November 25, 1622: "For my father hitherto hath done us more
hurt then good. I hope one day our fortune will change." No secure
corner of the world awaited them; they could not be impervious to
chaos and change around them.[55]
A brisk, pointed exchange between father and son-in-law in January and February 1623 intensified the difficulty of understanding
one another at such great distance. On January 23, James wrote to
Frederick admonishing and lecturing him. Nothing bothered James
more than to see all his efforts made in their behalf become fruitless
("n'y a il rien que nous afflige plus que de voir tous les efforts que
nous avons faits a cette fui, avoir resté jusqu' icy si infructurux").
An accusatory tone pervaded the letter. Stung, Frederick lashed
back in a letter of February 4—a rare moment when an extant letter
explicitly responds to another. Frederick complained that he had not
heard from James for a long time, although he had followed James's
counsel. He had received in the end, as always, new accusations
and censures instead of expressions of consolation and comfort ("je
n'y en reçois en fin que tousjours de nouvelles accusations et censures au lieu de consolations et soulayemens espressés"). This angry
exchange grew out of frustration on both sides. James doubtless held
Frederick responsible for creating intractable problems that had en-
sued from his acceptance of the Bohemian crown.[56]
James compelled Frederick by early fall 1623 to sign a treaty with
the emperor, as noted in Elizabeth's letter to Lord Edward Conway,
September 6: "By this time I hope his majesty is pleased with the
King who hath, to obey his command, signed the treaty." The terms
of the treaty required Frederick to renounce the Bohemian crown and
to stay out of the Palatinate for a specified period of time, plus other
humiliating conditions, all spelled out in James's letter to Frederick
on November 20. Elizabeth indicated to Conway that they had no
choice: "The king my father's will to us is law which we will ever obey

in that we can. . . . I hope his majesty will one day see the falsehood of our enemies." Perhaps a younger, more vigorous James might have, but the James of the 1620s had not the stamina, resources, or insight necessary to confront these problems successfully.[57]

Even when Frederick asked that one of their children be allowed to come to England and be brought up at court there, James refused, "thinking," said the Venetian ambassador, "there might be some understanding with his people to proclaim the boy king one day and depose him." As in the case of Elizabeth, James doubtless would have found the presence of this grandson a reproach to him, a tangible reminder of his fecklessness. Gratified that the Spanish Match of 1623 fell through, Elizabeth naively believed that their affairs would improve. She told the Venetian ambassador to the Netherlands in 1624 that "she did not trust her father, but now he is compelled to trust his son and Buckingham." Elizabeth's last few letters to her father contain nothing of a personal nature—perhaps she had finally despaired of significant help from him.[58]

Contemporary reaction condemned James for his neglect of his daughter and son-in-law. William Harris branded James's behavior simply "Strange conduct! un-heard of behaviour!" Welwood noted that in everything "the House of *Austria* [the Hapsburgs] outwitted him [James]; so that the poor Prince *Palatine* gain'd nothing by his Alliance with *England*, but the hard Fate to be abandon'd by those whose Honour and Interest it was to support him." About Frederick's acceptance of the Bohemian crown, Thomas Fuller wrote: "K. *James* privately foretold to some principal persons, that this matter would prove the ruine of *his Daughter*. There want not some who say, That he went about to verifie his *own Prediction*, by not sending seasonable succours for their assistance." Elizabeth and certainly Frederick made many mistakes, the most obvious being the headstrong action of accepting the Bohemian crown without first building a base of support or even dimly perceiving the consequences. Being in their early twenties and relatively inexperienced, they simply could not have anticipated the problems. Their political mistakes hardly warranted James's response to them. One cannot readily shake the image of the royal daughter's weeping bitterly in a dark room because of her father's treatment, or being refused entry into her native land because of his unfounded jealousy, or her bracing statement that she did not trust her father. Instead of adequate military and financial aid, they got lectures from James and his own naive hopes that the Spanish would bail him out. James shipped his portrait to Elizabeth but not his heart.[59]

In the meantime, Charles had his own struggles to secure his place in the esteem of his father and the public. He was trying to establish his own identity, wrestle with the prominence of Buckingham, reconcile the loss of his mother and the suffering of his sister, and endure the ambivalent feelings of his father toward him. The archbishop of Canterbury wrote to James about Charles: "And though, Sir, you have a large interest in the *Prince,* as the Son of your Flesh, yet hath the people a greater, as the Son of the Kingdom, upon whom (next after your Majesty) their Eyes are fixed, and Welfare depends." This definition recalls James's earlier assessment of Henry as belonging to the country, and it serves as a good description of the situation of the royal child: member of a family group but also a political figure belonging to the commonwealth—certainly in the case of the heir apparent. This definition expresses an inherent tension between the wishes of the sovereign-parent and the desires of the people. This strife also had existed in the case of Prince Henry, whose own agenda often conflicted with James's. For Charles, everything functioned on a lesser scale compared to his brother; he never stirred the passions, excitement, and expectation that Henry did. Although Anne grew close to Charles, James exhibited little interest in his only surviving son. Only in the last two years of his life did James finally begin noticeably to warm toward his son, even though this improvement carried residual notes of tension and jealousy. Probably Charles's blossoming friendship with Buckingham helped endear son to father.[60]

Initially, Charles resented Buckingham, just as Henry had disliked Carr. Without an especially strong personality, Charles must have smarted from the love and attention that Buckingham received. Even as the only surviving child still living in England, he experienced second-place status. Two incidents, minor in themselves, nevertheless depict the struggle in the relationship of the prince to the favorite. Edward Sherburn wrote to Carleton, March 1616, about the prince's taking a ring that belonged to Villiers, "and, putting it on his own [hand], forgot it and lost it, on which Villiers complained to the King, who chided the Prince so severely as to bring him to tears, and forbade him the presence till the ring was restored." Perhaps getting even, perhaps just having fun, Charles got in trouble again two months later. Sherburn reported, "The King boxed the Prince's ears, for turning a water-spout on Sir Geo. Villiers in jest, in the garden at Greenwich."[61]

In a letter, probably late 1618 or early 1619, Charles sought Buckingham's help in a problem with James. Some kind of misunderstanding had occurred, exactly what is unclear:

Ther is none that knows me so well as your selfe, what dewtiefull respect and love, I have ever & shall ever, carrie to kinge: and therfor ye may juge what greefe it is to me, to have the ill fortune as that anie of my actions should bring so ill an interpretation. . . . It doth greeve me much that the King should be so much moved with it as you say he is, for the least show of his displeasure, . . . I pray you to commend my most humble service to his M^tie & tel him that I ame verie sorre that I have done anie thing may offend him and that I will be content to have anie pennance inflicted upon me so he may forgive me.

Charles said that he had been trying to get his mother to make a will, although he did not say what precipitated the misunderstanding with James. Near the close of the letter Charles added, "Yet I deserve to be punniched for my ill fortune." These words emanated in a childish tone from a young man quite unsure about his standing with his father. Seeking Buckingham's help compounded the difficulty. One may even sense fear revealed in the letter.[62]

Buckingham and Charles in 1621 fought again, this time over the appointment of the bishop of London: each had his own candidate. According to the Venetian ambassador, Charles complained "very bitterly and angrily against the favourite and opened out on the subject very sharply to the king his father, quite contrary to his habit." James succeeded in mollifying him and settling the issue. The ambassador said that the argument "was of no slight importance." A long-lasting reconciliation between the prince and the favorite would not occur until the Spanish trip of 1623.[63]

In 1616, Charles came of age politically by being formally invested as Prince of Wales, an experience that Henry had enjoyed in 1610. The investiture took place in early November; it included, among other things, a street pageant prepared by London's citizens, the dramatist Thomas Middleton's *Civitatis Amor.* Like other pageants before it, this street entertainment also involved a complicity between royal family and the citizens in order to provide a "lively impression" of a stable kingdom that sanctioned a new heir apparent: "His Majesty, as well to show the bounty of his affection towards his royal son, as to settle in the hearts of his loving subjects a lively impression of his kingly care for continuance of the happy and peaceable government of this land in his issue and posterity" has thought fit to have these ceremonies. This festivity reinforced the archbishop's point that Charles belonged to the country.[64]

Arriving at Chelsea, Charles encountered a personification of London, who was accompanied by Neptune, and the rivers Thames and Dee; the figure London represented the "loves of many thousands" who spoke through her. London thus existed as an allegory and as a physical reality. This character referred to Charles as the "Treasure of hope, and jewel of mankind," a hope that truly rested in the future: "Thou whose most early goodness, fix'd in youth, / Does promise comfort to the length of time." Though anticipating a glorious future, London also commented on the glorious peace of the present, a fair assessment of England's situation in 1616. The pageant moved on to Whitehall, where Charles found the allegorical figures of Hope and Peace, both arising thematically out of the previous tableau. In her song Peace welcomed this "spring of joy and peace" to whom the city's love extended: such a prince and such a day, the song insisted. But the day did not include Queen Anne, who refused to participate. The Venetian ambassador claimed, "The festivities did not attain to the splendour of those which were celebrated for the dead prince." Charles endured constant comparison to his dead brother.[65]

In the investiture ceremony itself, Charles knelt before his father, who read the words of investment, put the robes on him, girded on the sword, gave him the patent that created him Prince of Wales, and kissed him. The full force of ceremony conferred a special legitimacy on Charles, made official what had already been known: he would succeed his father. The attendant lords of the realm confirmed their endorsement, as the citizens of London had earlier in the pageant. Charles took another large political step when James appointed him to the Privy Council in 1622, reported by Chamberlain: "On Sonday was sevenight the King caused the Prince to be sworne or admitted of the Privie Counsell commending him to them with many goode words and praises of his dutifull cariage and filiall demeanure." At last Charles at age twenty-two gained admission to the most important political body attached to the court, a sign that James had begun to understand that Charles needed to gain a political education and begin preparation for ruling.[66]

Charles manifested concern for politics and his sister when in 1622 he made an impassioned plea in behalf of her plight in the loss of Bohemia and the Palatinate. Joseph Mead described the episode in an October 1622 letter to Martin Stuteville: "The prince, before his father came down, besought him upon his knees, and with tears, to take pity upon his poor and distressed sister, her husband, and children, and to suffer himself no longer to be abused with treaties." Charles vowed to raise an army and lead it himself into the Palatinate, forgoing more diplomatic negotiations. He received no encouragement from his father.[67]

As with Henry, so with Charles: James often responded to his sons with jealousy, this jealousy growing not only out of James's personal character but also out of his political position. Even after Charles had assumed a place on the Privy Council, the Venetian ambassador would write: "The prince, brought up so as to be always at one with his father, never moves a step without looking up to him. His Majesty being naturally most jealous after the case of his other son, keeps him constantly at his side, and takes the utmost care that he shall not move except by his rule, and shall imbibe his ideas." The French ambassador reported in 1623: "His father for some time back has treated him with open and insupportable contempt. In order to avoid enduring this lesser evil, the Prince, like a man without judgement, hurls himself head foremost into the greatest of follies." The ambassador also offered a rationale for Charles's sudden decision to go to Spain to complete the marriage negotiation for the Infanta.[68]

Commenting on Charles's increasing prudence and stature, the Venetian ambassador, Alvise Valaresso, reported in April 1624: "The king undoubtedly knows this and resents it to such an extent that he can no longer keep silence. Last Sunday, as I know for certain, he [James] reproved him to some extent for making himself too popular, to which the prince replied modestly that he would always behave as an honourable man." There must have been a very low threshold of what constituted "too popular," a threshold known only to James.[69]

Trapped in an awkward bind, Charles struggled to find the right mixture of dutiful modesty and assertive curiosity. The earl of Kellie wrote the earl of Mar in May 1624, bemoaning the lack of harmony between the king and prince: "Not that the Prince hes done onye thing unbeseeming him to the Kings Majestie, but that out of a desyre to have all things goe weill. . . . he hes bein a lytill more populare then was fitting for him." The earl added that James has "spokin his mynd freelye to him, whitche I think did mutche woorke upone the Prince." Pesaro, the Venetian ambassador, reported in October 1624: "His Highness was summoned by his father who cannot bear to have his son far from his sight." A sentimental view would interpret James as merely desiring the friendly companionship of his son, but with James the matter was more complex. Aging, increasingly infirm, realizing that power was slipping from him, James retained a streak of jealousy that unfortunately permeated dealings with his family. To be fair, moments of genuine affection did occur; but James remained ironically torn between jealousy and neglect, a parent guilty of absence and guilty of a consuming presence.[70]

Giorlando Lando included a long assessment of Charles in a report to the Venetian Senate, September 21, 1622. He noted the basic tension between father and son: "Rule introduces some mistrust even in the natural affection between father and son. His Majesty has frequently shown that he does not wish others to touch the helm even if he abandoned it." We can call that jealousy of rule. The ambassador cited the goodwill of the people that Charles had earned, but "if they are in some parts lukewarm or not very zealous for him, it is because some would like to see him more bold and independent with his father, more zealous for his brother-in-law and sister." Ironically, the more Charles asserted himself, the more he risked his father's jealous reaction.

Modesty characterized Charles's personal habits. The ambassador noted: "So far as one knows he has not tasted certain youthful pleasures and apparently has not felt love except by some show of poetry; he even blushes like a modest maiden if he hears any scandalous conversation"—the latter certainly distinguished him from his father. Given the nature of court life, Charles's virtuous sexual behavior appeared as an anomaly. Only in 1623 with the pursuit of the Spanish Infanta do we begin to learn of Charles's response to love, although in this case a highly romanticized idea. In 1620, Lando had reported that Charles "has no inclination that way [toward marriage], but the influences surrounding him, prudence, the memory of things past, fear and every other consideration tend towards the satisfaction of his father," who had broached the subject of marriage. In a word, the ambassador in 1622 said, "He conducts himself with more decorum than the king, while equally gracious." Being more decorous in behavior than James may not have been Charles's greatest challenge.[71]

With regard to matters of state, Ambassador Lando said: "His Highness does not clearly disclose his opinions, so it would be presumptuous to give a judgment upon them." Lando added, "His special maxim is to adopt silence and sobriety of speech in affairs of state, so he proves most exemplary in that very worthy quality." But as the historian David Willson suggests, "His silence, praised by the court as wise and judicious, sprang partly from the fact that the young Prince had nothing to say." The Venetian ambassador found an appropriate metaphor: "He moves like a planet in its sphere, so naturally and quietly that one does not remark it." Charles held his opinions lightly: "If he hears his father or the favourite say anything

to the contrary, he immediately changes." The ambassador captured an essential problem: Charles behaved as if "the favourite
were prince and himself less than a favourite." Charles rightly felt
displaced or supplanted by Buckingham. Whatever hatred he may
have felt toward Buckingham transformed into a dependent friendship, especially during the 1623 trip to Spain, as we will see in more
detail below.[72]

John Chamberlain saw the prince in February 1624 and offered
this assessment in a letter to Carleton: "I went [to the gathering of
Parliament] specially to see the Prince who indeed is growne a fine
gentleman and beyond the expectation I had of him when I saw him
last which was not these seven yeares, and indeed I thincke he
never lookt nor became himself better in all his life." Charles stood
on the threshold of assuming power. But in the previous year James
had much less reason to feel sanguine. Bishop Goodman noted:
"King James did consider that his daughter being with the Holland-
ers, his son with the Spaniards, the two opposite factions of Christendom, and himself at home to be left destitute of children, what
the world would conceive of his judgment and of his natural affection. He considered the danger, himself being now aged, if he should
die, what then might befall his children." In 1623, James's plight, if
not the precise circumstances, resembled that of a king whose story
James had seen portrayed in Shakespeare's drama in the season pre-
ceding Elizabeth's wedding: Leontes in *The Winter's Tale*, whose wife
at the end of act 3 had presumably died, whose son had died, and
whose daughter, unknown to the king, had gone to Bohemia. James's
vulnerability in 1623 contained all the ingredients for a tragic winter's tale; but like *The Winter's Tale*, a child returns, and life opens at
the end with more possibilities than thought likely. A second chance
occurred, and Charles embodied the future of the Stuart royal
family.[73]

### George Villiers, duke of Buckingham

As this discussion of James's final years began with an examina-
tion of one of his favorites, so it ends with one: George Villiers,
eventually duke of Buckingham, James's last and greatest favorite.
The final twelve years of James's life thus began and ended with a
favorite. The royal family found itself drawn into this circular pattern, indeed often defined by James's reactions to his favorites.
Probably on the eve of Buckingham's departure to Spain in 1623,
James wrote: "I protest to God I rode this afternoon a great way in
the park without speaking to anybody and the tears trickling down

George Villiers, duke of Buckingham (c. 1616), King James's last and greatest favorite, in a painting attributed to William Larkin. National Portrait Gallery.

my cheeks, as now they do that I can scarcely see to write. But alas, what shall I do at our parting? . . . Remember thy picture." On February 28, 1623, James wrote to Buckingham as he journeyed with Charles to Spain: "I have no more to say but that I wear Steenie's picture in a blue ribbon under my waistcoat next my heart." James called him "Steenie," a version of the name Stephen, an apparent reference to the beauty of Saint Stephen. On the anniversary of James's accession, March 24, 1623, Buckingham wrote from Spain, thanking James for all his generosity and love and noting that he could "never satisfie the dett or detter in saying enough." Buckingham had learned that he was "increased in revenue, decresed in expence, my unworthie picture worne next the worthiest hart livinge, and all this in absence. . . . this effect . . . to teach me never to lous sight of that I love so pretiouslie againe." These powerful feelings, recollected in tranquility ("I, now in a chamber a lone"), confirm the genuine love that flowed between king and subject. The picture of Buckingham worn next to James's heart said precisely where he resided in the king's affection. The twenty-six years of age difference between the two apparently did not matter.[74]

George Villiers, born in Leicestershire in August 1592, possessed great charm and dazzling good looks, qualities that caught James's attention when they first met at Apethorpe in August 1614 while James was on progress. Roger Lockyer, author of the definitive biography of Buckingham, writes that this young man offered James "youth, beauty, high spirits, sensuality, sweetness of character, and devotion." Of course, Catherine Macaulay, writing in the eighteenth century, took a different perspective. She wrote that James found in "the disposition of the youth an unbounded levity, and a ductile licentiousness." One contemporary commented on Villiers's appearance thus: "From the nails of his fingers, nay, from the sole of his foot to the crown of his head, there was no blemish in him. And yet his carriage and every stoop of his deportment more than his excellent form were the beauty of his beauty." Even the restrained Bishop Goodman offered this assessment: "He had a very lovely complexion; he was the handsomest bodied man in England, his limbs were so well compacted, and his conversation so pleasing, and of so sweet a disposition." Some saw a feminine quality in Villiers's delicate features. Simonds D'Ewes in 1621 offered this assessment of Villiers: "I . . . most earnestly viewed him for about half an hour's space at the least; which I had opportunity the more easily to accomplish, because he stood all the time he talked bareheaded. I saw everything in him full of delicacy and handsome features; yea his hands and face seemed to me especially effeminate and curious."[75]

James was not alone in being smitten by this handsome young man; everyone saw him as an attractive means of ingratiating one-self with the king. Leading courtiers and churchmen sought Vil-liers's favor, starting with archbishop George Abbot, who wanted Villiers to think of him as his father. The fierce William Laud, even-tually archbishop of Canterbury, formed a close relationship with him, in fact served as his private confessor. Laud's diary contains a number of entries that provide information. For example, this some-what cryptic entry for June 9, 1621: "Being Whitsunday, my Lord Marquis Buckingham was pleased to enter upon a near respect to me. The particulars are not for papers." Laud exchanged letters with him during the Spanish trip of 1623 and watched by his sick bedside in 1624. In July 1625, Laud recorded a dream about the dead King James. But on August 21, 1625, Laud had quite another dream: "That night, in my sleep, it seemed to me that the Duke of Buck-ingham came into bed to me; where he behaved himself with great kindness towards me, after that rest, wherewith wearied persons are wont to solace themselves. Many also seemed to me to enter the chamber, who saw this." In September, Laud recorded yet another, less interesting, dream about Buckingham and his family. One can-not, of course, control one's dreams, but at the least, Laud's indicate a sensual fascination with Buckingham.[76]

Francis Bacon's letters contain dozens of references to Bucking-ham—not surprising given Bacon's several important governmental posts. But his letters also reveal a friendship with and dependence on Buckingham. Bacon signed a letter of February 19, 1616, to Buck-ingham as "Your true and affectionate servant"; and he added this postscript: "Sir, I kindly thank you for your inward letter; I have burned it as you commanded: but the flame it hath kindled in me will never be extinguished." Later in 1616, Bacon characterized Buck-ingham in a letter to James: "A safe nature, a capable mind, an hon-est will, generous and noble affections, and a courage well lodged; and one that I know loveth your Majesty unfeignedly." Such words James would have delighted in hearing. Thanking Buckingham for help in assisting him to be named Lord Keeper, Bacon wrote on March 7, 1617: "It is both in cares and kindness, that small ones float up to the tongue, and great ones sink down into the heart with silence. . . . in this day's work you are the truest and perfectest mir-ror and example of firm and generous friendship that ever was in court." Gratitude had provoked a momentary silence.[77]

Of course, Bacon did not always find Buckingham to be such a friend; their relationship certainly had its ups and downs. When Bacon lost his post as Lord Chancellor for accepting bribes, he threw himself on the good graces of Buckingham to help him and to soften the king's punishment. Buckingham did help. In disgrace and exile, Bacon wrote to Buckingham, wishing that he were beside him "in this stirring world" and professing a love that "can never cease." He added a postscript: "Being now out of use and out of sight, I recommend myself to your Lordship's love and favour, to maintain me in his Majesty's grace and good intention." When Buckingham safely returned from Spain in 1623, Bacon wrote: "How much I rejoice in your Grace's safe return, you will easily believe, knowing how well I love you, and how much I need you."[78]

Bacon did not of course shy from offering advice to Buckingham. In a long letter of 1616, he instructed Buckingham on his duties as "favorite": "You are now the King's Favourite, so voted, and so esteemed by all." It was no new thing, Bacon noted, "for Kings and Princes to have their privadoes, their favourites, their friends." Bacon correctly assessed the potential danger of the favorite's position. In 1617, a sharp exchange of letters between Bacon and James illustrated how sensitive James had become about Buckingham; he would not brook criticism of him. Bacon had professed his "parent-like affection" for Buckingham but worried "that the height of his fortune might make him too secure, and (as the proverb is) a looker-on sometimes seeth more than a gamester." James became incensed and used the word *jealousy* several times in his pointed reply to Bacon. James wrote bluntly: "Now we know not how to interpret this in plain English otherwise than that you were afraid that the height of his fortune might make him misknow himself." James found him "furthest from that vice of any courtier that ever we had so near about us, so do we fear that you shall prove the only phoenix in that jealousy of all the kingdom." The memory of Somerset had to be still fresh in James's mind, making him especially sensitive to the idea that yet another favorite had forgotten his place. If anyone was to talk about "parent-like affection" for Buckingham, it would be James himself.[79]

In 1615, when Villiers entered James's life, no one else offered such attractive qualities to James. Somerset stood on the verge of being exposed for his involvement in the Overbury murder and found in Villiers a natural rival and replacement. Surely the presence of Villiers encouraged James's desire to be rid of Somerset. With Queen Anne's help, Villiers became a Groom of the Bedchamber in April 1615, initially planted there by factions eager to speed Somerset's fall. Disaffected from Anne and Somerset, estranged from his daughter, uncertain in his relationship with the adolescent

Charles, James in 1615 appeared especially vulnerable to the charm of a handsome man, who fortunately also possessed intelligence and a pleasant disposition.

Each member of the royal family had to come to terms with Villiers (Buckingham); each became in some way dependent on him, especially Elizabeth and Charles. He occupied the center of James's devotion, a position one might have expected to be filled by a member of the family. The terms that James used for Buckingham—son, friend, sweetheart, wife, child—suggest possible confusion on James's part about exactly what role this young man played in his life. When James wrote that he was Buckingham's "economic father," we understand the term to mean that he oversaw Buckingham's welfare. When he addressed Buckingham as "my only sweet and dear child," we may be puzzled. After all, James had two healthy, living children—one even heir apparent to the throne. Had he forgotten them? What did James have in mind when he called Buckingham "wife"? Paradoxically, all these various terms could be valid in some way to characterize Buckingham's function. His handsome, even feminine features may have somewhat blurred sexual distinctions for James. One wonders in what way James and Charles both saw Buckingham as a substitute for the dead Prince Henry, only two years younger than Buckingham.

Ordinary familial terms did define the relationship between king and subject. Buckingham in his letters invariably used the term *dad* to refer to James. Clearly all such terms functioned as affectionate ones. James also expanded the concept of family to include Buckingham's family: his wife, their children, and other relatives. James insisted that he be godparent for each of the children and generally responded to them more affectionately than he did to his own family. Buckingham's children might have served as the grandchildren that James never got to know. In any event, James had found a family, even though it happened not to be his own. Buckingham's love may have unleashed these responses from James, whose advancing years and experience perhaps enabled him to bestow an unaffected love on Buckingham's family. That the children were not royal children may finally have removed the tension that James always felt with his own family.

Not only did Buckingham become a groom in the king's bedchamber in 1615, he also, according to Lockyer, satisfied in August of that year James's sexual longing. "Where the details of private relationships are concerned, nothing, of course, can be known for certain, but Buckingham himself provides the evidence that at Farnham he at last gave in to the King's importunity." An undated letter from Buckingham to James strongly implies a sexual encounter: "I intertain'd myself your unworthy Servant w$^t$ this Dispute, whether you loved me now . . . better, then, att y$^e$ time w$^c$ I shall never forgett at Farneham where y$^e$ Bed's hed could not be found betwene y$^r$ Master & his Doge." "Dog," we recall from Anne's correspondence, was one of the affectionate terms for Buckingham. The implications of this letter are not surprising, given what we already know about James's delight in handsome young men.[80]

A contemporary, commenting on Villiers's sudden rise to prominence, wrote: "And if the King had not received a new Impression thus, the old Character of *Somerset* that was imprinted in his *soul*, could not so soon (as many men thought) have been blotted out." Speaking of soul, Wotton offered a novel interpretation of James's designs on Buckingham: "He [James] resolved to make him a Masterpiece, and to mould him, as it were, Platonically to his own *Idea*. Neither was his Majesty content only to be the Architect of his fortune, without putting his Gracious hand likewise to some part of the work it self." One doubts that James ever had so grandiose a notion as making of Villiers a Platonic idea; on this score, James leaned more toward Aristotelian physical reality. Of course, he had tried to teach Robert Carr Latin. Perhaps part of James's imagination delighted in the prospect of shaping this person to suit his purposes. James relished the role of creator; he wanted to fashion the lives of others to suit his own image and function, as we have seen repeatedly. As the relationship developed, however, Buckingham asserted his own strong personality over a doting but aging king.[81]

Wilson wrote accurately, "To speak of his Advancement by *Degrees*, were to lessen the Kings Love; for *Titles* were heaped upon him, they came rather like *showers* than *drops*." Villiers rose to dizzying heights in record time. Typical of James, where he lavished titles and gifts, he gave prodigally. In 1616, for example, Villiers became Master of the Horse in January, a member of the Order of the Garter in April, and Viscount Villiers on August 27. In 1617, James created him earl of Buckingham in January and in February welcomed him as a member of the Privy Council—an honor Prince Charles did not receive until 1622. This year also saw him accompany James throughout the several-months' trip to Scotland. All such titles carried considerable financial rewards as well—outright gifts of money and property and also prerogatives that led to more financial gains. Buckingham was on his way to becoming one of the richest persons in the Stuart court.[82]

King James, a painting by Paul van Somer (1618) showing the symbols of power. Copyright reserved to Her Majesty Queen Elizabeth II.

Later in 1617 James told the assembled Privy Council:

> I, James, am neither a god nor an angel, but a man like any other. Therefore I act like a man, and confess to loving those dear to me more than other men. You may be sure that I love the Earl of Buckingham more than anyone else, and more than you who are here assembled. I wish to speak in my own behalf, and not to have it thought to be a defect, for Jesus Christ did the same, and therefore I cannot be blamed. Christ had His John and I have my George.

Breathtaking clarity characterizes this statement; none could have doubted James's regard for Buckingham. The theologian James did rather strain, however, for an analogy. Chamberlain summarized Buckingham's effect on James when he wrote to Carleton on December 20, 1617, anticipating a dull season at court because James had a "kind of morositie that doth either argue a great discontent in minde, or a distemper of humors in his body, yet he is never so out of tune but the very sight of my Lord of Buckingham doth settle and quiet all." When James learned that one of his guards had spoken slightingly of Buckingham, even suggesting that it would be a good thing to kill him, James punished the man's temerity by sending him "to the Tower of London, where the least harm that can come to him is that he will never come out so long as he lives," so reported the Venetian secretary in September 1617.[83]

The year 1618 dawned brightly for Buckingham: James gave him a new title, marquis. In fact, Buckingham had reason to look forward to each New Year's season with anticipation, so great were the rewards. Chamberlain reported: "The earle of Buckingham was created Marquis Buckingham a dignitie the King had not bestowed since his comming to the crowne, but he professed to do yt for the affection he bare him, more then ever he did to any man, and for the like affection, faith, and modestie that he had found in him." With such titles Buckingham vigorously set out to establish all the members of his family—brothers, cousins—in secure and lucrative posts. From his vantage point and increasing prestige, Buckingham extended his network of patronage. Something important began to happen with Buckingham's function. "The European crisis which marked the opening of the Thirty Years War turned Buckingham, willy-nilly, into a political figure. Up to 1618 he had simply been the King's favourite, a man upon whom fortune had smiled and who used his new-found favour to advance his friends and family. But from 1618 onwards he was seen in an altogether different light." He became a major adviser and participant in the two crucial political questions that gripped foreign policy of James's last years, namely, the Bohemian-Palatinate matter and the Spanish Match for Charles. Both issues involved James's children, who eagerly sought Buckingham's assistance. Even though he was already a member of the Privy Council, Buckingham had had minor impact on political policy; his function had been primarily to determine which way the wind was blowing and what James's wishes were. Then he assumed greater importance as a shaper of decisions, especially in the 1623–1625 period, when he became indispensable to political and diplomatic operations.[84]

In January 1619, Buckingham became Lord Admiral of the Navy, a job for which he possessed no special qualifications but one that he took seriously and performed admirably. In addition to being the favorite and an adviser, he now had an important, specific job to fulfill. James even wrote a poem to commemorate Buckingham's new status, which begins:

> Now let us [all] rejoice sing Peans all
> For Buckingham is now made Admirall
> And he that rules the horse our strenght by land
> Our strenght by sea the Navy doth command.

Also in January, James published *A Meditation upon the Lords Prayer,* which he dedicated to Buckingham. James wrote in the dedication: "I cannot surely find out a person to whom I can more fitly dedicate this short meditation of mine than to you, Buckingham, for it is made upon a very short and plain prayer and therefore the fitter for a courtier." Apparently, Buckingham had urged James "to put pen to paper" and give the world his thoughts on this prayer. James outlined the various reasons he dedicated this treatise to Buckingham. "As the person to whom we pray, it is our heavenly Father, so am I that offer it unto you not only your politic but also your economic father, and that in a nearer degree than unto others"—"economic" here referring to household management. "Receive then," James closed, "this New Year's gift from me as a token of my love."[85]

After nearly a year of negotiations, Buckingham married Katherine Manners, daughter of the earl of Rutland, on May 16, 1620. A contemporary reported on the conflict between Buckingham and the earl and the eventual intervention, at James's direction, by Bishop John Williams: "The Earl of *Rutland* was slow, or rather sullen, in giving way to this lusty Woer; who came on the faster. . . . Certain it is, that he kept not such distance in his Visits, as was required. Which put the Earl into so strong a Passion, that he could not be mitigated." Buckingham even appealed to James, urging him "by a straight charge upon my lord of rutland to caule whom [home] his daughter againe, . . . that in case I should marie her." He hoped that he "may have so much respitt of time given me as I may see some one act of wisdome in the foresayde lord as may put me in hope that of his stocke I may some time begett one able to serve you at least in some meane imployment." As Lockyer reports: "Under the terms of the agreement between Buckingham and Rutland, Katherine was to bring with her a dowry of £10,000 in cash and lands worth some £4,000 or £5,000 a year." With such a profitable marriage, Buckingham solidified his position as one of the wealthiest men in the Stuart court. James urged Buckingham to marry but did not favor this marriage until Katherine renounced her Catholicism.[86]

On the day after their wedding, James wrote this letter to Buckingham:

> My only sweet and dear child,
> Thy dear dad sends thee his blessing this morning and also to his daughter. The Lord of Heaven send you a sweet and blithe wakening, all kind of comfort in your sanctified bed, and bless the fruits thereof that I may have sweet bedchamber boys to play me with, and this is my daily prayer, sweet heart. When thou rises, keep thee from importunity of people that may trouble thy mind, that at meeting I may see thy white teeth shine upon me, and so bear me comfortable company in my journey.

In spite of his marriage, Buckingham would be expected to continue his intimate relationship with James. Even on the day after his wedding, he accompanied James on a trip. Fortunately, for their sake, Buckingham and Katherine developed a solid and loving relationship, as their letters to each other attest.[87]

James seems never to have felt threatened by Buckingham's marriage, and Katherine understood the mutual devotion of James and Buckingham. James, of course, believed in marriage, especially for political or economic reasons; but it need not interfere with one's life. Lee writes that James "never displayed any sexual jealousy of his favorites. He encouraged them to get married, was often actively involved in helping to arrange their marriages." Lee says this in part to explain away some of James's behavior. But in truth James simply saw nothing inconsistent between marriage and his own sexual practice, in part because sexuality did not define him. Certainly he displayed sexual jealousy but never toward women. The issue in Buckingham's marriage was not sex but religion: his proposed wife had to renounce Catholicism, which she eventually did. Perhaps the unresolved issue of Anne's Catholicism underlies James's insistence—what he could not control in his own wife, he controlled in his favorite's wife.[88]

As adviser to James, Buckingham became directly involved in the problems of Bohemia and the Palatinate. As early as 1619, Elizabeth had written to Buckingham seeking his intervention with James on her behalf. A draft letter, dated September 29, 1620, from Buckingham to Edward Herbert testified to the favorite's function in this political issue. James, Buckingham wrote, "hath resolved not to suffer his grandchildrens' [*sic*] patrimonie to be with held from them. But howsoever he meddle not with the matter of Bohemia yet he will prepare with all the speed that may be to succour those that are so neere unto him." A similar 1621 letter from Buckingham to the king of Denmark outlined James's political position. In many ways Buckingham had become the official spokesman, having become the most important figure in the Stuart court. James gave unstinting praise of Buckingham to sessions of Parliament.[89]

The solid relationship between James and Buckingham nevertheless ran into occasional personal difficulties. For example, James's wandering eye lit on Arthur Brett, Buckingham's cousin, who became Groom of the Bedchamber in the spring of 1622. D'Ewes recorded in his diary on November 22, 1622: "At court ther happened allsoe a strange accident which gave out the rumour of a new favourite; for the King did beginn to shew manye favours to one Brett, the Marquesses kinsman, and ther was some scuffling about it, but I heard as yett noe certaintye about it." Buckingham became alarmed and felt himself threatened, knowing how he had supplanted Somerset. Buckingham "heaped reproaches on the King and menaced the young man. There was clearly more than idle gossip behind these rumours" that Brett would replace Buckingham in James's favor. The Venetian ambassador, writing on December 23, confirmed the quarrel between James and Buckingham about Brett, but then added, "Matters have quieted down and the marquis seems more in favour than ever, and now has under seal a fresh gift from the king." Some think, the ambassador wrote, that the king's favor "is like the summer sky, from which, when quite serene, a thunderbolt sometimes falls unexpectedly." One cannot know whether James seriously liked Brett or just used the situation to remind Buckingham that his favored status could change. Buckingham took action and had Brett sent on a long journey: the best way to confront possible thunderbolts. No serious challenge to Buckingham's preferred status occurred again; if anything, the love between James and Buckingham deepened, even though quarrels would occur from time to time.[90]

## The Spanish Match

Most of 1623 focused on the trip to Spain taken by Prince Charles and Buckingham, a somewhat strange episode of seven months' duration. Apparently, although the historical record does not make it entirely clear, Charles decided on his own to make the trip in order to speed and conclude the marriage negotiations for the Infanta. Having secured a picture of her, Charles had convinced himself that he loved her and desperately wanted to marry her. At age twenty-three, Charles might understandably be deemed ready for marriage. As we recall, at age twenty-three James had married Anne. He, James, and Buckingham thought that such a match would result in possible restitution for Princess Elizabeth and Frederick by getting Spain to withdraw its troops from the Palatinate and to restore lands to Frederick. Such a hope proved vain, as it rested on ignorance of Spanish policy.

Charles sought Buckingham's help in convincing James to allow the trip. James did not initially like the idea; he asked Francis Cottington, who had been suggested as a companion for the journey, what he thought of the venture. He had many objections; "Upon which the King threw himself upon his bed, and said, 'I told you this before,' and fell into new passion and lamentation, that he was undone, and shall lose Baby Charles." Buckingham rebutted Cottington's objections, spoke rudely to James, told him that nobody would ever again believe him if he did not allow the prince to make the trip. James gave in but insisted that Buckingham accompany Charles. James remained uneasy and tearful about the trip, dreading the thought of his son and favorite, the two he loved most, leaving the kingdom on a dangerous journey. In an episode reminiscent of *King Lear,* James's fool Archy appeared to him, according to Coke, who had the story from his father. Archy "tells the King he must change Caps with him; Why? says the King: Why who, replies *Archy,* sent the Prince into *Spain*? But what, said the King, wilt thou say, if the Prince comes back again? Why then, said *Archy,* I will take my Cap from thy Head, and send it to the King of Spain: which was said troubled the King sore." James had much reason to be concerned about this extraordinary venture.[91]

On February 18, 1623, Charles (aged twenty-two) and Buckingham (aged thirty) donned false beards, wore different clothes to disguise their identities, and adopted the names Jack and Tom Smith, master and servant. Looking slightly ludicrous, they set out on the perilous trip by water to France and then overland to Spain. In a letter of February 27, James addressed them as "my sweet boys and dear venturous knights, worthy to be put in a new romance." The first flush of excitement might have led James to call the venture a "romance," but in subsequent months he contemplated a potential tragedy. He also wrote a poem "Off Jacke, and Tom" to commemorate the adventure. In it James referred to his own trip to Denmark to fetch Anne. He wrote in one stanza about the dangers:

> Love is a world of manye Spaynes
> where Coldest Hilles, and hottest playnes
> With Barren Rockes, and ffertyle ffeildes,
> by turne dispayre, and Comfort yeildes.
> Butt whoe can doubte of properous lucke
> where Love, and ffortune, doth conducte.

And James addressed the final stanza to himself:

> Kinde Sheappeardes, that have lov'd them longe
> bee not soe rashe, in Censuringe wronge
> Correct your ffeares, leave off to murne
> the Heavens will favour there returne,
> Remitt the Care, to Royall Pan
> of Jacke his Sonne, and Tom, his Man.

James tried to convince himself that all would turn out well; he had time to think about the paradoxes of Spain, a world of many wiles, hot passion, and cold cunning. The fertile fields of Spain did yield barren results finally.[92]

On February 21, Charles and Buckingham reached Paris; by averaging about sixty miles a day on horseback, they got to Madrid on March 7—to the complete surprise of the Spanish. The Spanish in fact did not quite know what to make of Charles's unexpected arrival into their kingdom. They accepted his testimony that he came to speed negotiations for the marriage. But it soon became clear to Charles and Buckingham that things would not proceed rapidly: the papal dispensation had to be waited for, for example. The major obstacle became, not surprisingly, religion. The Spanish decided that Charles had taken the extraordinary step of coming to Spain in order to embrace Catholicism, and such a conversion would definitely speed the marriage process. By the end of May, Buckingham stood in the way because he would not allow Charles to accept terms clearly unacceptable to his father. The Spanish also tried to separate Charles from Buckingham in order to increase their chances of pressuring Charles to convert. D'Ewes imaginatively captured the predicament in Spain in a diary entry of June 22, 1623: "Then wee had discourse of the picture at Rome, Twoe in a cage in splendid apparell resembling the Marquesse and the Prince, and an ancient man standing by, in a fooles coate resembling the King for letting them goe and yett a yong man with a key in his hand standing by the cage and a foles coate liing by him for the King of Spain, if having them now in possession hee lett them goe."[93]

After interminable delays and secretive strategies, the Spanish finally agreed to terms, which included assurance of freedom for English Catholics as well as allowing the Infanta complete freedom to practice her religion. "On 28 August the Prince and Philip [Philip IV of Spain] both took solemn oaths to put into effect the articles of marriage concluded between them. . . . the Prince signed the document authorising his marriage to take place by deputy. The authorisation was valid until Christmas." Despite their efforts, the English negotiators got no concessions from the Spanish about the Palatinate, and they did not get to take the Infanta back to England. But Charles and Buckingham did leave much wiser about Spanish trustworthiness. The venturous knights shook loose from romance and encountered something more nearly resembling a satire where words often meant the opposite of their presumed intention.[94]

On October 5, Charles and Buckingham landed safely on English soil at Plymouth; the next day they entered London and soon met James at Royston. Londoners responded with wild joy: the Prince and Buckingham had returned safely, and they did not bring the detested Infanta with them. Great bonfires of rejoicing lit up the skies. According to D'Ewes, "London never before saw soe many bonefires at one time, for a tast of other places, ther were 335 or thereabouts between Whitehall and Temple Barre." A service of celebration took place at St. Paul's, including, Chamberlain noted, the "singing of a new antheme . . . the 114th psalme, when Israell came out of Egipt and the house of Jacob from among the barbarous people."[95]

Chamberlain described the encounter at Royston succinctly: "The King going downe to receve them they met on the staires where the Prince and Duke beeing on theire knees the King fell on their neckes and they all wept." Tears of great joy welled in their eyes and their hearts overflowed: James's "sons" had returned. According to Hacket, "The Joy at the enterview was such, as surpasseth the Relation." He added:

His Majesty in a short while retir'd, and shut all out but his Son and the Duke; with whom he held Conference till it was four Hours in the

Night: They that attended at the Door sometime heard a still Voice, and then a loud; sometime they Laught, and sometime they Chafed, and noted such variety, as they could not gues what the close might prove: But it broke out at Supper, that the King appear'd to take all well. . . . And then that Sentence fell from him, which is in Memory to this Hour, *That he lik'd not to Marry His Son with a Portion of His Daughters Tears.* His Majesty saw there was no Remedy in this case but to go Hand in Hand with the Prince, and his now prepotent Favorite.

The Third Gentleman at the reunion of father and daughter in *The Winter's Tale* says: "I never heard of such another encounter, which lames report to follow it and undoes description to do it."[96]

In the elation of the moment one could forget that not many problems had been solved with the Spanish. But Chamberlain praised Buckingham's performance in Spain: "The Duke of Buckingams cariage in all the busines is much applauded and commended, and sure yf yt were altogether as is reported, yt was brave and resolute." Breathing the free air of England emboldened Charles and Buckingham to oppose the terms of the Spanish Match; simply put, they did not trust the Spanish. With their efforts and with the approval of Parliament in early 1624, James broke off negotiations with the Spanish: there would be no marriage. In response to the Spanish trip and the marriage negotiations an extraordinary event took place at the Globe Theatre in August 1624: namely, a production of Thomas Middleton's bitingly satirical play, *A Game at Chess.* Through its elaborate allegory it attacked James's pro-Spanish policy, and it represented Charles and Buckingham in two of the characters. The play was quite the rage in London until, after Spanish protests, James shut the play down. But the popular theater clearly reflected the political mood of the country.[97]

At least two personal things emerged out of the 1623 experience: an intimate record of the relationship of James and Buckingham and a deepened friendship between Charles and Buckingham. The evidence for the former comes from the extensive correspondence between king and favorite. Dozens of letters crossed the ocean; a few representative ones can provide a flavor of this extraordinary correspondence. Of course, many of the letters simply transact necessary business. In every letter James wished for Charles and Buckingham a safe and speedy return to their "dear dad." Buckingham typically signed his letters as "your humble slave and dog Steenie." His letters to James overflow with statements of gratitude, expressed in such varying ways that they avoid mere formulaic utterances. The choice of language conveys genuine love, not mere flattery. The playfulness, bawdy sauciness, and wit further indicate a secure position and an intimacy that could enjoy such seeming impertinence. These letters helped maintain the strong link of love, the fullest extant documentation of James's love for anyone. Of course, some interpreters of James have been annoyed by these letters. When Godfrey Davies cited one of Buckingham's letters, he characterized it as "repulsive," adding, "James's letters to Buckingham are few and not much less revolting." In a sense, Davies echoes what Catherine Macaulay had written in the eighteenth century when she characterized James's letters as "written in a style fulsomely familiar, many of them indecent, with very unusual expressions of love and fondness."[98]

A saucy impertinence runs through several letters as James and Buckingham banter back and forth. Letters in March and April 1623 touched on the matter of jewels that James would send to Spain for Buckingham and Charles to wear and distribute. In late April, Charles wrote his father to complain that he had not received any jewels. On April 25, Buckingham wrote, insisting on more jewels. He added a postscript that enumerated the rare presents that he had sent James from abroad, such as camels and elephants. He added a playfully threatening note: "If you doe not send you babie [Charles] jewels eneugh Ile stope all other presents therefore louke to it." Only a man secure in his relationship could have addressed the king in such a manner. James apparently enjoyed such sauciness and even once praised Buckingham for his "droll" letters. In a 1624 letter, Buckingham taunted James, irreverently suggesting that James was formed out of human excrement, what he called the philosopher's stone. He closed the letter: "Thus I conclude my sow [James] is helthfull, my divells luckie my selfe is happie, and neds no more then your blessing which is my trew felosephers stone upon which I build as on a rock. . . . I pray you burne this letter." James did not burn the letter; instead, he treasured it.[99]

As noted above, in February 1623, James wrote, saying that he wore Buckingham's picture next to his heart, a fact acknowledged in Buckingham's letter of March 24. Buckingham, alone reading over James's letters and contemplating their love, added: "I would faine give thankes, but alas what can I doe say or thinke; if I consider eyther the number of your favors or the paynefull time you tooke to doe them in, I may ese my hart in saying some thinge, but never satisfie the dett or detter in saying enough." And in May 1623, Buckingham had yet another reason for gratitude: James created him duke of Buckingham, the only duke in England without a trace of royal blood. Buckingham wrote in response that James would "never love none of your servants . . . better then Steenie." His position "may be a presedent of emulation hereafter to those that shall succed you to express as much love as you have done to me"; James had "filled a consuming purse, given me faire houses, more land then I ame worthie of . . . filled my coffers so full with patents of honer." Nevertheless, James added yet another honor, the title of duke; Buckingham signed his letter, "Your poure steenie as ducke of Buckingham." No greater titles existed: from groom of the bedchamber to duke—an extraordinary sign of James's love. [100]

James suffered from the separation from Buckingham and Charles. On June 14, 1623, James wrote to Buckingham and Charles, distressed at how the negotiations had been delayed, adding: "Alas, I now repent me sore that ever I suffered you to go away. I care for match nor nothing, so I may once have you in my arms again." He reminded them on July 31 of the serious political business: "After the contract, go as far as ye can before your parting upon the business of the Palatinate and Holland, that the world may see ye have thought as well upon the business of Christendom as upon the codpiece point." Reflecting his anguish, James wrote them on August 5: "I have no more to say but if ye hasten you not home I apprehend I shall never see you, for my extreme longing will kill me." [101]

Buckingham responded in kind to James's sense of longing in terms that carry sexual overtones. Early in the experience in Spain, Buckingham reported Charles's infatuation with the Infanta, wrongly interpreting this as a sign that they would soon return to England, thereby, he wrote to James, "getting libertie to make the speedier hast to lay my selfe at your feete, for never none longed more to be in the armes of his mistris." Months later Charles and Buckingham finally began preparations to depart from Spain. Buckingham responded to James on August 20, "I will not intreat you not to love him [Charles] the wors, nor him that thretens you that when he once getts hould of your bedpost againe never to quitt it." On August 29, Buckingham, recovering from an illness, wrote James again, disturbed that he and Charles had not been more successful and obviously weary of the whole Spanish venture. He lacked nothing, he wrote, "but meanes how to appere in som degree thankefull and worthie of your absent favors." He insisted that his love for James was greater than self-love: "I have tow [too] latelie saide I love you better then my selfe so in writeing longer to pleas my selfe I should give to what I have allredie said a contridiction." Leaving Spain finally, Buckingham wrote on September 1 of his expected joy: "My hart and verie sole dances for joy for the change will be no less then to leape from trouble to ese from sadness to merth nay from hell to heven, I can not now thinke of given thankes for frend wife or child my thoughts are onelie bent of haveing my dere dad and master legs sone in my armes." Perhaps this letter, though it could have been any number of others, prompted James to write: "My sweet Steenie and gossip [godson], Thy single letter was so sweet and comfortable unto me as I cannot forbear to pray God ever to bless and reward thee for it."[102]

One of the most extraordinary letters that James wrote to Buckingham cannot be dated accurately, although Akrigg makes a plausible case for December 1623, so that the sentiments reflect James's delight in having him back after so long an absence and a resolve never to let him leave again. James wrote:

> My only sweet and dear child,
> . . . And yet I cannot content myself without sending you this present, praying God that I may have a joyful and comfortable meeting with you and that we may make at this Christmas a new marriage ever to be kept hereafter; for, God so love me, as I desire only to live in this world for your sake, and that I had rather live banished in any part of the earth with you than live a sorrowful widow's life without you. And so God bless you, my sweet child and wife, and grant that ye may ever be a comfort to your dear dad and husband.

Marital terms pervade the letter, implying certainly that James saw his relationship to Buckingham as a marriage; at the same time, he looked upon the favorite as a son, his only "sweet and dear child." James apparently encountered no difficulty in the paradoxical accumulation of these terms; for him they served as terms of deep love: wife, child. Buckingham had become James's family, and everything that remained dear to him.[103]

James's solicitous care of Buckingham's family attests his love for the duke. James regularly reported on Buckingham's family matters, especially the news that Kate, Buckingham's wife, was apparently pregnant (March 25 and April 7, 1623), that their child, whom James referred to as his "grandchild," had four teeth. Later in August, James told of Kate's recent illness. James stayed in close contact with Buckingham's family, indulged, and enjoyed them. In return, Buckingham thanked James profusely for his great care. Letters and visits flowed regularly between the king and the duchess and her children. According to Weldon: "Little children did run up and downe the Kings Lodgings. . . . Here was a strange change, that the King, who formerly would not endure his Queen and children in his

Lodgings, now you would have judged, that none but women frequented them." Another contemporary recalled that James would
send for the children to come to his bedchamber and there would
play with them for hours. "And the King being once with the children, news was brought him that there was an ambassador come to
speak with him; whereupon he willed the nurse to stay there with
the children, and when he had spoken with the ambassador he
would come again to her. This the nurse herself told me."[104]

Lord Conway wrote to Buckingham in May 1623 of an episode in
which the king paid special attention to Mary, the oldest child of
Buckingham. James wittily remarked "that it was a miracle that such
an ugly deformed father should have so sweet a child; and all the
company agreed that it was a hard thing to find such a father and
such a child." Buckingham's family became the family that James as
royal parent had not allowed himself to have. Several things may
account for James's behavior: the mellowing effect of age, his great
love of Buckingham (something, for example, he had not felt for
Anne), the nonpolitical nature of these children (by not being royal
children, they carried no serious political consequences with them
and could be accepted as children).[105]

The experience in Spain strengthened the relationship between
Buckingham and Charles, a relationship, we recall, that had its understandably difficult moments early on. Lockyer writes: "The two
young men had been on close terms even before they left England,
but their time in Spain, despite occasional rifts, had created a bond
between them that turned out to be not only unbreakable but even
unshakeable." Bacon in 1624 offered this assessment of the relationship in a letter to Buckingham: "You are so dearly beloved both
of the King and Prince. . . . the King himself hath knit the knot of
trust and favour between the Prince and your Grace." Therefore,
Buckingham "enabled to be a noble instrument for the service, contentment, and heart's-ease both of father and son." Writing Buckingham and urging him to come visit James, Charles added: "All
this the King has dictated to me, I have onlie to add that I am verie
well if I had your companie." He had begun to call Buckingham
"Steenie," one of James's pet names for him. Advising Buckingham
on how he should behave himself regarding a political issue, Charles
wrote on April 26, 1624: "Now, sweet hart, if you thinke I am mis-
taken in my jugement in this, lett me know what I can doe in this or
anie thing else to serve thee, and then thou shalt see that all the
World shall daylie know more and more that I am and ever willbe,
Your faithful loving constant friend, CHARLES, P." Lee argues that

the close friendship between Charles and Buckingham "militates against the hypothesis that Villiers was the physical lover of Charles's father." But such a conclusion can neither be proved nor disproved—it is just another hypothesis to supplant the one that it argues against. In all likelihood, Charles simply accepted the relationship between his father and Buckingham, much as Queen Anne had, and developed a friendship because he, too, found Buckingham attractive in many ways.[106]

The Venetian ambassador saw a slight danger in this relationship in his report of November 3, 1623: "There is a strong alliance between the prince and Buckingham, and if it does not become too great and alarm the king, who perpetuates Buckingham's favour, it may go far to lead his Majesty towards taking good resolutions." As early as 1616, Bacon had seen the possibility of this problem when he offered Buckingham a letter of advice: "You serve a gracious Master and a good, and there is a noble and hopeful Prince, whom you must not disserve; Adore not him as the rising sun in such a measure, as that you put a jealousy into the father, who raised you." The threat of a jealous reaction from James lurked in the bond between Charles and Buckingham, but no evidence suggests that James actually responded in such a way. However deeply Charles felt about Buckingham, he may have seen Buckingham as a way of enhancing his relationship with his father and as a kind of brother substitute. In any event, from 1624 to the end of James's life these two constituted the primary political force, manipulating James to accept their ideas about Spain, for example. When Charles became king, he chose Buckingham as his most trusted adviser, a position Buckingham fulfilled until his assassination in 1628.[107]

The year 1624 had its precarious moments for Buckingham. First he had to explain and defend his actions in Spain before a gathering of Parliament where he handled himself superbly. Therefore, with Charles's help and James's eventual acquiescence, Buckingham helped terminate all negotiations with Spain about Charles's marriage. Later in the year, Buckingham served as a principal negotiator with the French for a marriage of Charles with Henrietta Maria—if not Spain, then France. "By December 1624 the two negotiations, for marriage and alliance, had both been brought to completion, though with a good deal of ill-feeling and suspicion on both sides." In a ceremony at Cambridge on December 12, James accepted the marriage articles.[108]

More troubling for Buckingham had been the accusations made by the Spanish against him in the spring of 1624. Basically they accused Buckingham of plotting to overthrow James, have his daughter marry Frederick and Elizabeth's son, and thereby ready his family to rule the kingdom. James, ever suspicious, became deeply disturbed; he did not want to believe such charges, but he had a keen ear for conspiracy. The incredible nature of the Spanish accusations made them, perversely, seem credible. James wavered; Buckingham became frightened. He vigorously protested his innocence, and he successfully survived all inquiries. Then, when his health broke in May, "all the clouds of suspicion and cross-purposes between him and James" vanished. Under great stress, as happened here in 1624, Buckingham's health often suffered; his fragile disposition buckled under the pressure of accumulating responsibilities and, in this case, accusations. All through the month of May, James ministered to Buckingham in his illness. "On the King's last visit to Wallingford House he had knelt by Buckingham's bedside with raised hands and called on God either to cure his beloved Steenie or else to transfer the sickness to himself." In a few more weeks Buckingham recovered fully. James's behavior and vigil at Buckingham's sickbed starkly contrast with his usual absences from the bedside of his own sick or dying children.[109]

Politically and personally, Buckingham ended the year better than he might have thought possible for a while. "By the end of 1624 Buckingham was clearly chief minister in all but name. Parliament had given him its confidence. His enemies in the Council had been routed. The Prince was content to leave the execution of policy in his hands because he trusted him, recognised his capacity for getting things done." In a word, Buckingham had become the major political force at court—with James's blessing, of course.[110]

Writing probably in June 1624, Buckingham observed: "I finde you, still one and the same dere and indulgent master you were ever to me." This statement may reflect the reconciliation that had occurred after the momentary rift earlier in the spring. Buckingham ended the letter: "I naturallie so love your person, and upon so good experience and knowledge adore all your other parts which are more than ever one man had, that were . . . all the world besids sett together on one side, and you alone on the other, I should to obey and please you displeas nay dispise all them." Certainly this letter conveys the devotion that Buckingham felt: James supplanted all others. The letter that opened this chapter raises the rhetorical question of how Buckingham could possibly respond to all the love that James had bestowed on him: "nothinge but silence." Buckingham then accumulated terms by which to define James's relation-

ship to him: "My pourvier [purveyor], my goodfellow, my phisi-
tion, my maker my frend my father my all." Buckingham also added
his gratitude. As inadequate as language and letter writing may be,
Buckingham had succeeded ably in conveying his gratitude to and
love for James, in part by a language whose simplicity connotes
sincerity.[111]

More recent historical interpretation has been much kinder to
Buckingham than that of earlier periods; Lockyer's biography especially offers a sympathetic analysis. Buckingham was not perfect,
nor was he a saint. Surely he possessed mixed motivations in his
dealings with James. He grabbed opportunities to enrich himself
and his family and accumulated great wealth by working a patronage system. He doubtless on occasion told James what James wanted
to hear. On the other hand, he might have lapsed into a sullen silence, such as Somerset had done, but he did not. The longevity of
the relationship between James and Buckingham and the bulk of the
evidence testify to a mutual love.

John Oglander, knighted by James in 1615, made this assessment of the king: "He loved young men, his favourites, better than
women, loving them beyond the love of men to women. I never yet
saw any fond husband make so much or so great dalliance over his
beautiful spouse as I have seen King James over his favourites, especially the Duke of Buckingham." Lockyer offers this analysis of
their relationship:

> Buckingham loved James—not, perhaps, in the same way, or with the
> same physical intensity, that James loved him, but with a depth of affec-
> tion that created a firm bond between them. Commentators, both at the
> time and since, have found the relationship between the aging King
> and his youthful and handsome favourite at times absurd, at times em-
> barrassing, and generally distasteful. No doubt it was all of these—as
> many human relationships are—but it was also genuine, profound,
> and, on occasions, moving.

James found in Buckingham a source of love that he did not find
elsewhere. Buckingham did not cause any particular disruption in
the royal family: Anne showed some affection for him, Elizabeth
wrote letters asking for his help, and Charles became a dear friend.
Each family member doubtless forgave James's fascination with
Buckingham. Thanks to his own personal strengths, Buckingham
incorporated himself into the royal family. He recognized that he
owed everything to James—"my all"—and he regularly expressed
his sincere gratitude. James, in turn, wore Buckingham's picture

next to his heart, signifying that he kept Buckingham in his heart of hearts.[112]

How did contemporaries regard James's relationship to Buckingham? The French ambassador, Tillières, reported on January 6, 1622, that James wished to be known as a friend to Buckingham "and to associate his name to the heroes of friendship of antiquity." But the ambassador added cynically: "Under such specious titles he [James] endeavours to conceal scandalous doings, and because his strength deserts him for these, he feeds his eyes where he can no longer content his other senses." Simonds D'Ewes, studying law in London, kept a diary and recorded this conversation with a friend in August 1622:

> Of things I discoursed with him that weere secrett as of the sinne of sodomye, how frequente it was in this wicked cittye, and if God did not provide some wonderfull blessing against it, wee could not but expect some horrible punishment for it; especially it being as wee had probable cause to feare, a sinne in the prince as well as the people, which God is for the most part the chastiser of himselfe, because noe man else indeed dare reprove or tell them of ther faults.

This link of James to sodomy is as explicit a reference as we find.[113]

Later writers, such as Weldon, Peyton, and Wilson, make clear their suspicions and disapproval of James's personal sexual behavior with Buckingham. The England of James's time certainly condemned homosexual practice, usually defined as sodomy, even as it tolerated it. James himself had warned Prince Henry about the grievous sin of sodomy in the pages of *Basilicon Doron*, whatever James may have precisely meant by the term. Overall, grumblings about the court's morality seldom pointed directly at James; doubtless his position as king kept him immune from such overt attack. A current position that lets James off the moral hook by ignoring evidence concludes that "James was one of those people, perhaps more numerous . . . than we suppose, who are simply not much interested in physical sex at all."[114]

"Some friendship between man and man prefer"—so went a line in a song in the 1613 wedding masque for Carr and Howard. Although writing long after James's death, Coke in his account for 1618 made an analogy between James's court and that of Edward II:

> Neither was it any great wonder, that *Edward* the II*d*, a young Man, should be governed by *Pierce Gaveston*, a Person of far more accomplished Parts than *Buckingham*, for *Gaveston* was bred up with *Edward*.

> . . . But for an old King, having been so for above fifty one Years, to dote so upon a young Favourite, . . . and to commit the whole Ship of the Common-wealth, . . . to such a *Phaeton,* is a Precedent without any Example.

Coke joined the example of Edward II and his favorite Gaveston, clearly a homosexual relationship, to James and Buckingham. Such an analysis of Edward and Gaveston had been made obvious in Christopher Marlowe's play *Edward II* of the early 1590s. Coke could excuse Edward but not James, whose age should have made him wiser.[115]

Sir Henry Yelverton, dismissed from the office of attorney-general for corruption, sought in 1621 to even the score with Buckingham, whom he believed responsible for his fate. In his impassioned defense before the House of Lords in May 1621, Yelverton linked the Jacobean court with Edward II's. The French ambassador reported: "At the conclusion, he compared Buckingham with Spenser, the favourite of Edward II, who brought his master to destruction, and himself to an evil end." Writing to Carleton, Chamberlain noted:

> He [Yelverton] indeavored to cast many aspersions upon the Lord of Buckingham and his regall authoritie (as he termed yt) and further comparing these times in some sort to those of Edward the second wherin the Spensers did so tirannise and domineer, wherupon the Prince (seeing him so transported with passion), asked leave of the Lords to interrupt him as not able to indure his fathers government to be so paralelled and scandalised.

Small wonder that Yelverton made a quick trip back to the Tower. What else might Yelverton say?[116]

He did not make explicit the sexual condemnation of Edward II, but few could have missed the implications. He scarcely needed to make the obvious point. James responded: "To reckon me with such a prince [Edward] is to esteem me a weak man, and I had rather be no king than such a one as King Edward II." But the unutterable had come perilously close to being spoken. James deflected the issue by simply referring to Edward as a "weak" king. Further, insofar as James recognized the sexual nature of his relationship with Buckingham, he knew that such behavior did not define him as either king or man. Secure as king, James continued to enjoy Buckingham's love, and he became ever more dependent on Buckingham's political and managerial skills. He trusted and loved Buckingham above all others. Writing from Spain on April 29, 1623, Buckingham had assured James, "For the faith of my selfe I shall soner lous life then in the least kind break it." Buckingham did not bring James down into some disaster; rather, he prevented a number of catastrophes and guided James as well as anyone else. Foreign policy failures grew out of James's own policy or lack thereof.[117]

• • •

In early March 1625, James got a "tertian ague," but no one regarded the illness as serious. The Venetian ambassador reported in April: "He [James] did not know his disease, which grew worse and became very serious three days ago, when he had an apoplectic fit, which affected his chin, loosening his jawbone and enlarging his tongue, and finally a violent dysentry carried him off." Buckingham, on the way to Dover in order to sail to France and complete marriage negotiations for Charles, got word of James's serious illness and returned immediately to London, where he kept vigil at the king's bedside. He and others shared the sacrament of communion with James on one of his last days. Despite the efforts of the royal physicians and a remedy provided by Buckingham and his mother, James grew worse and on Sunday, March 27, died. Charles visited him several times and received some advice about ruling from James. "On the following Saturday morning [March 26] the King lost the power of speech, and, although he made several efforts to address the Prince and members of the Privy Council who were present, he was unable to utter a single word which could be understood." He had earlier made a true confession of his religious faith.[118]

Princess Elizabeth wrote to Lord Conway in early April 1625: "You may easlie judge what an affliction it was to me to understand the evill newes of the loss of so loving a father as his late Matie was to me, it woulde be much more but that God hath left me so deare and loving a Brother as the King is to me." Elizabeth has uttered the expected words; however, knowing what we know of her relationship to her father, we may regard them as merely formulaic. A much harsher view came from Welwood: "King *James* went off the *Stage* not much lamented; and left in Legacy to his Son, *a discontented People; an unnecessary, expensive War; an incumbred Revenue, and an exhausted Treasury;* together with the Charge of his Grandchildren by the Queen of *Bohemia*, that were now divested of a large *Patrimony.*" Others joined in such bleak assessments.[119]

But they do not tell the full story either. James's funeral took place on May 7, "the greatest indeed that ever was knowne in England," according to Chamberlain. Over nine thousand persons wore black livery of mourning; the beautiful hearse had been fashioned by no less than Inigo Jones, best known for his collaboration with Ben Jonson and others in the court masques. The procession moved from Denmark House, where James's body had lain in state surrounded by the six silver candlesticks and black decoration throughout the house, to Westminster Abbey. It was five o'clock in the afternoon, according to Chamberlain, before all had entered the church. James, so averse to funerals—no evidence exists that he ever attended one—became the subject of the full display of a royal funeral. The world now imposed its ceremonies and fictions on the king. Bishop John Williams preached the funeral sermon, itself lasting over two hours. Chamberlain concluded, "In summe all was performed with great magnificence, but the order was very confused and disorderly." Magnificent but disorderly—what an apt image of and commentary on James himself, his government, and his personal life.[120]

Countering dire assessments or analogies made to Edward II, Bishop Williams took his text from the Old Testament account of the death of Solomon in 1 Kings 11:41–43. He developed a long and flattering comparison between Solomon and James: "King James shall first die in Salomons text, and Salomon shal then arise in King James his vertues." James had arisen phoenixlike out of Solomon's text, "For as he hath made a lively repraesentation of the vertues of Salomon, in the person of King James: so hath he done a like repraesentation of the vertues of King James, in the person of King Charles our gratious soveraigne." This subtle playing with the concept of representation grew from the lifelike effigy of James that rested atop his coffin. Williams reflected on the ways that James's life had been spared as an infant, child, and adult by divine providence, "A miracle of kings, and a king of miracles." In Williams's view, James "died like a saint." As James's life began to slip away, he experienced a calmness, and then "without any pangs, or convulsion at all, *Dormivit Salomon*, Salomon slept."[121]

A telling silence permeated the bishop's sermon: not a word about James's relationship with or love for his family. Two hours of sermon about James and nothing about the royal family. That silence underscores what we have seen in the unfolding narrative of this royal family. Neither Solomon nor Edward II, James finally and ironically could not reconcile his political responsibilities with familial demands. The man who had known neither father nor mother, brother nor sister never fully comprehended the role of parent or husband, torn by conflicting and irreconcilable desires.

In the hour of his funeral in 1625, King James lay quietly alone.

The sermon ended, the crowd went away, the candles burned out, and darkness claimed the cathedral. The rest is silence.

> Fear no more the heat o'th' sun
> Nor the furious winter's rages:
> Thou thy worldly task hast done,
> Home art gone and ta'en thy wages. . .
> Fear no slander, censure rash;
> Thou hast finished joy and moan.
> (*Cymbeline*, 4.2.258–73)

The "true novel" of this Stuart royal family thus has an ending.

# *Notes*

### *Notes to Chapter One: Introduction*

1. David Calderwood, *The History of the Kirk of Scotland*, 7:633. *William Shakespeare, The Complete Works*, general editor Alred Harbage (Baltimore: Penguin, 1969), 2.1.149. All quotations will be from this edition. Thomas Frankland, *The Annals of King James and King Charles*, 104.

2. David Calderwood, *The True History of the Church of Scotland*, 472, 473.

3. G. P. V. Akrigg, ed., *The Letters of King James VI & I*, 98.

4. Michel de Certeau, "Writing vs. Time: History and Anthropology in the Works of Lafitau," 62, 63.

5. Mark Poster, *Critical Theory of the Family*, ix.

6. Michael Anderson, *Approaches to the History of the Western Family, 1500–1914*. D. H. J. Morgan, *The Family, Politics and Social Theory*, esp. chap. 8, "Family History," 159–82. For an analysis that takes a dim view of most of the historians of the family, see Ferdinand Mount's *The Subversive Family: An Alternative History of Love and Marriage*. Poster, *Theory of the Family*, xvii.

7. Charles Carlton, *Royal Childhoods*. The chap. on Charles I is found on 78–99. Unfortunately, this chap. contains many factual errors and some dubious judgment. Patrick Morrah, *A Royal Family: Charles I and His Family*, 4.

8. Phillipe Ariès, *Centuries of Childhood*, 353, 403. Richard L. DeMolen, "Erasmus on Childhood," and "Childhood and the Sacraments in the Sixteenth Century."

9. *The Basilicon Doron*, ed. James Craigie, 1:11.

10. Jonathan Goldberg, *James I and the Politics of Literature*, 119; *The Political Works of James I*, ed. Charles H. McIlwain, 328.

11. Lawrence Stone, *The Family, Sex and Marriage in England 1500–1800*, 101–2.

12. British Library, Harleian MS. 6987, f. 56b.

13. Mount, *The Subversive Family*, 114. See Richard Marius, *Thomas More: A Biography*, esp. chap. on family life, 217–34.

14. Stone, *Family, Sex and Marriage*, 152; Schochet, *Patriarchalism in Political Thought*, 65; *Political Works*, ed. McIlwain, 272, 307; Frankland, *Annals*, 87.

15. *The Works of Francis Bacon*, ed. James Spedding et al., 4:283 (hereafter cited as *Works of Bacon*).

16. *Patriarcha: or, the Natural Power of Kings*, 20, 23, 24. Wing #F922.

17. Jonathan Goldberg, "Fatherly Authority: The Politics of Stuart Family Images," 4.

18. Stephen J. Greenblatt, *Sir Walter Ralegh: The Renaissance Man and His Roles*, 52. Especially in chap. 2 does Greenblatt explore Ralegh's self-conscious sense of drama. Alan Liu in "The Power of Formalism: The New Historicism," 721–71, has noted the predilection of that mode of literary theory called "new historicism" to rely on the theatrical metaphor as one of its essential paradigms (see 723). He observes, "Theatricality has been used primarily to model the *mentalité* of monarch-centered aristocracy or its overthrow" (723). He adds, "Theatricality in particular is the paradigm that stresses the slender control of dominance *over* plurality." Liu does allow, however, for the approach of Greenblatt that focuses on self-fashioned men. I agree with Liu that dangers do exist in the paradigm of theatricality, but the metaphor seems irresistible for James I and his family. *Basilicon Doron*, ed. Craigie, 1:163.

19. Stephen J. Greenblatt, *Renaissance Self-Fashioning: From More to Shakespeare*, 27, 13.

20. Liu, "Power of Formalism," 735.

21. *Political Works*, ed. McIlwain, 328.

22. George Marcelline, *The Triumphs of King James the First*, 47.

23. Spottiswoode, *The History of the Church of Scotland*, 547.

24. *Apology for Poetry*, in *English Literary Criticism: The Renaissance*, ed. O. B. Hardison, Jr. (New York: Appleton-Century Croft, 1963), 109; Frankland, *Annals*, sig. a3; Roger Coke, *A Detection of the Court and State of England during the Reigns of King James I*, 1:ix.

25. *Works of Bacon*, ed. Spedding et al., 4:336, 310–11.

26. *Tropics of Discourse: Essays in Cultural Criticism*, 94; *Historical Understanding*, 185, 196, 199; "The Character of James VI and I," 63.

27. Hayden White, *Tropics of Discourse*, 90; Paul Veyne, *Writing History: Essay on Epistemology*, 13; Albert Cook, *History/Writing*, 208.

28. White, *Tropics of Discourse*, 51, 62; Veyne, *Writing History*, 32, x; Michel de Certeau, *The Writing of History*, 10.

29. "The Inscription of the King's Memory: On the Metallic History of Louis XIV," 17, 18.

30. Northrop Frye, *Anatomy of Criticism*, 223, 224.

31. See the discussion that opens my *Shakespeare's Romances and the Royal Family*, 1. Arthur Wilson, *The History of Great Britain*, 192.

32. Frankland, *Annals*, 87. Speech given February 19, 1624.

33. E. M. Forster, *Howards End* (New York: Bantam, 1985), 267. Originally published in 1910.

### Notes to Chapter Two: Scotland (1566–1603)

1. See Caroline Bingham, *The Making of a King: The Early Years of James VI and I*, 26–27. This fine study offers much insight into James's first twenty years. For additional studies of James, see the following: G. P. V. Akrigg, *Jacobean Pageant or the Court of King James I*; Caroline Bingham, *James I of England* and *James VI of Scotland*; Antonia Fraser, *King James VI of Scotland I of England*; Samuel R. Gardiner, *History of England from the Accession of James I*

to the Outbreak of the Civil War 1603–1642; S. J. Houston, *James I*; William McElwee, *The Wisest Fool in Christendom: The Reign of King James I and VI*; David Mathew, *James I*; Otto J. Scott, *James I*; Alan G. R. Smith, ed., *The Reign of James VI and I*; Charles Williams, *James I*; David Harris Willson, *King James VI and I*; Maurice Lee, Jr., *Great Britain's Solomon: James VI and I in His Three Kingdoms*, which explicitly touches on issues of the Scottish period, in the first three chaps. See the discussion by Antonia Fraser, *Mary Queen of Scots*, 280–81. This superb biography of Mary offers a solid path to understanding James.

2. Bingham, *Making of a King*, 30.

3. Lord Herries, *Historical Memoirs of the Reign of Mary Queen of Scots*, 85. [Frances Erskine], *Memoirs Relating to the Queen of Bohemia*, 20–21. Erskine is the presumed editor of this account by a serving woman of Princess Elizabeth. Quotations from James's letters, unless indicated otherwise, are from Akrigg's edition of the *Letters*. This one occurs on 41. *Report on the Manuscripts of the Earl of Mar and Kellie*, 1:43. The letter dates from September 11, 1594. By this time the earl was himself custodian of James's son Henry.

4. *Calendar of State Papers Relating to Scotland . . . 1547–1603*, 3:57 (hereafter cited as *CSP Scot*).

5. Bingham, *Making of a King*, 82.

6. George F. Warner, "The Library of James VI," 1:xi–lxxv; Bingham, *Making of a King*, 84.

7. For a brief discussion of this pageant, see my *English Civic Pageantry 1588–1642*, 66–67.

8. Robert Johnston, *The Historie of Scotland during the Minority of King James*, 114.

9. Bingham, *Making of a King*, 129.

10. *CSP Scot*, 5:431; *The Correspondence of Robert Bowes*, ed. Joseph Stevenson, 78, 84, 115.

11. For the most recent assessment of Esmé Stuart's political and personal effect on James, see Lee, *Great Britain's Solomon*, 44–48, 235–38.

12. Willson, *King James VI and I*, 36; John Hacket, *Scrinia Reserata*, pt. 1:38.

13. John Boswell, *Christianity, Social Tolerance, and Homosexuality: Gay People in Western Europe from the Beginning of the Christian Era to the Fourteenth Century*, 42. This is an exceptionally valuable historical study that lays the foundation for similar work in the Renaissance. Bruce R. Smith, *Homosexual Desire in Shakespeare's England: A Cultural Poetics*, 11–12. The first chap., "Sexuality and the Play of Imagination," 3–29, spells out the terms of his study. Smith mentions King James occasionally. *Basilicon Doron*, ed. Craigie, 1:65.

14. *The Historie and Life of King James the Sext 1566–1596*, 64. Alan Bray, *Homosexuality in Renaissance England*. One should also consult James M. Saslow, *Ganymede in the Renaissance: Homosexuality in Art and Society*, and his discussion of legal and social attitudes toward homosexuality, 47–51. In the artists that Saslow discusses, one hears repeatedly of their perceived need to conceal homosexual interests or desires. Smith, *Homosexual Desire*, 48; legal discussion, 41–53.

15. Eve Kosofky Sedgwick, "Homophobia, Misogyny, and Capital: The Example of *Our Mutual Friend*," 127–28. See her expanded treatment of the subject in *Between Men: English Literature and Male Homosexual Desire* (New York: Columbia University Press, 1985). Smith, *Homosexual Desire*, 75.

16. Willson, *King James VI and I*, 33; Godfrey Davies, "The Character of James VI and I," 62; Lee, *Great Britain's Solomon*, 236. Otherwise, Lee is quite sympathetic about the relationship between James and Esmé as he emphasizes Esmé's positive contribution to James's maturation.

17. *Correspondence of Robert Bowes*, 185.

18. *CSP Scot*, 6:223–24.

19. Ibid., 294.

20. For a fascinating discussion of Michelangelo, see Saslow, *Ganymede in the Renaissance*, 17–62. The reference to the great-nephew's action occurs on 13.

21. *Phoenix*, in *The Poems of James VI of Scotland*, ed. James Craigie, 1:42, 44, 46, 48, 50, 52, 54, 58. All quotations of the poem will be from this edition.

22. Akrigg, *Letters*, 7.

23. *CSP Scot*, 9:701, 10:3; Akrigg, *Letters*, 91, 90. See the discussion in Lee, *Great Britain's Solomon*, chap. 8.

24. *CSP Scot*, 7:274.

25. Goldberg, *Politics of Literature*, 14; *The Winter's Tale*, 5.2.13–14.

26. *CSP Scot*, 3:56.

27. Johnston, *Historie of Scotland*, 112; Akrigg, *Letters*, 44; *CSP Scot*, 6:45.

28. *CSP Scot*, 6:115.

29. Akrigg, *Letters*, 46, 47.

30. *CSP Scot*, 6:262; *Correspondence of Robert Bowes*, ed. Stevenson, 426, 429, 430. The latest study of Mary's political skills has found her a failure. See Jenny Wormald, *Mary Queen of Scots: A Study in Failure.*

31. *CSP Scot*, 7:78. This may give some reason to date the letter a bit later since Fontenay's wonderful report of his visit with James comes in mid-August. He may have made several visits, of course. Akrigg, *Letters*, 55, 56.

32. *Calendar of the Manuscripts of the Marquess of Salisbury, Hatfield House*, 3:95; Fraser, *Mary Queen of Scots*, 462; *CSP Scot*, 8:23.

33. Sir Alexander Malet MS in *Historical Manuscripts Commission, Seventh Report*, 7:430b.

34. For a full discussion of this conspiracy and Mary's involvement, see Fraser's discussion in *Mary Queen of Scots*, 475–500; Akrigg, *Letters*, 73; *Extract from the Despatches of M. Courcelles, French Ambassador at the Court of Scotland*, ed. Robert Bell, 6.

35. *Salisbury MSS*, 13:317; Report of the French Ambassador Courcelles December 13, 1586, in Friedrich von Raumer, *History of the Sixteenth and Seventeenth Centuries*, 2:146; Akrigg, *Letters*, 71.

36. Akrigg, *Letters*, 78; Goldberg, *Politics of Literature*, 12; *Despatches of M. Courcelles*, 25; Annie I. Cameron, ed., *The Warrender Papers*, 1:253.

37. *Troilus and Cressida*, 5.3.108; Akrigg, *Letters*, 83; *CSP Scot*, 9:250.

38. Fraser, *Mary Queen of Scots*, 531–42; *CSP Scot*, 9:441.

39. *CSP Scot*, 9:300; *Salisbury MSS*, 13:334; Calderwood, *History of the Kirk*, 4:611; Robert S. Rait and Annie I. Cameron, eds., *King James's Secret: Negotiations between Elizabeth and James VI*, 194; Akrigg, *Letters*, 84–85.

40. British Library, Cotton MS. Julius. F. vi, f. 76b. I thank Donald Foster for calling my attention to this item.

41. *CSP Scot*, 12:359–60.

42. *The Faerie Queene*, ed. A. C. Hamilton (London: Longman, 1977), stanza 41. Quotations will be from this edition. Jonathan Goldberg has skillfully explored the implications of this dispute over Spenser's text in *James I and the Politics of Literature*, 1–17. This quotation is from 16.

43. *Basilicon Doron*, ed. Craigie, 1:14, 125, 18.

44. Akrigg, *Letters*, 75; *CSP Scot*, 4:531.

45. *CSP Scot*, 7:540; Akrigg, *Letters*, 64, 66.

46. Cameron, *Warrender Papers*, 1:210.

47. *Salisbury MSS*, 13:300, 305.

48. Willson, *King James VI and I*, 85.

49. Calderwood, *History of the Kirk*, 4:612; *Basilicon Doron*, ed. Craigie, 1:121.

50. *CSP Scot*, 10:97, 122.

51. Ibid., 129.

52. *CSP Scot*, 10:157. This letter of October 2 is written in French. I use Caroline Bingham's translation in her *James VI of Scotland*, 117. *Poems*, ed. Craigie, 2:68.

53. *CSP Scot*, 10:181; Akrigg, *Letters*, 98, 100; Calderwood, *History of the Kirk*, 5:67.

54. *Poems*, ed. Craigie, 2:165, 69.

55. For a discussion of this pageant, see my *English Civic Pageantry 1558–1642*, 67–69.

56. Akrigg, *Letters*, 127; *CSP Scot*, 11:237; *Antony and Cleopatra*, 2.2.114–16.

57. *CSP Scot*, 11:280.

58. Ibid., 319, 386–87, 397.

59. Cameron, *Warrender Papers*, 2:261, 266. For a full description of the festivities, see John Nichols, *Progresses of Queen Elizabeth* (London, 1823), 3:353–69.

60. *CSP Scot*, 11:545, 588, 610, 617, 626, 637.

61. Akrigg, *Letters*, 141–42; *CSP Scot*, 11:662–63.

62. *CSP Scot*, 12:22, 46, 74, 140.

63. *Poems*, ed. Craigie, 2:92.

64. *CSP Scot*, 12:336; Ethel Carleton Williams, *Anne of Denmark*, 60.

65. For a contemporary published account, see *The Earle of Gowries Conspiracie* (London, 1600), STC 21466.

66. *CSP Scot*, 13:719, 721, 723.

67. Ibid., 737, 748, 749. For further discussion, see Walter W. Seton, "The Early Years of Henry Frederick, Prince of Wales, and Charles, Duke of Albany."

68. Some scholarly works generate confusion about the date of Robert's birth. Caroline Bingham in *James VI of Scotland* has him born in 1601, and Ethel Williams, in *Anne*, has his birth as May 27, 1602 (66), which is actually

the date of his death. *CSP Scot,* 13:945, 996–97, 998; British Library, Lansdowne MS. 1236, f. 69.

69. Akrigg, *Letters,* 211; *Basilicon Doron,* ed. Craigie, 1:9.

70. J. W. Williamson, *The Myth of the Conquerer: Prince Henry Stuart: A Study in 17th Century Personation,* 19. See Williamson's discussion of Henry's childhood, 14–21. Akrigg, *Letters,* 214; Erskine, *Memoirs,* 18.

71. Maurice Lee, Jr., *Government by Pen: Scotland under James VI and I,* 23; Jenny Wormald, *Court, Kirk, and Community: Scotland, 1470–1625,* 158.

## Notes to Chapter Three: England (1603–1613)

1. *Calendar of State Papers Venetian, 1607–1610,* 11:423 (hereafter cited as *CSP Ven*).

2. McElwee, *Wisest Fool in Christendom,* 123; *Works of Bacon,* ed. Spedding et al., 6:276.

3. *The Letters and Life of Francis Bacon,* ed. James Spedding, 4:307; Marcelline, *The Triumphs of King James,* 14, 46.

4. John Nichols, *The Progresses, Processions, and Magnificent Festivities of King James the First,* 1:132, 277.

5. *Political Works,* ed. McIlwain, 269, 295.

6. Williams, *Anne,* 85; *CSP Ven,* 10:81.

7. Willson, *King James VI and I,* 95.

8. L. Hicks, S.J., "The Embassy of Sir Anthony Standen in 1603, Part II," 205. Hicks's several installments about Standen provide a wealth of material about Anne's Catholicism. See also A. W. Ward in *English Historical Review* 33 (1888): 795–98, in which he retracts the cautionary comments that he had written on this subject for the *Dictionary of National Biography.* Ward accepts the veracity of Abercromby's report.

9. L. Hicks, S.J., "The Embassy of Sir Anthony Standen in 1603, Part IV," 54, 71.

10. Williams, *Anne,* 85.

11. Fraser, *Mary Queen of Scots,* 552; John Harington, *Nugae Antiquae,* 2:118–19.

12. Akrigg, *Letters,* 326.

13. Fraser, *Mary Queen of Scots,* 552; Goldberg, *Politics of Literature,* 17.

14. Daniel, *The Vision of the Twelve Goddesses,* ed. Joan Rees, in *A Book of Masques,* ed. T. J. B. Spencer and S. W. Wells, 25, 37. All quotations are from this edition. Stephen Orgel, *The Illusion of Power: Political Theater in the English Renaissance,* 40.

15. This pageant is more fully discussed in my *English Civic Pageantry 1558–1642,* 71–89.

16. *CSP Ven,* 10:139.

17. *The Dramatic Works of Thomas Dekker,* ed. Fredson Bowers, 2:262. All quotations from Dekker's portion of the entertainment come from this edition.

18. Gilbert Dugdale, *The Time Triumphant,* sig. A3, B4, B2ᵛ, B2ᵛ-B3. See my discussion, "Gilbert Dugdale and the Royal Entry of James I (1604)."

19. For a discussion of these various political issues, see Willson, *King*

*James VI and I*, chaps. 12 and 15. Also consult for religious issues, Lee, *Great Britain's Solomon*, chap. 6, 164–95.

20. Ralph Winwood, *Memorials of Affairs of State in the Reigns of Q. Elizabeth and K. James I*, 2:57; *Prayers appointed to be used in the Church . . . for the Queenes safe deliverance* (London, 1605), sig. A2ᵛ. I thank Arthur Kinney for directing my attention to this item. One also notes that the same prayers were used in anticipation of another birth in 1606. Nichols, *Progresses of King James*, 1:505.

21. Ronald M. Meldrum, ed. *The Letters of King James I to King Christian IV, 1603–1625*, 44. This microfiche edition contains translations of James's Latin letters to Christian IV.

22. Nichols, *Progresses of King James*, 1:512; Phyllis M. Handover, *Arbella Stuart, Royal Lady of Hardwick and Cousin to King James*, 214.

23. Harington, *Nugae Antiquae*, 2:239–40. For discussion of the Gunpowder Plot, see Willson, *King James VI and I*, 223–28.

24. *Political Works*, ed. McIlwain, 281–286.

25. Williams, *Anne*, 112.

26. For discussion of this pageant, see my *English Civic Pageantry 1558–1642*, 91–92.

27. Nichols, *Progresses of King James*, 2:73.

28. Ibid., 154; *CSP Ven*, 11:39; *Salisbury MSS*, pt. 9:308.

29. *CSP Ven*, 10:513; Raumer, *History*, 2:197, 202.

30. Meldrum, *Letters of King James*, 9; Erskine, *Memoirs*, 56–57; Meldrum, *Letters of King James*, 21; *Salisbury MSS*, 19:14.

31. *Salisbury MSS*, 16:220; Frederick C. Dietz, *English Public Finances 1558–1641*, 2:103. Chaps. 6–9 provide much information about Stuart court finances.

32. *Memorials of the Holles Family 1493–1656*, ed. A. C. Wood, 100; Sully, *Memoirs of Maxmilian de Béthune, Duke of Sully*, trans. Charlotte Lennox, 2:188–89.

33. Sully, *Memoirs*, 2:213.

34. Ibid., 180–81.

35. *The Letters of John Chamberlain*, ed. Norman E. McClure, 1:249. All quotations from Chamberlain's letters will be from this edition. Two essays shed important light on James's transition from a Scottish king to an English one. First, Jenny Wormald argues persuasively in "James VI and I: Two Kings or One?" that to understand James I, we must first understand his rule in Scotland. She touches on the issue of James's favorites, most of whom, like Carr, were Scots. Neil Cuddy builds on Wormald's essay in his "The Revival of the Entourage: The Bedchamber of James I, 1603–1625." Cuddy documents the increasing power of the Bedchamber, an importance not wasted on Carr. Such power, however, interfered with James's dealings with Parliament, as did his favorites—so Cuddy argues. Willson, *King James VI and I*, 337. See his chap. on Carr, 333–56. See also Williams, *Anne*, 133–42, and Lee, *Great Britain's Solomon*, 240–47; Harington, *Nugae Antiquae*, 2:275, 272; Francis Osborne, *Traditional Memoirs* (1658), in *Secret History of the Court of James the First*, ed. Sir Walter Scott, 1:275.

36. *CSP Ven*, 10:513; Sully, *Memoirs*, 2:181.
37. Raumer, *History*, 2:209–10, 206.
38. *Salisbury MSS*, 15:347; British Library, Harleian MS. 6986, f. 186. Unfortunately, the letter is undated. It would be helpful to know when it was written. British Library, Add. MS. 19402, f. 55 (also undated); Erskine, *Memoirs*, 87.
39. Sanderson, *A Compleat History of the Lives and Reigns of Mary Queen of Scotland, and of Her Son and Successor, James*, 474; Osborne, *Traditional Memoirs*, 1:196; Nichols, *Progresses of King James*, 2:129.
40. *Chamberlain*, ed. McClure, 1:187, 245.
41. Godfrey Goodman, *The Court of King James the First*, ed. John S. Brewer, 1:168; *The Divine Catastrophe of the Kingly Family of the House of Stuarts*, in *Secret History*, 2:346, originally published in 1652; Anthony Weldon, *The Court and Character of King James*, 168.
42. McElwee, *Wisest Fool in Christendom*, 169.
43. Osborne, *Memoirs*, 1:262–63; James Welwood, *Memoirs of the Most Material Transactions in England for the Last Hundred Years*, 23; Coke, *A Detection of the Court of K. James*, 1:71.
44. Thomas Birch, *The Life of Henry Prince of Wales*, 23; British Library, Harleian MS. 7007, f. 242.
45. *CSP Ven*, 10:513. Strong, *Henry, Prince of Wales and England's Lost Renaissance*, 74. This most recent study of Henry offers an excellent and full portrait of this fascinating young man. *Political Works*, ed. McIlwain, 319.
46. Samuel R. Gardiner, *History of England from the Accession of James I to the Outbreak of the Civil War, 1603–1642*, 2:73; Francis Bacon, "Memorial of Henry Prince of Wales," in *Works of Bacon*, ed. Spedding et al., 6:327. All quotations from Bacon's account are from this edition. Elkin Calhoun Wilson, *Prince Henry and English Literature*; J. W. Williamson, *The Myth of the Conqueror: Prince Henry Stuart: A Study of 17th Century Personation*; Strong, *Henry*.
47. Jonson, *Prince Henry's Barriers*, in Stephen Orgel and Roy Strong, *Inigo Jones: The Theatre of the Stuart Court*, 1:163. These glorious volumes offer all of Jones's drawings for masques and entertainments plus the appropriate texts. Strong, *Henry*, 141. See Strong's illuminating discussion of these festivities in his chap., "The Prince's Festivals," 138–83. *Chamberlain*, ed. McClure, 1:293.
48. Strong, *Henry*, 76. See for example British Library, Harleian MS. 6986, f. 178, 179. In these letters Henry notes his servants who are being sent to the French Court, and he asks for the French King's continuation of friendship.
49. *Pageants and Entertainments of Anthony Munday: A Critical Edition*, ed. David M. Bergeron, 41, 42.
50. See British Library, Add. MS. 36932.
51. Strong, *Henry*, 155; Orgel & Strong, *Inigo Jones*, 1:193.
52. Orgel, *Illusion of Power*, 67; Strong, *Henry*, 171; *Oberon, the Fairy Prince*, ed. Richard Hosley, in *A Book of Masques*, 61, 63.
53. Osborne, *Traditional Memoirs*, 1:259–60.

54. Sanderson, *Compleat History,* 379–80; *Works of Bacon,* ed. Spedding et al., 6:327, 328.

55. Marcelline, *Triumphs,* 66, 67, 73; *Minerva Britanna,* 17. This 1612 emblem book is dedicated to Prince Henry.

56. Peacham, *Minerva Britana,* sig. A2. For a good summary of Henry as patron of the arts, see Graham Parry, *The Golden Age Restor'd: The Culture of the Stuart Court, 1603–42,* 64–94; and Strong, *Henry,* 86–137 and 184–219. W. H., *The True Picture and Relation of Prince Henry,* 31. Strong argues in *Henry* that W. H. "is almost certainly William Haydon, the senior groom of the Prince's bedchamber" (227). The account contains exceptionally rich anecdotes about Henry. *CSP Ven,* 10:513.

57. *The Autobiography of Phineas Pett,* ed. W. G. Perrin, 50, 98.

58. Strong, *Henry,* 26.

59. "A Collection of Several Speeches and Treatises of the Late Lord Treasurer Cecil and of Several Observations of the Lords of the Council Given to King James Concerning His Estate and Revenue in the Years 1608, 1609, and 1610," ed. Pauline Croft, in *Camden Miscellany 29,* 259.

60. *Works of Bacon,* ed. Spedding et al., 6:328; Birch, *Life of Henry,* 370, 380–81; *The Laudable Life, and Deplorable Death of our late peerlesse Prince Henry,* sig. B2ᵛ; Nichols, *Progresses of King James,* 2:162; British Library, Harleian MS. 7007, f. 176.

61. British Library, Lansdowne MS. 1236, f. 59; Nichols, *Progresses of King James,* 2:265–66. Original in British Library, Harleian MS. 7007, f. 316.

62. W. H., *Picture of Prince Henry,* 3.

63. Harington, *Nugae Antiquae,* 3:305; Goodman, *Court,* ed. Brewer, 1:250.

64. *CSP Ven,* 10:513–14, 11:507, 516.

65. Strong, *Henry,* 54, 56; Wilson, *History of Great Britain,* 55.

66. Francis Bacon, "Memorial of Henry Prince of Wales," in *Works of Bacon,* ed. Spedding et al., 6:328; Charles Cornwallis, *A Discourse of the most Illustrious Prince Henry,* 2:222. For additional discussion of the marriage negotiations for Henry, see Roy Strong, "England and Italy: The Marriage of Henry Prince of Wales." W. H., *Picture of Prince Henry,* 24.

67. British Library, Harleian MS. 7008, f. 118; MS. 6986, f. 180b; Copy in Add. MS. 39288, f. 7b-8a.

68. W. H., *Picture of Prince Henry,* 4; Cornwallis, *Discourse,* 2:223.

69. British Library, Harleian MS. 7007, f. 21; MS. 7007, f. 62; *Shakespeare,* 1.1.26–29.

70. W. H., *Picture of Prince Henry,* 9; *The Life and Death of our late most incomparable and Heroique Prince Henry.* Traditionally, this tract has been assigned to Charles Cornwallis, but Strong argues that the author may be John Hawkins (*Henry,* 227).

71. *CSP Ven,* 12:449; *Chamberlain,* ed. McClure, 1:390.

72. Meldrum, *Letters of King James,* 142; *CSP Ven,* 12:472, 521.

73. Weldon, *Court and Character,* 78. See my note on this problem in *Shakespeare's Romances and the Royal Family,* 233–34.

74. *Salisbury MSS,* 16:111; James Maxwell, *Laudable Life,* sig. B3; Thomas

Ross, *Idae sive De Jacobi* (London, 1608), 322–23. An enumeration of the several virtues of James's family may be found on 240–330. The translation of this passage I take from Mary Anne Everett Green, *Elizabeth Electress Palatine and Queen of Bohemia*, rev. S. C. Loman, 15–16. For additional studies on Princess Elizabeth see: Elizabeth Ogilvy Benger, *Memoirs of Elizabeth Stuart, Queen of Bohemia*; Alice Buchan, *A Stuart Portrait*; Carole Oman [Lenanton], *Elizabeth of Bohemia*; Marie Hay, *The Winter Queen Being the Unhappy History of Elizabeth Stuart*; Jessica Gorst-Williams, *Elizabeth the Winter Queen*.

75. British Library, Lansdowne MS. 90, f. 77, recorded in Green, *Elizabeth*, 17; Erskine, *Memoirs*, 107–8; British Library, Harleian MS. 6986, f. 89.

76. British Library, Harleian MS. 6986, f. 87, reprinted in *The Letters of Elizabeth Queen of Bohemia*, ed. L. M. Baker, 26; Harleian MS. 6986, f. 111, reprinted *Letters of Elizabeth*, ed. Baker, 29–30; Harleian MS. 6986, f. 146.

77. Peacham, *Minerva Britanna*, 14; *Report on the Manuscripts of the Duke of Portland*, ed. R. F. Isaacson, 9:26. *CSP Ven*, 12:405–6; *Chamberlain*, ed. McClure, 1:381.

78. Raumer, *History*, 2:227; *Chamberlain*, ed. McClure, 1:404, 427.

79. *Chamberlain*, ed. McClure, 1:416.

80. Nichols, *Progresses of King James*, 2:542–43, 544.

81. Ibid., 546.

82. *Chamberlain*, ed. McClure, 1:424, 425.

83. *The Lords' Masque*, ed. I. A. Shapiro, in *A Book of Masques*, 117; Orgel & Strong, *Inigo Jones*, 1:260, 262; *The Masque of the Inner Temple*, ed. Philip Edwards, in *A Book of Masques*, 135, 142.

84. *John Donne: The Epithalamions, Anniversaries and Epicedes*, ed. W. Milgate, 63–66, 64, 7, 10. Quotations from Donne are from this edition.

85. *Letters of Elizabeth*, ed. Baker, 32–33.

86. *Salisbury MSS*, 16:163.

87. *The Memoirs of Robert Carey*, ed. F. H. Mares, 68. For Charles's early life, see Charles Carlton, *Charles I*, 1–21.

88. *Memoirs of Robert Carey*, ed. Mares, 69.

89. *CSP Ven*, 11:95; Goodman, *Court*, ed. Brewer, 1:251.

90. Marcelline, *Triumphs*, 67, 73; Peacham, *Minerva Britanna*, 18; Maxwell, *Laudable Life*, sig. B3.

91. *Letters to King James the Sixth*, ed. Alexander MacDonald, facsimile; British Library, Harleian MS. 6986, f. 182.

92. Akrigg, *Letters*, 329.

93. *Letters to King James*, ed. MacDonald, xxxviii; British Library, Harleian MS. 6986, f. 176; Strong, *Henry*, 196, 220.

94. British Library, Harleian MS. 6986, f. 78; *CSP Ven*, 10:514.

95. These and other events in Arbella's life are discussed by David N. Durant, *Arbella Stuart: A Rival to the Queen*, and by P. M. Handover, *Arbella Stuart, Royal Lady of Hardwick and Cousin to King James*. See also Ian McInnes, *Arabella: The Life and Times of Lady Arabella Seymour, 1575–1615*. Goodman, *Court*, ed. Brewer, 1:210, 209.

96. British Library, Landsdowne MS. 1236, f. 60; Handover, *Arbella Stuart*, 288.

97. Wilson, *History of Great Britain*, 61.

*Notes to Chapter Four: England (1613–1625)*

1. National Library of Scotland, Advocates MS. 33.1.7, XXII, no. 79.

2. *CSP Ven,* 15:79, 80.

3. Ibid., 388, 389.

4. Ibid., 392, 393.

5. *Chamberlain,* ed. McClure, 1:443; *Letters of Bacon,* ed. Spedding, 5:287.

6. *Chamberlain,* ed. McClure, 1:495, 496; Nichols, *Progresses of James,* 2:713; Akrigg, *Jacobean Pageant,* 187. See Akrigg's interesting discussion of Somerset and his fortunes in chaps. 15 and 16. *Chamberlain,* ed. McClure, 1:548.

7. Akrigg, *Letters,* 338, 337.

8. Ibid.

9. Ibid., 338.

10. Ibid., 336, 339.

11. Ibid., 340.

12. Akrigg, *Jacobean Pageant,* 189.

13. Akrigg, *Letters,* 343–345.

14. Wilson, *History of Great Britain,* 81.

15. Akrigg, *Letters,* 353; Akrigg, *Jacobean Pageant,* 204.

16. *CSP Ven,* 14:315; Orgel & Strong, *Inigo Jones,* 1:273.

17. Nichols, *Progresses of James,* 3:309; *Chamberlain,* ed. McClure, 2:63.

18. Nichols, *Progresses of James,* 3:322

19. British Library, Sloane MS. 3213, f. 4ᵛ.

20. Wilson, *History of Great Britain,* 79.

21. Nichols, *Progresses of King James,* 2:749, 750.

22. *Chamberlain,* ed. McClure, 1:586, 593, 2:32.

23. Ibid., 2:47, 129, 152.

24. Coke, *A Detection of the Court of K. James,* 1:83, 84, 146.

25. British Library, Harleian MS. 6986, f. 188, f. 192; David Dalrymple Hailes, *Memorials and Letters Relating to the History of Britain in the Reign of James the First,* 58.

26. *CSP Ven,* 15:207, 307.

27. Ibid., 420, 464.

28. National Library of Scotland, Advocates MS. 33.2.31, f. 156, f. 157; *Chamberlain,* ed. McClure, 2:219–20.

29. *CSP Ven,* 15:494–95; *Chamberlain,* ed. McClure, 2:220.

30. Akrigg, *Letters,* 369, 370, 369, 370n.

31. *Letters of Elizabeth,* ed. Baker, 47; James Maxwell, *Carolanna . . . A Poeme in Honour of Our King, Charles-James, Queene Anne, and Prince Charles,* sig. C4ᵛ.

32. *Poems,* ed. Craigie, 2:174. The editor discusses the different versions of the poem, on 2:257–58.

33. *Chamberlain,* ed. McClure, 2:224, 232, 237.

34. Wilson, *History,* 129; *CSP Ven,* 15:495.

35. *Chamberlain,* ed. McClure, 2:242; Thomas Birch, *The Court and Times of James the First,* 2:146; *Parliamentary History of England,* ed. William Cobbett and John Wright, 1:1373.

36. *CSP Ven*, 16:137, 14:225.

37. Weldon, *Court and Character*, 168.

38. *Letters of Elizabeth*, ed. Baker, 39–40; Public Record Office (hereafter cited as PRO), State Papers, Germany States, SP/81/14, f. 71.

39. *Letters of Elizabeth*, ed. Baker, 43; PRO, State Papers, Germany States, SP/81/14, f. 199.

40. PRO, State Papers, Germany States, SP/81/14, f. 252–53; *Historical Manuscripts Commission Second Report, Fortescue MSS*, 52.

41. *The Life and Letters of Sir Henry Wotton*, ed. Logan Pearsall Smith, 2:88, 89, 90.

42. Lee, *Great Britain's Solomon*, 269. Lee frequently refers to Frederick as "stupid." See his discussion of the Bohemian-Palatinate problem, 269–93. Willson, *King James VI and I*, 414. For a fine summary and analysis of the Bohemian question, see Willson's chap. on the topic, 399–424. See also, Akrigg, *Jacobean Pageant*, 334–44.

43. Hacket, *Scrinia Reserata*, pt. 1:167.

44. *Letters of Elizabeth*, ed. Baker, 50.

45. *Chamberlain*, ed. McClure, 2:266; *CSP Ven*, 16:53; Battista Nani, *The History of the Affairs of Europe in this Present Age*, trans. Robert Honywood, bk. 4:136; *Chamberlain*, ed. McClure, 2:284–85.

46. *Letters of Elizabeth*, ed. Baker, 51; PRO, State Papers, Germany States, SP/81/17, f. 59b, f. 192; *Parliamentary History*, 1:1179; Green, *Elizabeth*, 153. This remains one of the best studies of Elizabeth.

47. Samuel Gardiner, ed. *The Fortescue Papers, Consisting Chiefly of Letters Relating to State Affairs*, 138; *Letters of Elizabeth*, ed. Baker, 54.

48. PRO, State Papers, Holland, SP/84/98, f. 85; *Letters of Elizabeth*, ed. Baker, 55.

49. *CSP Ven*, 17:37; PRO, Germany States, SP/81/21, f. 30.

50. John Rushworth, *Historical Collections of Private Passages of State*, 1:57–58.

51. Green, *Elizabeth*, 175; Raumer, *History*, 2:253.

52. PRO, Germany States, SP/81/20, f. 313, f. 329; PRO, Germany States, SP/81/21, f. 18–19.

53. PRO, Germany States, SP/81/21, f. 155.

54. *Letters of Elizabeth*, ed. Baker, 61; *CSP Ven*, 17:146.

55. PRO, Germany States, SP/81/26, f. 179–80; George Bromley, *A Collection of Original Royal Letters*, 16, 18; PRO, Germany States, SP/81/27, f. 192.

56. PRO, Germany States, SP/81/28, f. 23–26, f. 48–52.

57. *Letters of Elizabeth*, ed. Baker, 66; Akrigg, *Letters*, 429–31; *Letters of Elizabeth*, ed. Baker, 67.

58. *CSP Ven*, 17:414, 18:185.

59. *An Historical and Critical Account*, 157; Welwood, *Memoirs*, 25; *Church-History of Britain*, bk. 10:111.

60. Arthur Wilson, *History*, 236.

61. *Calendar of State Papers Domestic, 1611–18*, 9:354, 370.

62. British Library, Harleian MS. 6986, f. 196a–196b.

63. *CSP Ven*, 17:88.

64. *The Works of Thomas Middleton*, ed. A. H. Bullen, 7:271.

65. Ibid., 274, 276; *CSP Ven*, 14:350.

66. *Chamberlain*, ed. McClure, 2:429.

67. Birch, *Court and Times*, 2:344.

68. *CSP Ven*, 17:443; Raumer, *History*, 2:277.

69. *CSP Ven*, 18:268.

70. *Report on the Manuscripts of the Earl of Mar and Kellie*, 2:202, 203; *CSP Ven*, 18:468.

71. *CSP Ven*, 17:451, 450, 451, 16:238, 17:452.

72. *CSP Ven*, 17:451–52; Willson, *King James VI and I*, 406–7; *CSP Ven*, 17:451.

73. *Chamberlain*, ed. McClure, 2:546; Goodman, *Court*, ed. Brewer, 1:367.

74. Akrigg, *Letters*, 386–87, 392; British Library, Harleian MS. 6987, f. 37.

75. *Buckingham: The Life and Political Career of George Villiers, First Duke of Buckingham*, 22. See also Lockyer's "An English *Valido*? Buckingham and James I"; Donald Wilkinson, "George Villiers, Duke of Buckingham"; Catherine Macaulay, *The History of England from the Accession of James I to the Elevation of the House of Hanover*, 1:96; Willson, *King James VI and I*, 384; Goodman, *Court*, ed. Brewer, 1:225–26; *Letters of Bacon*, ed. Spedding, 5:226.

76. *The Works of William Laud*, ed. James Bliss, 3:139, 170.

77. *Letters of Bacon*, ed. Spedding, 5:249, 6:8, 152.

78. Ibid., 7:293, 432.

79. Ibid., 6:14, 239, 244, 244.

80. Lockyer, *Buckingham*, 22. British Library, Harleian MS. 6987, f. 214 copy. Reprinted in Hugh Ross Williamson, *George Villiers, First Duke of Buckingham*, 235.

81. Wilson, *History of Great Britain*, 80; *The Life and Death of George Villiers*, in Henry Wotton, *Reliquiae Wottonianae*, 210.

82. Wilson, *History of Great Britain*, 104.

83. Ross Williamson, *George Villiers*, 68; *Chamberlain*, ed. McClure, 2:121; *CSP Ven*, 15:5.

84. *Chamberlain*, ed. McClure, 2:125; Lockyer, *Buckingham*, 83.

85. *Poems*, ed. Craigie, 2:176; Akrigg, *Letters*, 367–68.

86. Hacket, *Scrinia Reserata*, pt. 1:41; British Library, Harleian MS. 6986, f. 198; Lockyer, *Buckingham*, 60.

87. Akrigg, *Letters*, 374.

88. Lee, *Great Britain's Solomon*, 248–49.

89. Moray MSS in *Historical Manuscripts Commission Tenth Report*, 10:104.

90. *The Diary of Sir Simonds D'Ewes*, ed. Elisabeth Bourcier, 106; Lockyer, *Buckingham*, 122; *CSP Ven*, 17:530.

91. Edward Hyde Clarendon, *The History of the Rebellion and Civil Wars in England*, ed. W. Dunn Macray, 1:21; Coke, *A Detection of the Court of K. James*, 1:131.

92. Akrigg, *Letters*, 388; *Poems*, ed. Craigie, 2:193.

93. Lockyer, *Buckingham*, 151. For an excellent discussion of the whole experience in Spain, see 125–64. See also Charles Carlton, *Charles I: The Personal Monarch*, 34–47. For a contemporary account, see Hacket, *Scrinia Reserata*, pt. 1:109–62. *Diary of Sir Simonds D'Ewes*, 142.

94. Lockyer, *Buckingham*, 163.
95. *Diary of Sir Simonds D'Ewes*, 162; *Chamberlain*, ed. McClure, 2:516.
96. *Chamberlain*, ed. McClure, 2:516; Hacket, *Scrinia Reserata*, pt. 1:165; *The Winter's Tale*, 5.2.54–56.
97. For a convenient analysis, see Thomas Cogswell, "Thomas Middleton and the Court, 1624: *A Game at Chess* in Context," and the recent study by Albert Tricomi, *Anticourt Drama in England, 1602–1642*, 142–52.
98. Davies, "The Character of James VI and I," 60; Macaulay, *History of England*, 1:265n.
99. British Library, Harleian MS. 6987, f. 79; National Library of Scotland, Advocates MS. 33, f. 7, vol. 22, no. 70. Reprinted in Ross Williamson, *George Villiers*, 260–61. Unfortunately, Ross Williamson misread "sow" as "son" and then launched an explanation about how this must be some kind of obscure reference.
100. British Library, Harleian MS. 6987, f. 37, f. 153a–153b.
101. Akrigg, *Letters*, 416, 420, 421.
102. British Library, Harleian MS. 6987, f. 23, f. 149b, f. 157, f. 158, f. 164b; Akrigg, *Letters*, 425.
103. Akrigg, *Letters*, 431.
104. Ibid., 405, 423; Weldon, *Court and Character of King James*, 125; Wilson, *History of Britain*, 147, offers similar testimony; Goodman, *Court*, ed. Brewer, 1:385.
105. Goodman, *Court*, ed. Brewer, 2:290.
106. Lockyer, *Buckingham*, 168–69; *Letters of Bacon*, ed. Spedding, 7:448; British Library, Harleian MS. 6987, f. 204, f. 211b. See also Harleian MS. 6011, f. 22b; *Great Britain's Solomon*, 248. For additional discussion of Charles and Buckingham, see Carlton, *Charles I*, 22–33.
107. *CSP Ven*, 8:143; *Letters of Bacon*, ed. Spedding, 6:25.
108. Lockyer, *Buckingham*, 208.
109. Ibid., 196, 197.
110. Ibid., 216.
111. National Library of Scotland, Advocates MS. 33.1.7, vol. 22, no. 88, no. 79.
112. John Oglander, *A Royalist's Notebook: The Commonplace Book of Sir John Oglander*, ed. Francis Bamford, 196; Lockyer, *Buckingham*, 234.
113. Raumer, *History*, 2:265–66; *The Diary of Sir Simonds D'Ewes*, 92–93.
114. Lee, *Great Britain's Solomon*, 249. This argument completes what I see as Lee's triadic defense of James. First, he argues that since James encouraged his favorites to marry there can be no problem. Second, Charles's relationship to Buckingham disproves that James and Buckingham could have been lovers. And now, third, James simply was not interested in sex. Lee is trying to counter the prejudice and prudishness of earlier historians. But he has succeeded in creating a kind of alternative fiction that the historical facts, in my judgment, do not warrant.
115. Coke, *A Detection of the Court of K. James*, 1:97–98.
116. Raumer, *History*, 2:254; *Chamberlain*, ed. McClure, 2:369.
117. Lockyer, *Buckingham*, 102; British Library, Harleian MS. 6987, f. 92.

118. *CSP Ven,* 18:627; Salvetti correspondence in Henry Duncan Skrine MSS, *Historical Manuscripts Commission, Eleventh Report,* 11:2.

119. PRO, Germany States, SP/81/32, f. 149; Welwood, *Memoirs,* 20.

120. *Chamberlain,* ed. McClure, 2:616.

121. The text of the sermon appears in John Somers, *A Collection of Scarce and Valuable Tracts,* ed. Walter Scott, 2:35, 53, 45, 51, 52.

# Bibliography

*Primary Sources*

British Library Manuscripts.
  Additional MSS 1589, 5832, 12497, 12507, 15227, 18201, 19398, 19401, 19402, 19969, 22591, 28032, 35832, 36932, 39288.
  Cotton Julius. F. vi.
  Egerton MS. 2592.
  Harleian MSS 38, 366, 852, 4761, 6011, 6356, 6986, 6987, 7006, 7007, 7008.
  Lansdowne MS 1236, 1238.
  Sloane MSS 30, 174, 1775, 1786, 1792.
  Stowe MSS 150, 156, 183.
National Library of Scotland. Advocates MSS 19.3.29; 33.1.7, vol. 22; 33.1.10, vol. 27; 33.1.12, vol. 26; 33.1.12, vol. 29; 33.1.14, vol. 31.
Public Record Office, London. State Papers, Germany States, SP/81, vols. 12–32. State Papers, Holland, SP/84, vols. 91 and 98.
A. D. B. *The Court of the Most Illustrious and Most Magnificent James the First.* London, 1619.
Akrigg, G. P. V., ed. *The Letters of James VI and I.* Berkeley and Los Angeles: University of California Press, 1984.
Alberti, Leon Battista. *The Albertis of Florence: Leon Battista Alberti's "Della Famiglia".* Translated by Guido A. Guarino. Lewisburg, Pa.: Bucknell University Press, 1971.
Andrewes, Lancelot. *Ninety-six Sermons.* 5 vols. Oxford: John Henry Parker, 1843–1861.
Bacon, Francis. *The History of the Reign of King Henry the Seventh.* Edited by F. J. Levy. Indianapolis: Bobbs-Merrill, 1972.
———. *The Letters and the Life of Francis Bacon.* Edited by James Spedding. Vols. 3–7. London: Longmans, Green, Reader & Dyer, 1868–1874.
———. *The Works of Francis Bacon.* Edited by James Spedding, Robert Ellis, and Douglas Heath. 14 vols. London: Longmans, 1868–1890.
Balfour, James. *Annales of Scotland in the Historical Works of Sir James Balfour.* Edited by James Haig. 4 vols. Edinburgh, 1824–1825.

Battista, Nani. *The History of the Affairs of Europe in This Present Age.* Translated by Robert Honywood. London, 1673.

Birch, Thomas. *The Court and Times of James the First.* 2 vols. London: Henry Colburn, 1849.

————. *The Life of Henry Prince of Wales.* London, 1760.

Bowes, Robert. *The Correspondence of Robert Bowes.* Edited by Joseph Stevenson. London: Nichols; Edinburgh: Laing and Forbes, 1842.

Bromley, George. *A Collection of Original Royal Letters.* London: John Stockdale, 1787.

Buccleuch, Duke of. *Report on the Manuscripts of the Duke of Buccleuch: The Montagu Papers.* Vols. 1 and 2. London: HMSO, 1899, 1926.

Calderwood, David. *The History of the Kirk of Scotland.* Edited by Thomas Thomson. 8 vols. Edinburgh: Wodrow Society, 1842–1849.

————. *The True History of the Church of Scotland.* Edinburgh, 1678.

*Calendar of State Papers Domestic, 1603–1625.* Vols. 8–11. London: Longman, Brown, Green, Longmans, & Roberts, 1857–1859.

*Calendar of State Papers Relating to Scotland and Mary, Queen of Scots, 1547–1603.* 13 vols. Edinburgh: H M General Register House, 1898–1969.

*Calendar of State Papers Scotland.* 2 vols. Edited by John Thorpe. London: Ferguson, Treen et al., 1858.

*Calendar of State Papers Venetian, 1603–1625.* Vols. 10–18. London: HMSO, 1900–1912.

Camden, William. *Annales: The True and Royall History of Elizabeth.* London, 1625.

————. *The Annals of Mr. William Camden in the Reign of King James I, 1603–1623.* In *A Complete History of England,* vol. 2. London, 1706.

Cameron, Annie I., ed. *The Warrender Papers.* 2 vols. Edinburgh: Scottish History Society, 1931–1932.

Carey, Robert. *The Memoirs of Robert Carey.* Edited by F. H. Mares. Oxford: Clarendon Press, 1972.

Chamberlain, John. *The Chamberlain Letters: A Selection of the Letters of John Chamberlain Concerning Life in England from 1597 to 1626.* Edited by Elizabeth McClure Thomson. London: John Murray, 1966.

————. *The Letters of John Chamberlain.* Edited by Norman E. McClure. 2 vols. Philadelphia: American Philosophical Society, 1939.

Clarendon, Edward Hyde. *The Characters of Robert Earl of Essex . . . and George D. of Buckingham.* London, 1706.

————. *The History of the Rebellion and Civil Wars in England.* Edited by W. Dunn Macray. 6 vols. Oxford: Clarendon, 1888.

Clifford, Lady Anne. *The Dairy of the Lady Anne Clifford.* Introduction by V. Sackville-West. London: Heinemann, 1923.

Cobbett, William, and John Wright, eds. *Parliamentary History of England.* Vol. 1. London, 1806.

Coke, Roger. *A Detection of the Court and State of England during the Reigns of King James I.* 4th ed. 3 vols. Originally published in 1694. London, 1729.

"A Collection of Several Speeches and Treatises of the late Lord Treasurer Cecil, and of several observations of the lords of the Council given to King James concerning his estate and revenue in the years 1608, 1609, and 1610." Edited by Pauline Croft, in *Camden Miscellany 29*, Camden 4th series, 34:245–317. London: Royal Historical Society, 1987.

Cornwallis, Charles. *A Discourse of the most Illustrious Prince Henry, Late Prince of Wales.* (London, 1641). In *A Collection of Scarce and Valuable Tracts*, edited by Lord John Somers, vol. 2. London, 1809.

———. [John Hawkins]. *The Life and Death of our late most incomparable and Heroique Prince Henry* (1641). In *A Collection of Scarce and Valuable Tracts*, edited by Lord John Somers, vol. 2. London, 1809.

Dalyell, John Graham, ed. *The Diary of Robert Birrel.* In *Fragments of Scottish History.* Edinburgh, 1798.

Dekker, Thomas. *The Dramatic Works of Thomas Dekker.* Edited by Fredson Bowers. Vol. 2. Cambridge: Cambridge University Press, 1955.

"Descriptive List of State Papers, Foreign: Germany States." London: Typescript, 1934.

"Descriptive List of State Papers, Foreign: Holland." London: Typescript, 1939.

D'Ewes, Sir Simonds. *The Autobiography and Correspondence of Sir Simonds D'Ewes, Bart., during the Reigns of James I and Charles I.* Edited by James O. Halliwell. 2 vols. London: Richard Bentley, 1845.

———. *The Diary of Sir Simonds D'Ewes 1622–1624.* Edited by Elisabeth Bourcier. Paris: Didier, 1974.

Donne, John. *John Donne: The Epithalamians, Anniversaries and Epicedes.* Edited by W. Milgate. Oxford: Clarendon Press, 1978.

D'Orleans, F. J. *The History of the Revolutions in England under the Family of the Stuarts.* London, 1711.

Dugdale, Gilbert. *The Time Triumphant.* London, 1604.

*The Earle of Gowries Conspiracie.* London, 1600.

Elizabeth, Queen of Bohemia. *The Letters of Elizabeth Queen of Bohemia.* Edited by L. M. Baker. London: Bodley Head, 1953.

*England as Seen by Foreigners in the Days of Elizabeth and James the First.* Edited by William Brenchley Rye. London: J. R. Smith, 1865.

*England's Wedding Garment.* London, 1603.

[Erskine, Frances]. *Memoirs Relating to the Queen of Bohemia.* London, 1753.

*Extract from the Despatches of M. Courcelles, French Ambassador at the Court of Scotland.* Edited by Robert Bell. Edinburgh: Bannatyne Club, 1828.

Filmer, Robert. *Patriarcha: or the Natural Power of Kings*. London, 1680.
Frankland, Thomas. *The Annals of King James and King Charles the First*. London, 1681.
Fuller, Thomas. *The Church-History of Britain*. London, 1655.
Gardiner, Samuel Rawson, ed. *The Fortescue Papers: Consisting Chiefly of Letters Relating to State Affairs, Collected by John Packer.* London: Camden Society, 1871.
———, ed. and trans. *Narrative of the Spanish Marriage Treaty*. London: Camden Society, 1869.
Goodman, Godfrey. *The Court of King James the First*. Edited by John S. Brewer. 2 vols. London: Richard Bentley, 1839.
"The Gordon Letters." In *The Miscellany of the Spalding Club,* vol. 3, 213–16. Aberdeen, 1846.
Greville, Fulke. *The Five Yeares of King James*. London, 1643.
Hacket, John. *Memoirs of the Life of Archbishop Williams*. London, 1715.
———. *Scrinia Reserata: A Memorial offer'd to the Great Deservings of John Williams*. London, 1692.
Hailes, David Dalrymple. *Memorials and Letters Relating to the History of Britain in the Reign of James the First*. 2d ed. Glasgow, 1766.
———. *The Secret Correspondence of Sir Robert Cecil with James VI: King of Scotland*. Edinburgh, 1766.
Hardwicke, Philip Y., ed. *Miscellaneous State Papers from 1501 to 1726*. Vol. 1. London, 1778.
Harington, John. *The Letters and Epigrams of Sir John Harington*. Edited by Norman E. McClure. Philadelphia: University of Pennsylvania Press, 1930.
———. *Nugae Antiquae*. 2d ed. 3 vols. London, 1779.
Harris, William. *An Historical and Critical Account of the Life and Writings of James the First, King of Great Britain*. London, 1753.
Harrison, G. B., ed. *A Jacobean Journal . . . 1603–1606*. New York: Macmillan, 1941.
———. *A Second Jacobean Journal . . . 1607 to 1610*. London: Routledge & Kegan Paul, 1958.
H[aydon], W[illiam]. *The True Picture and Relation of Prince Henry*. Leyden, 1643.
Herbert, Edward Lord. *The Autobiography of Edward, Lord Herbert of Cherbury.* Introduction by Sidney Lee. London: John Nimmo, 1886.
Herries, John Maxwell. *Historical Memoirs of the Reign of Mary Queen of Scots, and King James the Sixth*. Edited by Robert Pitcairn. Edinburgh: Abbotsford Club, 1836.
*Historical Manuscripts Commission, Second–Fifteenth Reports*. London, 1874–1899.
*The Historie and Life of King James the Sext, 1566–1596*. Edinburgh: Bannatyne Club, 1835.

Hoby, Lady Margaret. *Diary of Lady Margaret Hoby, 1599–1605.* Edited by Dorothy M. Meads. London: Routledge, 1930.

Holles, Gervase. *Memorials of the Holles Family, 1493–1656.* Edited by A. C. Wood. London: Camden Society, 1937.

James I. *A Meditation upon the Lord's Prayer.* London, 1619.

———. *The Poems of James VI of Scotland.* Edited by James Craigie. 2 vols. Edinburgh: Blackwood, 1955–1958.

———. *The Political Works of James I.* Edited by Charles H. McIlwain. Cambridge: Harvard University Press, 1918.

———. *A Remonstrance of the Most Gratious King James I.* London, 1616.

[James I]. *The Peace-Maker; or, Great Brittaines Blessing.* London, 1619.

———. *Two Meditations of the King's Maiestie.* London, 1620.

James VI. *The Basilicon Doron of King James VI.* Edited by James Craigie. Scottish Text Society. 2 vols. Edinburgh and London: Blackwood, 1944.

———. *The Workes of the most high and mightie prince, James.* London, 1616.

Jesse, John Heneage. *Memoirs of the Court of England during the Reign of the Stuarts.* 3 vols. London: Bohn, 1857.

Johnston, Robert. *The Historie of Scotland during the Minority of King James.* Translated by T. M. [Thomas Middleton?]. London, 1646.

Laud, William. *The Works of William Laud.* Edited by James Bliss. Vol. 3. Oxford: Parker, 1853.

*Letters from and to Sir Dudley Carleton.* 2d ed. London, 1775.

*Letters to King James the Sixth.* Edited by Alexander MacDonald. Edinburgh: Maitland Club, 1835.

*The Life of George Villiers, Duke of Buckingham.* London, 1740.

Macaulay [Graham], Catherine. *The History of England from the Accession of James I to the Elevation of the House of Hanover.* 2 vols. London, 1766.

Mar, Earl of. *Report on the Manuscripts of the Earl of Mar and Kellie.* London: HMSO, 1904.

Marcelline, George. *The Triumphs of King James the First.* London, 1610.

Maxwell, James. *Carolanna, That is to say, A Poeme in Honour of Our King, Charles-James, Queene Anne, and Prince Charles.* London, 1619.

———. *The Laudable Life, and Deplorable Death, of our late peerlesse Prince Henry.* London, 1612.

Meldrum, Ronald M., ed. *The Letters of King James I to King Christian IV, 1603–1625.* Brighton: Harvester Press, 1977.

Melville, James. *Memoirs of Sir James Melville of Halhill, 1535–1617.* Edited by A. Francis Steuart. London: Routledge & Sons, 1929.

Middleton, Thomas. *The Works of Thomas Middleton.* Edited by A. H. Bullen. Boston: Houghton Mifflin, 1885.

Moyses [Moysie], David. *Memoirs of the Affairs of Scotland.* Edinburgh, 1755.

Munday, Anthony. *Londons Love to the Royal Prince Henrie*. London, 1610.

————. *Pageants and Entertainments of Anthony Munday: A Critical Edition*. Edited by David M. Bergeron. New York: Garland, 1985.

————. *The Triumphs of Re-United Britannia*. London, 1605.

Nichols, John. *The Progresses, Processions, and Magnificent Festivities of King James the First*. 4 vols. London: J. B. Nichols, 1828.

Oglander, John. *A Royalist's Notebook: The Commonplace Book of Sir John Oglander*. Edited by Francis Bamford. London: Constable, 1936.

Osborne, Francis. *Traditional Memoirs* (1658). In *Secret History of the Court of James the First*. Edited by Sir Walter Scott. 2 vols. Edinburgh: Ballantyne, 1811.

*Papers Relative to the Marriage of King James the Sixth of Scotland, with the Princess Anna of Denmark*. Edinburgh: Bannatyne Club, 1828.

Peacham, Henry. *Minerva Britanna*. London, 1612.

Pett, Phineas. *The Autobiography of Phineas Pett*. Edited by W. G. Perrin. London: Navy Records Society, 1918.

Peyton, Edward. *The Divine Catastrophe of the Kingly Family of the House of Stuarts* (1652). In *Secret History of the Court of James the First*. Edited by Sir Walter Scott. 2 vols. Edinburgh: Ballantyne, 1811.

*Prayers appointed to be used in the Church . . . for the Queenes safe deliverance*. London, 1605.

Rait, Robert S. *Five Stuart Princesses*. Westminster: Constable, 1902.

Rait, Robert S., and Annie I. Cameron, eds. *King James's Secret: Negotiations between Elizabeth and James VI . . . from the Warrender Papers*. London: Nisbet, 1927.

Raumer, Friederich Ludwig Georg von. *History of the Sixteenth and Seventeenth Centuries*. 2 vols. London: John Murray, 1835.

Ross, Thomas. *Idae sive De Jacobi*. London, 1638.

Rushworth, John. *Historical Collections of Private Passages of State*. Vol. 1. London, 1729. Originally published in 1659.

Rutland, Duke of. *The Manuscripts of the Duke of Rutland at Belvoir Castle*. London: HMSO, 1905.

Sackville, Major-General Lord. *Calendar of the Manuscripts of Major-General Lord Sackville: Cranfield Papers, 1551–1612*. 2 vols. London: HMSO, 1940, 1966.

Salisbury, Marquess of. *Calendar of the Manuscripts of the Marquess of Salisbury, Hatfield House*. Parts 15–24. London: HMSO, 1930–1976.

Sanderson, William. *A Compleat History of the Lives and Reigns of Mary Queen of Scotland, and of Her Son and Successor, James*. London, 1656.

*Secret History of the Court of James the First*. Edited by Sir Walter Scott. 2 vols. Edinburgh: Ballantyne, 1811.

Shakespeare, William. *The Complete Works.* General editor Alfred Harbage. Baltimore: Penguin, 1969.

Spanheim, Friedrich. *Memoires sur la vie et la mort de la Princesse Loyse Juliane.* Leyden, 1645.

Sparke, Michael. *The Narrative History of King James, for the first fourteen years.* London, 1651.

Spencer, T. J. B., and S. W. Wells, eds. *A Book of Masques in Honour of Allardyce Nicoll.* Cambridge: Cambridge University Press, 1967.

Spottiswoode, John. *The History of the Church of Scotland.* London, 1655. Reprint. Menston: Scolar, 1972.

Stow, John. *Annales or a Generall Chronicle of England.* London, 1631.

Sully. *Memoirs of Maximilian de Béthune, Duke of Sully.* 3 vols. Translated by Charlotte Lennox. London, 1756.

Thomson, Thomas, ed. *Letters and Papers Relating to Patrick Master of Gray.* Edinburgh: Bannatyne Club, 1835.

Weldon, Anthony. *The Court and Character of King James.* London, 1651.

Welwood, James. *Memoirs of the Most Material Transactions in England, for the Last Hundred Years.* 4th ed. Originally published in 1700. London, 1702.

*Wentworth Papers, 1597–1628.* Edited by J. P. Cooper. Camden 4th series, vol. 12. London: Royal Historical Society, 1973.

Whitaker, Thomas Dunham. *The Life and Original Correspondence of Sir George Radcliffe.* London: John Nichols, 1810.

Wilson, Arthur. *The History of Great Britain, Being the Life and Reign of King James the First.* London, 1653.

Winwood, Ralph. *Memorials of Affairs of State in the Reigns of Q. Elizabeth and K. James I.* Edited by Edmund Sawyer. 3 vols. London, 1725.

Wotton, Sir Henry. *The Life and Letters of Sir Henry Wotton.* Edited by Logan Pearsall Smith. 2 vols. 1907. Reprint. Oxford: Clarendon Press, 1966.

———. *Reliquiae Wottonianae.* 3d ed. London, 1672.

### Secondary Sources

Abbott, Philip. *The Family on Trial: Special Relationship in Modern Political Thought.* University Park: Pennsylvania State University Press, 1981.

Aikin, Lucy. *Memoirs of the Court of King James the First.* 3d ed. 2 vols. London: Longman, Brown, & Green, 1823.

Akrigg, G. P. V. *Jacobean Pageant or the Court of King James I.* London: Hamish Hamilton, 1962.

Amussen, S[usan] D. "Gender, Family, and the Social Order, 1560–1725." In *Order and Disorder in Early Modern England,* edited by

Anthony Fletcher and John Stevenson, 196–217. Cambridge: Cambridge University Press, 1985.

Anderson, Judith. *Biographical Truth: The Representation of Historical Persons in Tudor-Stuart Writing.* New Haven and London: Yale University Press, 1984.

Anderson, Michael. *Approaches to the History of the Western Family, 1500–1914.* London: Macmillan, 1980.

Ariès, Phillipe. *Centuries of Childhood.* Translated by Robert Baldick. London: Jonathan Cape, 1962. Originally published as *L'Enfant et la vie familiale sous l'ancien régime.* Paris, 1960.

Benger, Elizabeth Ogilvy. *Memoirs of Elizabeth Stuart, Queen of Bohemia.* 2 vols. London: Longman, Green, 1825.

Bergeron, David M. *English Civic Pageantry 1558–1642.* London: Edward Arnold; Columbia: University of South Carolina Press, 1971.

———. "Gilbert Dugdale and the Royal Entry of James I (1604)." *Journal of Medieval and Renaissance Studies* 13 (1983): 111–25.

———. "Prince Henry and English Pageantry." *Tennessee Studies in Literature* 13 (1968): 109–16.

———. *Shakespeare's Romances and the Royal Family.* Lawrence: University Press of Kansas, 1985.

Bingham, Caroline. *James I of England.* London: Weidenfeld & Nicolson, 1981.

———. *James VI of Scotland.* London: Weidenfeld & Nicolson, 1979.

———. *The Making of a King: The Early Years of James VI and I.* London: Collins, 1968.

Boswell, John. *Christianity, Social Tolerance, and Homosexuality: Gay People in Western Europe from the Beginning of the Christian Era to the Fourteenth Century.* Chicago: University of Chicago Press, 1980.

Bowen, Catherine Drinker. *The Lion and the Throne: The Life and Times of Sir Edward Coke (1552–1634).* Boston: Little, Brown, 1956.

Bradley, E. T. *Life of the Lady Arabella Stuart.* 2 vols. London: Bentley, 1889.

Bray, Alan. *Homosexuality in Renaissance England.* London: Gay Men's Press, 1982.

Buchan, Alice. *A Stuart Portrait.* London: Peter Davies, 1934.

Carlton, Charles. *Charles I: The Personal Monarch.* London: Routledge and Kegan Paul, 1983.

———. *Royal Childhoods.* London: Routledge and Kegan Paul, 1986.

Certeau, Michel de. *The Writing of History.* Translated by Tom Conley. New York: Columbia University Press, 1988.

———. "Writing vs. Time: History and Anthropology in the Works of Lafitau." In *Rethinking History: Time, Myth, and Writing,* 37–64. Yale French Studies 59. New Haven: Yale University, 1980.

Cogswell, Thomas. "Thomas Middleton and the Court, 1624: *A Game at Chess* in Context." *Huntington Library Quarterly* 47 (1984): 374–88.

Cook, Albert. *History/Writing.* Cambridge: Cambridge University Press, 1988.

Cuddy, Neil. "The Revival of the Entourage: The Bedchamber of James I, 1603–1625." In *The English Court from the Wars of the Roses to the Civil War,* edited by David Starkey et al., 173–225. London: Longman, 1987.

Davies, Godfrey. "The Character of James VI and I." *Huntington Library Quarterly* 5 (1941–1942): 33–63.

———. *The Early Stuarts, 1603–1660.* 2d ed. Oxford: Clarendon Press, 1959.

DeMolen, Richard L. "Childhood and the Sacraments in the Sixteenth Century." *Archiv für Reformationsgeschichte* 66 (1975): 49–71.

———. "Erasmus on Childhood." *Erasmus of Rotterdam Society Yearbook Two* (1982): 25–46.

Dietz, Frederick C. *English Public Finance, 1558–1641.* 2d ed. Vol. 2. London: Frank Cass, 1964.

Disraeli, Isaac. *An Inquiry into the Literary and Political Character of James the First.* London: John Murray, 1816.

Donaldson, Gordon. *Scotland: James V to James VII.* Edinburgh and London: Oliver & Boyd, 1965.

Dray, William H. "J. H. Hexter, Neo-Whiggism and Early Stuart Historiography." *History and Theory* 26 (1987): 133–49.

Durant, David N. *Arbella Stuart: A Rival to the Queen.* London: Weidenfeld & Nicolson, 1978.

Elliott, J. H. "Power and Propaganda in the Spain of Philip IV." In *Rites of Power: Symbolism, Ritual, and Politics Since the Middle Ages,* edited by Sean Wilentz, 145–73. Philadelphia: University of Pennsylvania Press, 1985.

Flandrin, Jean-Louis. *Families in Former Times: Kinship, Household and Sexuality.* Translated by Richard Southern. Cambridge: Cambridge University Press, 1979.

Fraser, Antonia. *King James VI of Scotland I of England.* New York: Alfred A. Knopf, 1975.

———. *Mary Queen of Scots.* New York: Delacorte Press, 1969.

Fritz, Paul S. "From 'Public' to 'Private': The Royal Funerals in England, 1500–1830." In *Mirrors of Mortality: Studies in the Social History of Death,* edited by Joachim Whaley, 61–79. London: Europa, 1981.

Frye, Northrop. *Anatomy of Criticism: Four Essays.* Princeton: Princeton University Press, 1957.

Gardiner, Samuel R. *History of England from the Accession of James I to the Outbreak of the Civil War, 1603–1642.* 10 vols. 1883–1884. Reprint. New York: AMS Press, 1965.

Gay, Peter. *Style in History.* New York: Basic Books, 1974.

Geertz, Clifford. "Centers, Kings, and Charisma: Reflections on the Symbolics of Power." In *Local Knowledge: Further Essays in Interpretive Anthropology,* 121–46. New York: Basic Books, 1983.

Goldberg, Jonathan. "Fatherly Authority: The Politics of Stuart Family Images." In *Rewriting the Renaissance: The Discourses of Sexual Difference in Early Modern Europe,* edited by Margaret W. Ferguson, Maureen Quilligan, and Nancy J. Vickers, 3–32. Chicago and London: University of Chicago Press, 1986.

———. *James I and the Politics of Literature: Jonson, Shakespeare, Donne, and Their Contemporaries.* Baltimore and London: Johns Hopkins University Press, 1983.

Goody, Jack. *The Character of Kinship.* Cambridge: Cambridge University Press, 1973.

Goody, Jack, Joan Thirsk, and E. P. Thompson, eds. *Family and Inheritance: Rural Society in Western Europe, 1200–1800.* Cambridge: Cambridge University Press, 1976.

Gorst-Williams, Jessica. *Elizabeth the Winter Queen.* London: Abelard, 1977.

Green, Mary Anne Everett (Wood). *Elizabeth Electress Palatine and Queen of Bohemia.* Revised by S. C. Lomas. 1855. Reprint. London: Methuen, 1909.

Greenblatt, Stephen. *Renaissance Self-Fashioning: From More to Shakespeare.* Chicago and London: University of Chicago Press, 1980.

———. *Sir Walter Ralegh: The Renaissance Man and His Roles.* New Haven: Yale University Press, 1973.

Handover, Phyllis M. *Arbella Stuart, Royal Lady of Hardwick and Cousin to King James.* London: Eyre & Spottiswoode, 1957.

Hardy, Blanche C. *Arbella Stuart: A Biography.* London: Constable, 1913.

Hay, Marie. *The Winter Queen, Being the Unhappy History of Elizabeth Stuart.* London: Constable, 1910.

Henderson, Thomas F. *James I and VI.* Paris, London, and New York: Goupil, 1904.

Hexter, J. H. *Reappraisals in History: New Views on History and Society in Early Modern Europe.* 2d ed. Chicago and London: University of Chicago Press, 1979.

Hicks, L., S.J. "The Embassy of Sir Anthony Standen in 1603, Part II." *Recusant History* 5 (1960): 184–222.

———. "The Embassy of Sir Anthony Standen in 1603, Part IV." *Recusant History* 7 (1963): 50–81.

Hill, Christopher. *Change and Continuity in Seventeenth-Century England.* London: Weidenfeld & Nicolson, 1974.

Hirst, Derek. *Authority and Conflict: England, 1603–1658.* London: Edward Arnold, 1986.

Houston, S. J. *James I*. London: Longman, 1973.

Hunt, David. *Parents and Children in History: The Psychology of Family Life in Early Modern France*. New York: Basic Books, 1970.

Javitch, Daniel. *Poetry and Courtliness in Renaissance England*. Princeton: Princeton University Press, 1978.

Kenyon, J. P. *Stuart England*. 2d ed. Harmondsworth: Penguin, 1985.

Laing, R. D. *The Politics of the Family and Other Essays*. New York: Random House, 1971.

Laslett, Peter. *Family Life and Illicit Love in Earlier Generations: Essays in Historical Sociology*. Cambridge: Cambridge University Press, 1977.

———. *Household and Family in Past Time*. Cambridge: Cambridge University Press, 1972.

———. *The World We Have Lost*. 2d ed. London: Methuen, 1971.

Lee, Maurice, Jr. *Government by Pen: Scotland under James VI and I*. Urbana: University of Illinois Press, 1980.

———. *Great Britain's Solomon: James VI and I in His Three Kingdoms*. Urbana: University of Illinois Press, 1990.

[Lenanton], Carola Oman. *Elizabeth of Bohemia*. London: Hodder & Stoughton, 1938.

Lévi-Strauss, Claude. "The Family." In *Man, Culture, and Society*, edited by Harry L. Shapiro, 333–57. Revised edition. London: Oxford University Press, 1971.

Liu, Alan, "The Power of Formalism: The New Historicism," *ELH* 56 (1989): 721–71.

Lockyer, Roger. *Buckingham: The Life and Political Career of George Villiers, First Duke of Buckingham, 1592–1628*. London: Longman, 1981.

———. *The Early Stuarts: A Political History of England, 1603–1642*. London and New York: Longman, 1989.

———. "An English *Valido*? Buckingham and James I." In *For Veronica Wedgwood: These Studies in Seventeenth Century History*, edited by Richard Ollard and Pamela Tudor-Craig, 45–58. London: Collins, 1986.

McElwee, William. *The Wisest Fool in Christendom: The Reign of King James I and VI*. New York: Harcourt Brace, 1958.

McInnes, Ian. *Arabella: The Life and Times of Lady Arabella Seymour, 1575–1615*. London: Allen, 1968.

Marin, Louis. "The Inscription of the King's Memory: On the Metallic History of Louis XIV." In *Rethinking History: Time, Myth, and Writing*, edited by Marie Rose Logan and John Frederick Logan, 17–36. Yale French Studies 59. New Haven: Yale University Press, 1980.

Marius, Richard. *Thomas More: A Biography*. New York: Alfred A. Knopf, 1984.

Mathew, David. *James I*. London: Eyre & Spottiswoode, 1967.

Mink, Louis D. *Historical Understanding*. Edited by Brian Fay, Eugene

O. Golob, and Richard T. Vann. Ithaca: Cornell University Press, 1987.

Mitterauer, Michael, and Reinhard Sieder, eds. *The European Family: Patriarchy to Partnership from the Middle Ages to the Present.* Translated by Karla Oosterveen and Manfred Horzinger. Chicago: University of Chicago Press, 1982.

Morrah, Patrick. *A Royal Family: Charles I and His Family.* London: Constable, 1982.

Morgan, D. H. J. *The Family, Politics and Social Theory.* London: Routledge and Kegan Paul, 1985.

Morgan, John. *Godly Learning: Puritan Attitudes towards Reason, Learning and Education, 1560–1640.* Cambridge: Cambridge University Press, 1986.

Morris, Christopher. *Political Thought in England: Tyndale to Hooker.* London: Oxford University Press, 1953.

Mount, Ferdinand. *The Subversive Family: An Alternative History of Love and Marriage.* London: Jonathan Cape, 1982.

Murstein, Bernard I. *Love, Sex, and Marriage through the Ages.* New York: Springer, 1974.

Notestein, Wallace. *The House of Commons, 1604–1610.* New Haven and London: Yale University Press, 1971.

Orgel, Stephen. *The Illusion of Power: Political Theater in the English Renaissance.* Berkeley and Los Angeles: University of California Press, 1975.

Orgel, Stephen, and Roy Strong. *Inigo Jones: The Theatre of the Stuart Court.* 2 vols. Berkeley and Los Angeles: University of California Press, 1973.

Parry, Graham. *The Golden Age Restor'd: The Culture of the Stuart Court, 1603–42.* Manchester: Manchester University Press, 1981.

Patrides, C. A. "'The Greatest of the Kingly Race': The Death of Henry Stuart." *The Historian* 47 (1985): 402–8.

Pinchbeck, Ivy, and Margaret Hewitt. *Children in English Society.* Vol. 1, *From Tudor Times to the Eighteenth Century.* London: Routledge and Kegan Paul; Toronto: University of Toronto Press, 1969.

Poster, Mark. *Critical Theory of the Family.* New York: Seabury, 1978.

Rabb, Theodore K., and Robert I. Rothberg, eds. *The Family in Interdisciplinary Essays.* New York: Octagon, 1976.

Randall, Dale B. J. *Jonson's Gypsies Unmasked: Background and Theme of "The Gypsies Metamorphos'd."* Durham: Duke University Press, 1975.

Raumer, Friedrich Ludwig Georg von. *The Political History of England during the 16th, 17th, and 18th Centuries.* 2 vols. London: Richter, 1837.

*Rethinking History: Time, Myth, and Writing.* Yale French Studies 59.

Edited by Marie Rose Logan and John Frederick Logan. New Haven: Yale University, 1980.

Rosenberg, Charles E., ed. *The Family in History.* Philadelphia: University of Pennsylvania Press, 1975.

Ross Williamson, Hugh. *George Villiers, First Duke of Buckingham: Study for a Biography.* London: Duckworth, 1940.

Rowse, A. L. *Simon Forman: Sex and Society in Shakespeare's Age.* London: Weidenfeld & Nicolson, 1974.

Saslow, James M. *Ganymede in the Renaissance: Homosexuality in Art and Society.* New Haven: Yale University Press, 1986.

Schochet, Gordon J. *Patriarchalism in Political Thought.* Oxford: Basil Blackwell, 1975.

Scott, Otto J. *James I.* New York: Mason Charter, 1976.

Sedgwick, Eve Kosofsky. "Homophobia, Misogyny, and Capital: The Example of *Our Mutual Friend.*" *Raritan* 2 (1983): 126–51.

Seton, Walter W. "The Early Years of Henry Frederick, Prince of Wales, and Charles, Duke of Albany." *The Scottish Historical Review* 13 (1916): 366–79.

Sharpe, Kevin. *Criticism and Compliment: The Politics of Literature in the England of Charles I.* Cambridge: Cambridge University Press, 1987.
———. *Sir Robert Cotton, 1586–1631: History and Politics in Early Modern England.* Oxford: Oxford University Press, 1979.

Shorter, Edward. *The Making of the Modern Family.* New York: Basic Books, 1975.

Smith, Alan G. R., ed. *The Reign of James VI and I.* London: Macmillan, 1973.

Smith, Bruce R. *Homosexual Desire in Shakespeare's England: A Cultural Poetics.* Chicago: University of Chicago Press, 1991.

Smuts, R. Malcolm. *Court Culture and the Origins of a Royalist Tradition in Early Stuart England.* Philadelphia: University of Pennsylvania Press, 1987.

Stone, Lawrence. *The Family, Sex and Marriage in England, 1500–1800.* London: Weidenfeld & Nicolson, 1977.

Strong, Roy. *Britannia Triumphans: Inigo Jones, Rubens and Whitehall Palace.* London: Thames & Hudson, 1980.
———. "England and Italy: The Marriage of Henry Prince of Wales." In *For Veronica Wedgwood: These Studies in the Seventeenth-Century History,* edited by Richard Ollard and Pamela Tudor-Craig, 59–87. London: Collins, 1986.
———. *The English Icon: Elizabethan and Jacobean Portraiture.* London: Routledge & Kegan Paul; New York: Pantheon, 1969.
———. *Henry, Prince of Wales and England's Lost Renaissance.* London: Thames and Hudson, 1986.

Tawney, R. H. *Business and Politics under James I: Lionel Cranfield as Merchant and Minister.* Cambridge: Cambridge University Press, 1958.

Thomas, Keith. "Age and Authority in Early Modern England." *Proceedings of the British Academy* 62 (1976): 205–48.

Trevelyan, G. M. *England under the Stuarts.* Rev. ed. 1949. Reprint. London: Methuen, 1972.

Tricomi, Albert H. *Anticourt Drama in England, 1602–1642.* Charlottesville: University Press of Virginia, 1989.

Vaughan, Robert. *The History of England under the House of Stuart.* London: Baldwin & Cradock, 1840.

Veyne, Paul. *Writing History: Essay on Epistemology.* Translated by Mina Moore-Rinvolucri. Middletown, Conn.: Wesleyan University Press, 1984. Originally published in 1971.

Warner, George F. "The Library of James VI." In *Miscellany of the Scottish History Society,* 1:xi–lxxv. Edinburgh, 1893.

Wedgewood, C. V. *Poetry and Politics under the Stuarts.* Cambridge: Cambridge University Press, 1960.

Wheaton, Robert, and Tamara K. Hareven, eds. *Family and Sexuality in French History.* Philadephia: University of Pennsylvania Press, 1980.

White, Hayden, *Tropics of Discourse: Essays in Cultural Criticism.* Baltimore: Johns Hopkins University Press, 1978.

Wilentz, Sean. *Rites of Power: Symbolism, Ritual, and Politics since the Middle Ages.* Philadelphia: University of Pennsylvania Press, 1985.

Wilkinson, Donald. "George Villiers, Duke of Buckingham." In *Statesmen and Politicians of the Stuart Age,* edited by Timothy Eustace, 37–60. London: Macmillan, 1985.

Williams, Charles. *James I.* 1934. Reprint. London: Arthur Barker, 1951.

Williams, Ethel Carleton. *Anne of Denmark: Wife of James VI of Scotland: James I of England.* London: Longman, 1970.

Williamson, J. W. *The Myth of the Conqueror: Prince Henry Stuart: A Study of 17th Century Personation.* New York: AMS Press, 1978.

Willson, David Harris. *King James VI and I.* London: Jonathan Cape, 1956.

Wilson, Elkin Calhoun. *Prince Henry and English Literature.* Ithaca: Cornell University Press, 1946.

Wormald, Jenny. *Court, Kirk, and Community: Scotland, 1470–1625.* London: Edward Arnold, 1981.

———. "James VI and I: Two Kings or One?" *History* 68 (1983): 187–209.

———. *Mary Queen of Scots: A Study in Failure.* London: George Philip, 1988.

# *Index*

Abbot, George, 137–38, 163
Akrigg, G. P. V., 35, 128, 178
Anderson, Michael, 4
Anne, Queen, wife of James, 48–62, 69–71, 88, 135–43: Catholicism, 72–73; childhood, 53; conflict about royal children, 53, 54–58, 62, 88, 139; coronation in England, 71–72; coronation in Scotland, 52–53; Danish family, 52, 53; marriage, 51–52, 58, 59, 89–91, 139; sickness and death, 139–43
Ariès, Phillipe, 5
Arran, James Stewart, earl of, 28, 34–35, 39
Asheby, William, 49, 50, 51
Aston, Roger, 56, 57, 60
Atkins, Henry, 117

Bacon, Francis, 1, 93, 98, 102–3, 105, 127, 137, 179, 180: *Advancement of Learning*, 8, 13; *De Augmentis*, 13, 17; friendship with Buckingham, 163–64; *History of Great Britain*, 67–68; views on history, 13–14
Beaumont, Francis, 115
Beaumont, Harley de, 83–84
Bingham, Caroline, 21, 27
Boswell, John, 29
Bowes, Robert, 27, 32, 39–40, 45, 53, 55, 56, 57, 58
Bray, Alan, 29
Brett, Arthur, 171
Buchanan, George, 22–24
Buckingham, countess of, 6–7

Buckingham, duke of. *See* Villiers, George
Busino, Horatio. *See* Venetian ambassadors

Calderwood, David, 44, 49, 51
Campion, Thomas, 115, 128
Carey, Robert, 61, 117–19
Carleton, Dudley, 87, 90, 107–9, 134, 136–37, 139, 142, 148, 150, 151, 155, 160, 168
Carlton, Charles, 4
Carr, Robert (earl of Somerset), 105: involvement in Overbury scandal, 127, 131–32; loss of James's favor, 131–32; marriage to Frances Howard, 127–28; relationship with James, 86–88, 104–5, 126–32, 164; trial, 132
Cecil, Robert (Salisbury), 55, 60, 61, 72, 82, 83, 85, 102, 105
Cecil, William (Burghley), 27, 45, 53, 58, 59, 60
Certeau, Michel de, 3, 15, 74
Chamberlain, John, 87, 90, 94, 107–9, 113–14, 115, 126–27, 128, 134, 136–37, 139, 140, 142, 148, 157, 160, 168, 174, 185, 186
Chapman, George, 115–16
Charles, Prince, 117–21, 155–60: arrival in England, 117; birth, 60; made Prince of Wales, 156–57; relationship with Buckingham, 155–56, 179–80; relationship to Henry, 121; relationship with James, 120, 155–58; the Spanish Match and trip to Spain, 172–75